POLITICS AND SPACE

POLITICS AND SPACE

Image Making by NASA

MARK E. BYRNES

Westport, Connecticut
London

Library of Congress Cataloging-in-Publication Data

Byrnes, Mark E.
        Politics and space : image making by NASA / Mark E. Byrnes.
            p.   cm.
        Includes bibliographical references and index.
        ISBN 0–275–94950–8 (alk. paper)
        1. United States. National Aeronautics and Space Administration—
Public opinion.   2. United States—Politics and government.
3. Mass media—United States—Influence.   I. Title.
TL521.312.B95   1994
353.0087′8—dc20   94–13727

British Library Cataloguing in Publication Data is available.

Library of Congress Catalog Card Number: 94–13727
ISBN: 0–275–94950–8

First published in 1994

Praeger Publishers, 88 Post Road West, Westport, CT 06881
An imprint of Greenwood Publishing Group, Inc.

Printed in the United States of America

The paper used in this book complies with the
Permanent Paper Standard issued by the National
Information Standards Organization (Z39.48–1984).

10 9 8 7 6 5 4 3 2 1

To my parents, Virginia W. Byrnes and John F. Byrnes

and my brothers, Jeff and Matt

Contents

Tables and Figures

Acknowledgments

I have been fortunate to receive abundant help and encouragement throughout the long process of writing this book. I owe special thanks to Donald F. Kettl for his invaluable advice at virtually every stage of the project. John R. Vile also provided beneficial recommendations and encouragement. Michael Nelson, Erwin C. Hargrove, Robert H. Birkby, and Daniel Cornfield read drafts of the manuscript and made helpful comments.

Many people facilitated my research for this book. I received a great deal of assistance from the staff of the Vanderbilt University library, particularly from the government documents section and the inter-library loan department, and from the Middle Tennessee State University library staff. Thanks also to the people at the NASA History Office in Washington, D.C., and to Al Tompkins of WSMV-TV in Nashville. I am especially grateful to Rhea Seddon and James Fletcher for meeting with me, and for their candor and graciousness in our interviews.

This book would not have been possible without generous support from Vanderbilt University, the Eisenhower Institute, and MTSU. I want to thank my brother, Matthew C. Byrnes, for his extensive counseling on computer matters, and my mother, Virginia W. Byrnes, for her moral support and editorial advice. Thanks to my friends and colleagues in the MTSU Department of Political Science for their support. Finally, thanks to James Dunton, Liz Leiba, and Frances Rudner at Praeger.

Introduction

On July 20, 1969, people around the world watched in awe as Neil Armstrong became the first human to walk on the moon. The event symbolized, as Armstrong laconically radioed to earth, a "giant leap for mankind." In fact, the achievement was so overwhelming that a few people refused to believe it actually occurred, claiming that it must have been a hoax staged on some studio back lot. A U.S. government agency—the National Aeronautics and Space Administration (NASA)—made that hard-to-believe feat happen.

The Apollo program, and the lunar landing it produced, brought NASA considerable glory. The American public was thrilled with the achievement, as were Congress and the media. President Richard Nixon went so far as to call the mission "the greatest week in the history of the world since the Creation."[1] NASA had attained, only eleven years after its birth, one of humankind's most impressive accomplishments. The agency seemed omnipotent.

Yet two decades after the triumphant moon landing, NASA's situation had changed radically. The agency was still suffering after-shocks from its worst disaster, the 1986 explosion of the space shuttle *Challenger*, when a new set of embarrassing troubles appeared. Despite a post-accident overhaul of the entire shuttle system, the program continued to be plagued by problems and delays. In addition, NASA discovered after the long-awaited launch of the Hubble Space Telescope that one of the telescope's mirrors had been manufactured incorrectly, seriously blurring its vision. NASA's numerous stumbles made it the butt of jokes.

NASA's technical problems aggravated the political difficulties it experienced throughout much of the post-Apollo period. In general, the public perception of NASA was much less positive than it had been during the 1960s. According to observers, NASA in its early years was seen as "the embodiment of Yankee ingenuity and derring-do, the pride of the U.S. and the envy of the world" and as "a superhuman agency."[2] That "can-do" image, which had helped politically empower NASA, was tarnished by the troubles in the shuttle program and by the agency's other problems.[3] The public's attitude toward NASA seemed to shift from the idea that the agency was invincible to the notion that it could not do anything quite right. In short, NASA underwent a precipitous fall from political grace.

This change in public perception has undoubtedly been painful for NASA. The agency has always been quite sensitive to its public image because it has relied heavily on public support in its quest for political backing.[4] NASA's programs have naturally engendered greater public interest than those of most government agencies,[5] giving NASA the opportunity to communicate to the public the message that the agency deserves support. A favorable public image helps NASA capitalize on that opportunity and therefore plays a vital part in the agency's efforts to win political support. The troubles that have beset NASA since the glory days of Apollo have made managing the agency's public image a definite challenge.

AGENCIES, THEIR IMAGES, AND POLITICAL SUPPORT

This brief look at NASA's history raises some interesting political questions: Has NASA changed over time the images it projects to the public to try to win political support? If so, how and why? In studying those issues, this book addresses a basic theoretical question: How and why do bureaucratic agencies change over time the images they project in trying to build political support?

Agencies must have political support to function; that simple fact underlies virtually all agency activity.[6] The fates of agency programs—and of the agencies themselves—are determined in the political arena, where political support is a prerequisite for success. Bureaucratic agencies need political support because it enables them to obtain the two resources all agencies must have: the authority to run programs and the money to pay for them.[7] Agencies seek political backing from numerous sources: Congress, the president, other bureaucratic agencies, interest groups, and the general public.[8]

One way agencies try to tap these sources of political support is by manipulating their public images. Scholars have frequently noted that agencies worry about their public images and how those images affect their political standing.[9] Images are vital because they influence the way other political actors perceive the agencies. Agencies therefore carefully construct and promulgate favorable public images of themselves.

Scholars have pointed out that differences in agencies and their political environments greatly affect the kinds of images they employ.[10] The question of how and why agencies change their images over time, however, has not been fully answered. Based on a case study of NASA, this book suggests that agencies carefully adjust their images in response to changes in their political environments.

The notion that agencies adapt to changes in their political environments falls within an established body of scholarly work. Researchers have indicated that agencies exist within a larger political environment that determines their fates.[11] If agencies are to survive and prosper, they must be able to adapt to changes in their political environment.[12] If agencies do not adapt, argue three scholars of the bureaucracy, they "will cease to exist for they will lose the support necessary for their continuance."[13]

NASA's Images

NASA has used three images—nationalism, romanticism, and pragmatism—to build political support over its history. Nationalism has appealed to Americans' patriotism and love of country. Nationalist statements have emphasized that the space program should be supported because it is good for America as a nation. In general, NASA has contended, space capability helps America protect its national interests. Specifically, such capability bolsters American national pride, national prestige, national strength (both military and economic), and peaceful international relations. Nationalism was NASA's primary image during the late 1950s and into the 1960s.

Romanticism has played to the emotional aspect of the human character. It has highlighted the excitement and adventure inherent in NASA's activities and described how space exploration fulfills some basic human yearnings. Romanticism has noted that space activity allows humans to continue to explore, requires the efforts of heroic people, provides a variety of emotional rewards, and helps satisfy human curiosity. NASA employed romanticism often during the middle to late 1960s.

Pragmatism has emphasized that the space program produces practical benefits for all citizens, thus appealing to individuals' material self-interest. This image has asserted that activity in space pays down-to-earth dividends. According to pragmatism, the space program stimulates technological advances, generates new products and techniques, delivers economic returns, enhances scientific knowledge, offers educational opportunities, and provides a space transportation system. NASA stressed pragmatism throughout the 1970s and well into the 1980s.

NASA has used all of its images to varying degrees throughout its existence, but it has clearly emphasized certain images at certain times. This book argues that NASA, seeking to maximize its political support, has altered its use of images as the agency's political environment has changed.

NOTES

1. Eugene M. Emme, "Presidents and Space," in *Between Sputnik and the Shuttle: New Perspectives on American Astronautics*, ed. Frederick C. Durant III (San Diego: American Astronautical Society, 1981), 101. In his memoirs, Nixon recalls that his friend Billy Graham later told him that the comment "may have been a little excessive." See Richard M. Nixon, *RN: The Memoirs of Richard Nixon* (New York: Grosset & Dunlap, 1978), 429-30.

2. Leon Jaroff, "Spinning Out of Orbit," *Time*, 6 August 1990, 26; Thomas R. McDonough, *Space: The Next 25 Years* (New York: John Wiley & Sons, 1987), 38.

3. See James A. Skardon, "The Apollo Story: What the Watchdogs Missed," *Columbia Journalism Review* 6 (Fall 1967): 12; Alex Roland, "The Shuttle: Triumph or Turkey?" *Discover*, November 1985, 38-41; Philip M. Boffey, "Space Agency Image: A Sudden Shattering," *New York Times*, 5 February 1986, A1; Tom Wicker, "Icons and O Rings," *New York Times*, 18 February 1986, 31.

4. David Howard Davis, *How the Bureaucracy Makes Foreign Policy: An Exchange Analysis* (Lexington, Mass.: Lexington Books, 1972), 41; National Commission on Space, *Pioneering the Space Frontier* (Toronto: Bantam Books, 1986), 169; Astronaut Rhea Seddon, interview by author, Murfreesboro, Tennessee, 23 November 1989; Dr. James C. Fletcher, interview by author, Washington, D.C., 5 October 1990.

5. Jon D. Miller, "Is There Public Support for Space Exploration?" *Environment*, June 1984, 26-29; National Academy of Public Administration, *Effectiveness of NASA Headquarters* (Washington, D.C.: NAPA, 1988), 3; Davis, *How the Bureaucracy Makes Foreign Policy*, 41; Seddon interview.

6. See, for example, Francis E. Rourke, *Bureaucracy, Politics, and Public Policy*, 3d edn. (Boston: Little, Brown & Co., 1984), 48, 116; David B. Truman, *The Governmental Process: Political Interests and Public Opinion* (New York: Alfred A. Knopf, 1971), 467; Paul R. Schulman, *Large-Scale Policy Making* (New York: Elsevier, 1980), 17; and Harold W. Stoke, "Executive Leadership and the Growth of Propaganda," *American Political Science Review* 35 (June 1941): 493.

7. Herbert A. Simon, Donald W. Smithburg, and Victor A. Thompson, *Public Administration* (New York: Alfred A. Knopf, 1950), 401; Rourke, *Bureaucracy, Politics, and Public Policy*, 66, 117.

8. See Simon et al., *Public Administration*, 402-22; Rourke, *Bureaucracy, Politics, and Public Policy*, 48-87.

9. See Francis E. Rourke, *Secrecy and Publicity: Dilemmas of Democracy* (Baltimore: Johns Hopkins University Press, 1961); Rourke, *Bureaucracy, Politics, and Public Policy*, 50-53; Anthony Downs, *Inside Bureaucracy* (Boston: Little, Brown & Co., 1967), 237-46; Steven Thomas Seitz, *Bureaucracy, Policy, and the Public* (St. Louis: C. V. Mosby Co., 1978), 90; George J. Gordon, *Public Administration in America*, 3d edn. (New York: St. Martin's Press, 1986), 70; Dean L. Yarwood and Ben J. Enis, "Advertising and Publicity Programs in the Executive Branch of the National Government: Hustling or Helping the People?" *Public Administration Review* 42 (January/February 1982): 37-46; Louis C. Gawthorp, *Bureaucratic Behavior in the Executive Branch: An Analysis of Organizational Change* (New York: Free Press, 1969), 179-80; Murray J. Edelman, *Politics as Symbolic Action: Mass Arousal and Quiescence* (New York: Academic Press, 1971), 7; Frank M. Sorrentino, *Ideological Warfare: The FBI's Path Toward Power* (Port Washington, N.Y.: Associated Faculty

Press, 1985), 16-26; and W. Henry Lambright, *Governing Science and Technology* (New York: Oxford University Press, 1976), 52-53.

10. Downs, *Inside Bureaucracy*, 237-46; Rourke, *Bureaucracy, Politics, and Public Policy*, 50-52.

11. See Charles Perrow, *Complex Organizations: A Critical Essay*, 3d edn. (New York: Random House, 1986); Daniel Katz and Robert L. Kahn, *The Social Psychology of Organizations*, 2d edn. (New York: John Wiley & Sons, 1978); James D. Thompson, *Organizations in Action* (New York: McGraw-Hill, 1967); Rourke, *Bureaucracy, Politics, and Public Policy*; Peter M. Blau and Marshall W. Meyer, *Bureaucracy in Modern Society*, 3d edn. (New York: Random House, 1987); Philip Selznick, *TVA and the Grass Roots: A Study in the Sociology of Formal Organization* (New York: Harper Torchbooks, 1966); Chester I. Barnard, *The Functions of the Executive* (Cambridge: Harvard University Press, 1940); and Kenneth J. Meier, *Politics and the Bureaucracy: Policymaking in the Fourth Branch of Government*, 2d edn. (Monterey, Calif.: Brooks/Cole Publishing Co., 1987).

12. See, for example, Gawthorp, *Bureaucratic Behavior*; Truman, *Governmental Process*; Herbert Kaufman, *The Administrative Behavior of Federal Bureau Chiefs*, (Washington, D.C.: Brookings Institution, 1981); Sorrentino, *Ideological Warfare*; Seitz, *Bureaucracy, Policy, and the Public*; Frederic A. Bergerson, *The Army Gets an Air Force: Tactics of Insurgent Bureaucratic Politics* (Baltimore: Johns Hopkins University Press, 1980); Richard J. Stillman, *The American Bureaucracy* (Chicago: Nelson-Hall, 1987); and Harold F. Gortner, Julianne Mahler, and Jeanne Bell Nicholson, *Organization Theory: A Public Perspective* (Chicago: Dorsey Press, 1987).

13. Simon et al., *Public Administration*, 389.

1

Nationalism

Testifying before Congress in 1960, NASA's Wernher von Braun compared the space efforts of America and the Soviet Union and then issued this ominous warning: "I fear it is later than we think, and our position in the world is gravely endangered."[1] Von Braun contended that the Soviet Union's lead in space threatened American national security, and he urged Congress to respond to that threat by strongly backing NASA and the American space program. Such a response, von Braun maintained, would contribute greatly to America's well-being.

Von Braun's argument exemplifies nationalism, an image based on the idea that the space program benefits America as a nation. Nationalism has sought to gain political support for NASA by explaining how the space program helps America and by stressing the importance of those national benefits. The image has thus appealed primarily to Americans' love of their country.

In its most general form, nationalism has emphasized that America must be active in space in order to protect its national interest, however defined. NASA has named the space program's broadest and most important objective as "the establishment and maintenance of a strong national capability to operate in space and to use space fully in the national interest."[2] Such a capability would give the nation "freedom of choice to carry out whatever missions the national interest may require—be they for national prestige, military requirements, scientific knowledge, or other purposes."[3] Proficiency in space would also "prevent any other power from denying us the utilization of space in our interests."[4]

NASA has used nationalism to varying degrees throughout its history, but never more prominently than during its early years of existence. The agency's efforts to gain political support for its major program of 1958-63, Project Mercury, and for space exploration in general relied heavily on nationalism. NASA's political environment in the late 1950s and early 1960s made nationalism the appropriate image.

MAJOR THEMES IN NATIONALISM

Nationalism has highlighted the space program's role in pursuing four specific goals: national pride, national prestige, national strength, and international peace and cooperation. NASA's explanations of its contributions to attaining each of these vital aims constitute four subsidiary themes within nationalism. The agency has stressed different themes at different times.

National Pride

Space exploration can engender great national pride in the citizens of the exploring nation, NASA has asserted. Due to the difficulty and the highly public nature of the endeavor, America stands to enhance its national pride through its program of space exploration. Success in space results in a feeling of accomplishment and heightened national vitality. Conversely, failures in space can tarnish the nation's pride. A 1969 NASA brochure maintained that "the morale of the United States rose and fell" with the fortunes of its space program.[5]

The space program has tended to evoke national pride because it is a highly visible, publicly funded, and pioneering national effort. Americans, a proud and patriotic people, would probably look with pride on such an endeavor even if NASA did nothing to encourage them to do so. Of course, through words and symbols, NASA has tried to tie its activities to national pride. NASA has contended that national pride is good for America, and that increased national pride is an intangible benefit of the space program.[6]

One way has NASA promoted the connection between national pride and the space program is by using the American flag. The ultimate use of this cherished national symbol came in 1969 when Apollo 11 astronauts planted the American flag on the surface of the moon, yet NASA has always extensively employed the flag. Flags have adorned the space vehicles, the astronauts' spacesuits, and myriad other items. The agency has also prominently displayed the letters "USA" and "NASA" in close proximity to the flag, intensifying the connection.

NASA has also encouraged pride in the space program by giving some of its spacecraft names that foster feelings of patriotism. Alan Shepard's Mercury capsule was called *Freedom 7*, while Gus Grissom's was known as *Liberty Bell 7*. The names of several Apollo craft carried patriotic connotations, including *Columbia*, *Eagle*, and *America*.[7] In addition, NASA named the proposed space station *Freedom*.

Since the space program is linked with national pride, the results of the program can carry considerable emotional punch to the public. As a 1988 NASA brochure said, the nation's success in space "affects the confidence with which Americans face the future."[8] A notable example of this phenomenon was the upswell of pride after NASA landed men on the moon in 1969. Another instance occurred twenty years later, when nearly half a million people went to California's Edwards Air Force Base to witness the landing of the shuttle *Discovery*, one of the first shuttle flights after the *Challenger* tragedy. As *Discovery* landed, the crowd applauded and spontaneously sang the national anthem. As one member of the crowd remarked, "The patriotic spirit here is really something. I even bought a new flag for this."[9] In both cases, the increased national pride helps explain the rise in public support for NASA and its programs that occurred at the time of those events.[10]

While Americans have taken great pride in the nation's space achievements, they have also bemoaned its failures. The *Challenger* explosion was a definite blow to America's national pride. Administrator James Fletcher promised that the agency would work diligently to overcome the failure and to "make America proud again."[11] He explained, "The American people deserve and expect no less."[12] After NASA successfully resumed shuttle operations with the flight of *Discovery* in September 1988, Fletcher declared that the event "made many people glad to be Americans."[13] Fletcher's comments underscored the notion that successful space ventures do engender national pride.

A passage from one 1988 NASA publication epitomizes the theme of national pride:

The space program of the United States is extraordinary. Technologically superb, intellectually rewarding, rich in heritage, witness to tragedy yet filled with triumph, the space program is a reflection of our country at its best. It is a success story of which we can all be proud.[14]

Tying the space program to feelings of national pride and patriotism has been a powerful type of nationalistic appeal.

National Prestige

NASA has frequently argued that the space program influences American prestige around the globe.[15] A "national space capability will help to maintain our standing in the eyes of the world," according to a representative statement.[16] Conversely, NASA has asserted, a nonexistent or sluggish space effort indicates weakness and tarnishes the national reputation. Prestige is important because it helps shape other nations' opinions of the United States, and those opinions affect America's ability to attain its international goals. Because NASA and the space program influence America's success abroad, according to this argument, it is vital to keep the nation's prestige high through determined efforts in space.

NASA has argued that space exploration demonstrates leadership in science and technology, which generates an especially potent type of national prestige because it reflects military and economic might. An agency official explained to Congress in 1967, "In the real terms of today's world it is that kind of leadership that is important in causing other peoples of the world, other nations of the world, to assess our real strength."[17] The message is that nations with the ability to conquer space also possess the kind of national strength that commands respect on earth. As Administrator James Beggs remarked in 1984, NASA programs are "a vivid demonstration of America's power."[18]

Yet the manner in which a nation conducts its space program also affects its prestige, NASA has contended. A 1970 agency brochure expressed it this way:

Americans who have recently traveled abroad can appreciate the impact our space program makes on other nations around the world. People in all parts of the world are impressed by ambitious objectives stated openly in advance, by missions conducted openly, and by results that are made available to all.[19]

By operating its space program in the open, NASA said, the United States gains admiration as well as respect.

National Strength

Throughout its history, NASA has stressed that leadership in space exploration is a vital component of national strength. This has probably been the most frequently used type of nationalist appeal. The agency has emphasized that, by striving to achieve space leadership, it makes a great contribution to American national strength. As NASA's director of manned space flight once said, the agency's manned space programs "are designed to achieve and maintain U.S. space leadership."[20]

Maintaining leadership in space is no easy task because, as the agency has noted, "The competition for leadership in space is keen."[21] Many other nations pursue space programs. A 1988 NASA publication remarked: "The United States is not alone in its attempts to tame space. Many nations see a bright future in exploring and exploiting the space frontier for world prominence, national strength, and commercial profit."[22] In addition to the long-standing Russian program, the Japanese, Europeans, and Chinese have all become active in space.[23]

NASA has continually assessed the nation's status in space. Those assessments have changed, of course, over the space program's history. NASA issued numerous dire pronouncements on America's relative position in the late 1950s and early 1960s. By 1964, however, the agency's tone had brightened. James Webb told Congress in that year, "NASA has made substantial progress toward insuring enduring preeminence in space for the United States."[24] The many American space successes later in the decade seemed to confirm NASA's optimistic assessment.

In the 1970s and 1980s, NASA's estimates of American space leadership were inconsistent. Many statements of the time spoke of America maintaining its lead in space exploration, clearly implying that the United States did indeed hold the lead.[25] Yet other comments in the same period warned that the nation was in imminent danger of losing its advantage. NASA reported to Congress in 1971 that there was "every indication" the United States would lose its leadership in space.[26] In 1987 an agency publication cautioned, "Today, United States leadership in space is being challenged."[27] That same year, James Fletcher said that the United States "may have lost the competitive edge" in manned space flight to the Soviet Union.[28] A 1988 NASA brochure remarked, "U.S. leadership among spacefaring nations has eroded."[29]

Two factors help explain this inconsistency. First, regardless of other nations' space activities, NASA has been most optimistic when things are going well for the American program. Second, and more important, NASA has often used the specter of the United States trailing in space to lobby for increased support. Fletcher gave an excellent example of this in defending the increases in NASA's proposed fiscal year 1989 budget: "Failure to provide the funds required in fiscal year 1989 . . . will cut the space program off at the knees and effectively keep the United States from achieving leadership in space."[30] Fletcher also told Congress that inadequate funding would mean that "the goal of long-term U.S. leadership in space will become an idle dream."[31]

Yet NASA has also expressed confidence about America's ability to lead in space, contending that the nation has the skill needed to excel in space. According to a 1987 NASA publication, "No nation can match our experience in space or our technical capabilities."[32] An agency brochure published a year later said, "Today, the United States is uniquely capable of leading the exploration and development of space."[33]

If the United States has the capability to lead in space, what else is needed? NASA's answer has been that the nation must make the effort necessary to lead. That message has recurred throughout NASA's nationalist appeals. In 1964, NASA Deputy Administrator Hugh Dryden declared to Congress, "We must not delude ourselves or the Nation with any thought that leadership in this fast-moving age can be maintained with anything less than determined, wholehearted, sustained effort."[34]

Similarly, James Fletcher told Congress in 1977 that developing "the full potentials of space in the face of determined competition abroad is calling for our very best national efforts."[35] In 1988, a NASA publication describing the recovery from the *Challenger* disaster also broached the subject:

We must decide if the twenty-first century will see the United States as the preeminent spacefaring nation or simply one of several nations in space. We have the capability to be what we want to be. We can lead as we have done in the past, or we can simply remain a principal player. The choice is ours.[36]

NASA has made clear its eagerness to do all it can to ensure American leadership in space. In 1964 the agency said, "The ultimate objective of the manned space flight program is to provide the capability for a broad program of exploration which will achieve and maintain a position of space leadership for the United States."[37] The next year James Webb vowed that NASA was dedicated "to achieving and maintaining supremacy in all areas of space."[38] By 1983, the agency was bragging about its success: "There can be no doubt that NASA's quarter century of effort has preserved the nation's leadership role and strengthened its posture" in space.[39]

How does leadership in space contribute to American national strength? One way, discussed above, is by enhancing American national prestige and shaping foreign perceptions of American strength. In addition, NASA has argued, the nation's ability to operate in space affects two other crucial determinants of national strength: national security and economic vitality.

National Security. In the Mercury era, NASA repeatedly emphasized the importance of space expertise to national security. That idea lived on in NASA's post-Mercury statements. In 1965 James Webb spoke of the "inextricable linkage" between progress in space and national security.[40] A 1968 NASA statement to Congress maintained that the United States needs "skill in the mastery of space for national protection" from the variety of potential threats that would arise if another nation were dominant.[41]

James Fletcher testified to Congress in 1971:

Every major advance in technology—in ships, land transport, and aircraft—has had a significant and often decisive impact on relations between Nations. We cannot ignore the real likelihood that this will also be true in space.[42]

Indeed, NASA has contended that the national security benefits alone justify NASA's budget. Webb said in 1968, "In my view our national security gains more than this program costs."[43]

Having space capability boosts national security, NASA has asserted, even though it may not be possible to specify in advance how such capability will be employed. The military potential of space demands that America be active there. Yet NASA has been careful to emphasize that it is a civilian agency, and that its military role, while important, is mainly indirect. According to the agency, its major military contribution stems from the basic scientific and technological research it conducts in space. James Webb explained in 1965:

The future of man in space cannot yet be distinguished from his possible military value there. Even purely scientific inquiries into the nature of the spatial environment may be necessary for the employment of military systems in space. So, while seeking to maximize the peaceful uses of outer space, we have no choice but to acquire a known and understood capability in space in our own most fundamental interest.[44]

Thus the space program "contributes very largely to our national military capability" by performing the basic scientific and technical development work that must precede military applications.[45]

NASA has occasionally remarked on the direct role it plays in national security. The agency sold the space shuttle in the early 1970s partly on its potential military use, particularly the deployment and maintenance of surveillance satellites. In 1986, James Fletcher said one purpose of the space program was to "help the military when necessary."[46]

Pointing to the Soviet Union's impressive space ability and the concomitant threat to the United States has been a prominent part of NASA's focus on national security. This was especially true during the first few years of NASA's existence, when the agency asserted that the Soviets planned to use their space expertise in their quest to dominate the world. Yet even after the Cold War fizzled, NASA sometimes conjured up a disturbing image of the heavens controlled by the Russians.

NASA often stressed the Soviet Union's dedication to its space program. James Webb gave a typical statement in 1966: "It should now be entirely clear that the Soviets have a continuing major commitment to a long-term, large-scale program in space."[47] He and other NASA officials repeatedly made this observation up to the final days of the Soviet Union.[48] Those statements frequently contended that, compared with the United States, the Soviet Union devoted a proportionally greater share of its resources to space exploration.[49]

The Soviet Union's dedication to its space program required an equal level of commitment from the United States, NASA argued. America must at least match the Soviets' efforts, James Webb said in 1966, "to keep them from forging ahead as the unchallenged leader" in space.[50] Even after the triumphant Apollo 11 flight, NASA's Wernher von Braun cautioned that the United States had to maintain its exertions: "If we start resting on our laurels, and wait, and don't start new programs, we may be bracing ourselves for another surprise of the Sputnik category [a] few years hence."[51]

Many of NASA's announcements warned that the Soviets either held the lead in space or would achieve the lead shortly. James Webb announced in 1964, "We are still behind in manned space flight."[52] That same year Webb told Congress an anecdote featuring prominent scientist Edward Teller. When asked what he thought what Americans would find on their first moon landing, Teller supposedly replied, "Russians."[53] Webb did not want to see that prediction come true. Even in 1968, when the Apollo program was well under way, he was still warning that the Soviets were building a superior space capability.[54]

By 1971, NASA admitted that the United States probably was leading the Soviets, but nevertheless worried that "today there is every indication that we will lose this leadership; and once we do, we may not again have the capacity to catch up."[55] NASA has regularly issued similar warnings.[56] In the 1980s,

the agency sought support for its proposed space station by noting that the Soviets had two manned space stations in orbit.[57]

Economic Vitality. NASA has also emphasized that space activity exerts
great influence on the national economy. Space, according to the agency, is an
important economic venue. The United States must continue to explore the
economic aspects of space because its competitors certainly are going to do so.
A 1988 NASA publication said:

Today, space represents a new competitive territory for commercial opportunity and
economic expansion. Other nations—Japan, France, Germany, and the Soviet Union
among them—also recognize the alluring commercial potential of space. They are
strongly challenging the United States for leadership in the industrial application of
space science and technology.[58]

As another agency publication phrased it, "Space is a place of profit and of
competition."[59]

How does the space program influence the nation's economic competitiveness? NASA has asserted that the key is its programs' effect on scientific and
technological progress. The agency has pointed out that the requirements of an
active space program force scientific and technological advances.[60] These advances, in turn, contribute to America's economic productivity. Therefore,
since "economic prosperity in a competitive world depends upon productivity,"
NASA contends that its programs exercise a positive influence on America's
competitive position.[61] Spending on NASA not only produces direct benefits
from its programs, but also bolsters the nation's overall economic strength.
Administrator James Beggs stated in 1984, "NASA alone cannot assure our
competitiveness, but the agency's programs can be—and I believe must be—
an element in our nation's investment strategy."[62]

This emphasis on the economic impact of science and technology has been
a common NASA theme. Administrator James Fletcher said in 1977, "The
importance of our retaining leadership in science and technology cannot be
overemphasized, for science and technology represent the cornerstone of our
economic well-being."[63] Fletcher made a similar point during his second tenure as administrator. He told Congress in 1988 that if the United States fails to
"pursue aggressively science and advanced technologies, we will not have the
technical foundation we need for future achievements."[64]

NASA has noted other ways that the space program pays national economic dividends. A nation active in space enjoys the opportunity to compete in
the often lucrative worldwide markets of space-related services. These markets
include satellite launching and servicing, materials processing, remote observations of the earth, and transportation of payloads into space.[65] Much of the
activity in these markets comes in the form of exports, which help improve
America's balance of trade.[66] In addition, the new or improved products and
services that result from the space program[67] also have a propitious effect on

the overall economy.[68] Finally, the space program is said to act as a dramatic "symbol of American competitiveness in the world."[69]

NASA has stressed that it works hard to cooperate with American industry in bringing about these economic benefits for the nation. The agency vowed that it was "forging a working partnership with the U.S. private sector" to pursue those gains.[70] A 1988 agency publication promised, "NASA's cooperative efforts with U.S. industry offer hope for new economic strength from America's space enterprise."[71]

International Peace and Cooperation

A final theme, usually employed under political conditions that differ from the preceding ones, has described how space exploration can foster international peace and cooperation. Nations can and should peacefully cooperate with one another in space exploration, NASA has contended, because such cooperation eases tensions among nations.[72] The agency asserted that its own efforts to cooperate in space "have served the cause of international understanding and, ultimately, of peace."[73]

It seems somewhat contradictory that NASA would use this theme, which stresses the pacific aspect of space, as well as the preceding ones, which emphasize space's competitive side. There are several explanations for this inconsistency. First, because the prevailing political situation has influenced which approach NASA accentuates, some contradiction is to be expected due to fluctuations in international affairs. Second, some people have argued that peace is best preserved by preparing for war—in this case, ensuring that no one side has an overwhelming superiority in space. Thus, perhaps the contradiction is not as strong as it may appear. Third, even if the United States were competing with a particular country, it could still simultaneously cooperate with other nations and boost world harmony in that way. Finally, speaking of world peace and cooperation sounds good even when taking action toward that goal is not feasible.

In 1964, James Webb noted the potential for working together: "Space is one of the few areas in which it has been possible for the East and West to find areas of common interest which can be cooperatively developed."[74] A 1975 NASA publication also described the healthy effects of international space cooperation: "The mutual confidence and trust developed in joint space ventures may be significant not just for what peoples working together may accomplish in orbit but also from what peoples working together may achieve on Earth."[75] Joint space endeavors encourage nations to concentrate more on peaceful earthly pursuits. In the words of NASA Administrator James Beggs, they "redirect creative human brains from the prospects of dealing with armed conflict to the prospects of planning and carrying out a peaceful, stimulating, and ultimately more valuable" program.[76]

NASA has argued that teamwork in space can help patch up differences between friends, such as the coolness between the United States and France during the 1950s and 1960s, as well as reduce hostility between competitors, such as the United States and the Soviet Union.[77] Cooperation in space will not solve all the world's problems, NASA admitted, but it can help. As James Webb remarked, "The potential of these beginnings, as the first step toward further cooperation in other fields, is not to be overlooked."[78] NASA has always made it clear that it works hard to promote international cooperation in space and that any limits to such cooperation come from other nations.[79]

In addition to reducing international tensions, NASA commented, space cooperation can also lower space costs for the participating nations.[80] For instance, participation in the space shuttle program by Canada and some European nations reduced America's fiscal burden. Moreover, cooperation brings the best minds from all over the world to work on the challenging problems inherent in space exploration.[81] As a result, NASA said, "International cooperation in space has produced scientific achievements of consequence."[82]

Developing nations especially stand to gain from working with the United States, according to NASA. Cooperation enables those countries to be active in space, something they could not afford on their own.[83] Such programs provide for "the extension of very real benefits to the developing countries," said James Webb in 1965.[84] That is in keeping, remarked one of Webb's successors, with the long-standing NASA ideal that "the fruits of civil space research are to be shared with all mankind."[85]

Another way that space exploration promotes peace on earth, NASA has claimed, is by giving people confidence that difficult problems can be solved. The moon landing, for example, provided such a psychological boost. "Having attained what had seemed impossible," a NASA brochure stated, "men became instilled with a belief that other apparently unyielding problems could also be overcome through similarly single-minded, dedicated effort."[86] According to this argument, humans can use this pride and confidence to tackle such life-threatening problems as war, poverty, pollution, and overpopulation.[87]

NASA has professed that human activity in space contributes to world harmony by drawing the people on earth closer together. Not only do the people on earth identify with the men and women exploring space, they come to realize that we all share the same fragile planet. A 1988 NASA publication summarized the spirit: "We are all human beings. Our lives are intertwined. Our future is one. . . . Space exploration expresses a profound sense of brotherhood."[88] NASA quoted poet Archibald MacLeish's comment that photographs of our planet taken from space vividly show that we are all "riders on the Earth together."[89]

In general, NASA has argued that space exploration has the potential to improve relations among people on earth. In 1984, NASA Administrator James Beggs presented his sanguine vision of the future:

Continued exploration and development of space holds the promise of a new era of progress, peace and prosperity for all mankind. I believe that promise is unlimited. If we can preserve the peace and build on the existing foundation of international understanding and cooperation on earth and in space, we will have the opportunity to build an enduring world order—a golden age such as history has never known.[90]

Peaceful cooperation in space, a major tenet of NASA's image of nationalism, is at the heart of that beguiling vision.

STYLES OF NATIONALIST APPEALS

NASA has frequently used two kinds of stylistic techniques—historical analogies and sports metaphors—in making nationalist appeals.

Historical Analogies

NASA officials have often drawn historical analogies to explain the importance of the space program. For example, in 1964 Hugh Dryden told Congress that America needlessly imperils itself by not vigorously pursuing its technological breakthroughs. He noted that in the early 1900s Americans built and flew the first airplanes but so neglected further development that no planes designed and built by Americans took part in World War I. Similarly, despite American Robert Goddard's discoveries in rocketry, the United States did little to develop missiles in the 1940s and 1950s, allowing the Soviets to beat America into space. Dryden wondered whether the United States would repeat the mistake in the field of space exploration. He said, "The decisions which confront us today are those which will determine whether this kind of history will repeat itself a few years hence."[91]

In 1979, NASA Administrator Robert Frosch made the same basic point even more starkly. Musing about the historical lessons of space, he asked:

Where else in the twentieth-century history of our nation is more clearly encapsulated our dangerous national trait of international roulette—of a deep-seated complacency that can be penetrated only by extreme challenge: World War I and the too-late founding of NACA [NASA's predecessor]; World War II and the belated threefold expansion of NACA; the Cold War and scrambling from behind to NASA and Apollo?[92]

Frosch contended that a steady space program was a far safer and more rational approach.

A similar kind of analogy was made in a 1968 NASA statement. The agency argued that nations become dominant because of technological feats:

Two millenia ago Rome was preeminent because, in considerable degree, of its road network. A half millenium ago England grew almost overnight from a small island kingdom to a world power because of its new skills at ocean navigation. . . . In our own time, spanning the few decades from Kitty Hawk to the supersonic transport, there has been this same close association between demonstrated competence in flight technology and primacy among nations. . . . A similar association will prove equally true in space.[93]

The lesson was clearly that America had to persevere in space if it wanted to be a world power.

Sports Metaphors

NASA has frequently employed sports metaphors in describing space exploration, particularly its competitive aspects. The metaphors were especially prominent in the late 1950s and early 1960s. Americans are generally competitive people as well as avid sports fans, and are therefore likely to use and respond to sports images. Talk of American politics is replete with sports metaphors: political races, front-runners, dark horse candidates, and so on.

The notion of competition in space and concern with who is leading in that competition is a fundamental kind of sports metaphor, and such references have abounded in NASA statements. For example, an agency official said in 1966, "The competition for leadership in space is keen."[94] Administrator Fletcher warned in 1987 that the country was losing its "competitive edge."[95] In 1989, another NASA leader declared that the United States would have to fight to achieve competitiveness.[96]

Where does this competition take place? In the "arena" of space, according to several NASA statements.[97] Not everyone can enter this arena; because of the expense and complexity of space exploration, this competition "is a game that only big nations can play."[98] In 1966, James Webb warned that the Soviet Union might "forge ahead as the unchallenged contestant in the field" if the United States were not careful.[99]

NASA's assessments of the American-Soviet rivalry drew extensively on the language of sports. In 1960, Administrator T. Keith Glennan compared "the score" in the number of launches made by the two nations.[100] He also contended that the Soviets' main goal in space was to "beat America."[101] NASA's George Low said that same year that failure to proceed with the Mercury program would "keep us in second place."[102] In 1961, Wernher von Braun remarked that Alan Shepard's Mercury flight put the United States "back in the solar ball park. We may not be leading the league, but at least we are out of the cellar."[103] In 1971, Fletcher warned that continued cuts in NASA's budget would force the America to play catch-up, just as it had to do after Sputnik.[104]

A frequently used sports metaphor was the "space race." Keith Glennan commented in 1959, "I never envisioned my assignment as one where I would always be driving the second place entry in this race."[105] NASA's director of manned space flight downplayed the early Soviet lead in space by noting that "being ahead in the first lap in a race is not necessarily the key to winning the overall race."[106] Although NASA officials did periodically use this metaphor, they sometimes said it was not entirely accurate. A race has a single starting line, parallel tracks, and a common objective, NASA pointed out, and that was not necessarily true of the competition in space. Glennan suggested an alternate sports metaphor for the competition between the Americans and the Soviets: a "tug of war."[107]

CONCLUSION

Nationalism has emphasized that the space program benefits America as a nation. It does so, NASA has argued, by bolstering national pride, enhancing national prestige, increasing national strength, and promoting international peace and cooperation. In general, the agency has contended, an active space program serves the national interest.

Although NASA has employed nationalism throughout its history, it used the image most heavily in the late 1950s and early 1960s. Stiff competition from the Soviet Union in those years largely drove America's space effort, making nationalism a natural image for NASA and its major program—Project Mercury.

NOTES

1. Congress, Senate, Committee on Aeronautical and Space Sciences, Subcommittee on NASA Authorization, *NASA Authorization for Fiscal Year 1961*, Part 1, 86th Cong., 2d sess., 29 March 1960, 241.

2. Congress, Senate, Committee on Aeronautical and Space Sciences, *NASA Authorization for Fiscal Year 1968*, 90th Cong., 1st sess., 19 April 1967, 436.

3. Congress, House, Committee on Science and Astronautics, Subcommittee on Manned Space Flight, *1965 NASA Authorization*, Part 2, 88th Cong., 2d sess., 18 February 1964, 364.

4. NASA, *America's Next Decades in Space* (Washington, D.C.: GPO, 1969), 72.

5. NASA, *Man in Space*, by David A. Anderton, EP-57 (Washington, D.C.: GPO, 1969), 25.

6. NASA, *Questions About Aeronautics and Space* (Washington, D.C.: GPO, 1976), 6.

7. Helen T. Wells, Susan H. Whiteley, and Carrie E. Karegeannes, *Origins of NASA Names*, SP-4402 (Washington, D.C.: GPO, 1976), 100, 107-108.

8. NASA, *Space Shuttle: The Journey Continues*, by Richard Truly, NP-117 (Washington, D.C.: GPO, 1988), 3.

9. "Fans Stream into Shuttle Landing Area," *Murfreesboro (Tenn.) Daily News Journal*, 19 March 1989, 10A.

10. Louis Harris, "Public, in Reversal, Now Backs Landing on Moon, 51 to 41 Pct.," *Washington Post*, 14 July 1969; Congress, Office of Technology Assessment, *Civilian Space Policy and Applications* (Washington, D.C.: GPO, 1982), 142; Jon D. Miller, "Is There Public Support for Space Exploration?" *Environment* 26 (June 1984): 26; National Commission on Space, *Pioneering the Space Frontier* (Toronto: Bantam Books, 1986), 178-79.

11. Robert C. Cowen, "Tough Choices Ahead for NASA," *Technology Review* 89 (August/September 1986): 21.

12. Congress, Senate, Committee on Appropriations, Subcommittee on HUD— Independent Agencies, *Department of Housing and Urban Development—Independent Agencies Appropriations for Fiscal Year 1988*, 100th Cong., 1st sess., 9 April 1987, 1035.

13. Mdu Lembede, "Fletcher Says NASA Gains Support," *Washington Post*, 19 October 1988, A21.

14. NASA, *The Journey Continues*, NP-117, 24.

15. For example, Senate Committee on Aeronautical and Space Sciences, 19 April 1967 hearing, 437; NASA, *Man in Space*, EP-57, i; Congress, House, Committee on Science and Technology, Subcommittee on Space Science and Applications, *1978 NASA Authorization*, Part 2, 95th Cong., 1st sess., 9 February 1977; and Congress, Senate, Committee on Appropriations, Subcommittee on HUD—Independent Agencies, *Department of Housing and Urban Development—Independent Agencies Appropriations for Fiscal Year 1987*, 99th Cong., 2d sess., 16 September 1986, 986.

16. NASA, *America's Next Decades*, 73.

17. Senate Committee on Aeronautical and Space Sciences, 19 April 1967 hearing, 134.

18. NASA, *Space Station: The Next Logical Step*, by James M. Beggs (Washington, D.C.: GPO, 1984), 1.

19. NASA, *Space Station: Key to the Future*, EP-75 (Washington, D.C.: GPO, 1970), 40.

20. Congress, House, Committee on Science and Astronautics, Subcommittee on Manned Space Flight, *1964 NASA Authorization*, 88th Cong., 1st sess., 6 March 1963, 128.

21. Congress, Senate, Committee on Aeronautical and Space Sciences, *NASA Authorization for Fiscal Year 1967*, 89th Cong., 2d sess., 1 March 1966, 106.

22. NASA, *Space Station Freedom: A Foothold on the Future*, by Leonard David, NP-107 (Washington, D.C.: GPO, 1988), 2.

23. NASA, *The Journey Continues*, NP-117, 3; NASA, *Foothold on the Future*, NP-107, 2, 15.

24. Congress, House, Committee on Appropriations, Subcommittee on Independent Offices, *Independent Offices Appropriations for 1965*, Part 2, 88th Cong., 2d sess., 7 April 1964, 934.

25. For example, see Congress, House, Committee on Science, Space, and Technology, Subcommittee on Space Science and Applications, *1988 NASA Authorization*, 100th Cong., 1st sess., 14 February 1987, 15; Congress, House, Committee on Appropriations, Subcommittee on HUD—Independent Agencies, *Department of Housing and Urban Development—Independent Agencies Appropriations for 1986*, Part 6, 99th

Cong., 1st sess., 2 April 1985, 8; Congress, Senate, Committee on Appropriations, Subcommittee on HUD—Independent Agencies, *Department of Housing and Urban Development—Independent Agencies Appropriations for Fiscal Year 1987*, 99th Cong., 2d sess., 15 May 1986, 921; and Congress, House, Committee on Appropriations, Subcommittee on HUD—Independent Agencies, *Department of Housing and Urban Development—Independent Agencies Appropriations for 1989*, Part 7, 100th Cong., 2d sess., 19 April 1988, 17.

26. Congress, Senate, Committee on Aeronautical and Space Sciences, *NASA Authorization for Fiscal Year 1972*, 92d Cong., 1st sess., 30 March 1971, 15.

27. NASA, *Space Station: Leadership for the Future*, by Franklin D. Martin and Terence T. Finn, PAM-509 (Washington, D.C.: GPO, 1987), 8.

28. Congress, Senate, Committee on Commerce, Science, and Transportation, Subcommittee on Science, Technology, and Space, *NASA Authorization*, 100th Cong., 1st sess., 3 February 1987, 26.

29. NASA, *The Journey Continues*, NP-117, 3.

30. House Committee on Appropriations, 19 April 1988 hearing, 6.

31. Congress, Senate, Committee on Commerce, Science, and Transportation, Subcommittee on Science, Technology, and Space, *NASA Authorization*, 100th Cong., 2d sess., 22 March 1988, 204.

32. NASA, *Leadership for the Future*, PAM-509, 8.

33. NASA, *Discovering Space for America's Economic Growth* (Washington, D.C.: GPO, 1988), 5.

34. Congress, House, Committee on Science and Astronautics, Subcommittee on Manned Space Flight, *1965 NASA Authorization*, Part 1, 88th Cong., 2d sess., 4 February 1964, 18.

35. Congress, House, Committee on Appropriations, Subcommittee on HUD—Independent Agencies, *Department of Housing and Urban Development—Independent Agencies Appropriations for 1978*, Part 5, 95th Cong., 1st sess., 29 March 1977, 12.

36. NASA, *The Journey Continues*, NP-117, 24.

37. House Committee on Appropriations, 7 April 1964 hearing, 1070.

38. Congress, Senate, Committee on Aeronautical and Space Sciences, *National Space Goals for the Post-Apollo Period*, 89th Cong., 1st sess., 23 August 1965, 12.

39. NASA, *National Aeronautics and Space Administration: Twenty-fifth Anniversary, 1958-1983*, NF-200 (Washington, D.C.: GPO, 1983), 1.

40. James E. Webb, "The Challenge and Promise of the Space Age," speech at the University of Miami, 25 January 1965, NASA History Office, Washington, D.C., 3.

41. Congress, Senate, Committee on Aeronautical and Space Sciences, *NASA Authorization for Fiscal Year 1969*, 90th Cong., 2d sess., 29 February 1968, 362.

42. Congress, Senate, Committee on Appropriations, *Department of Housing and Urban Development, Space, and Science Appropriations for Fiscal Year 1972*, 92d Cong., 1st sess., 23 June 1971, 471.

43. Congress, House, Committee on Appropriations, Subcommittee on Independent Offices and the Department of Housing and Urban Development, *Independent Offices and Department of Housing and Urban Development Appropriations for 1969*, Part 2, 90th Cong., 2d sess., 11 March 1968, 1024.

44. Webb, "Challenge and Promise," 4.

45. House Committee on Appropriations, 11 March 1968 hearing, 1024.

46. Congress, House, Committee on Appropriations, Subcommittee on HUD—Independent Agencies, *Department of Housing and Urban Development—Independent Agencies Appropriations for 1987*, Part 7, 99th Cong., 2d sess., 13 May 1986, 33-34.

47. Senate Committee on Aeronautical and Space Sciences, 28 February 1966 hearing, 16.

48. See, for example, Congress, Senate, Committee on Aeronautical and Space Sciences, *NASA Authorization for Fiscal Year 1966*, 89th Cong., 1st sess., 8 March 1965, 24; Congress, House, Committee on Science and Astronautics, *1968 NASA Authorization*, Part 1, 90th Cong., 1st sess., 28 February 1967, 13; Congress, House, Committee on Science and Astronautics, *1970 NASA Authorization*, Part 1, 91st Cong., 1st sess., 4 March 1969, 15; NASA, *Space for Mankind's Benefit*, SP-313 (Washington, D.C.: GPO, 1972), 14; NASA, *The Journey Continues*, NP-117, 13; and Congress, House, Committee on Science, Space, and Technology, Subcommittee on Space Science and Applications, *1990 NASA Authorization*, 101st Cong., 1st sess., 2 February 1989, 15.

49. NASA, *Space for Mankind's Benefit*, SP-313, 15; Congress, House, Committee on Science and Astronautics, *1970 NASA Authorization*, Part 1, 91st Cong., 1st sess., 4 March 1969, 15.

50. "Russian Space Gain Seen by NASA Chief," *New York Times*, 20 May 1966, 51.

51. Congress, House, Committee on Science and Astronautics, *1971 NASA Authorization*, 91st Cong., 2d sess., 17 February 1970, 40.

52. House Committee on Appropriations, 7 April 1964 hearing, 935.

53. House Committee on Science and Astronautics, 4 February 1964 hearing, 11.

54. Congress, Senate, Committee on Aeronautical and Space Sciences, *NASA Authorization for Fiscal Year 1969*, 90th Cong., 2d sess., 27 February 1968, 14.

55. Senate Committee on Aeronautical and Space Sciences, 30 March 1971 hearing, 15.

56. For example, Congress, Senate, Committee on Aeronautical and Space Sciences, *NASA Authorization for Fiscal Year 1974*, Part 1, 93d Cong., 1st sess., 28 February 1973, 212; Congress, House, Committee on Science and Technology, Subcommittee on Space Science and Applications, *United States Civilian Space Policy*, 96th Cong., 2d sess., 24 July 1980, 75.

57. See, for example, NASA, *Leadership for the Future*, PAM-509, 7; NASA, *Space Station: A Research Laboratory in Space*, PAM-512 (Washington, D.C.: GPO, 1988), 1.

58. NASA, *Discovering Space for America's Economic Growth*, 6.

59. NASA, *The Journey Continues*, NP-117, 2.

60. For a more detailed explanation of this phenomenon, see the section on technological stimulus in Chapter 5.

61. Beggs, *Space Station*, 1. See also Fletcher testimony in Senate Committee on Appropriations, 23 June 1971 hearing, 470.

62. Beggs, *Space Station*, 1.

63. Congress, House, Committee on Appropriations, Subcommittee on HUD—Independent Agencies, *Department of Housing and Urban Development—Independent Agencies Appropriations for 1978*, Part 5, 95th Cong., 1st sess., 29 March 1977, 12.

64. Senate Committee on Commerce, Science, and Transportation, 22 March 1988 hearing, 204.

65. NASA, *Discovering Space for America's Economic Growth*, 6.

66. NASA, *This Is NASA*, EP-155 (Washington, D.C.: GPO, 1979), 35.

67. For a more detailed explanation of this phenomenon, see the section on spinoffs in Chapter 5.

68. NASA, *STS 26: Flight of Discovery*, PAM-515 (Washington, D.C.: GPO, 1988), 6.

69. Congress, House, Committee on Science, Space, and Technology, Subcommittee on Space Science and Applications, *1988 NASA Authorization*, 100th Cong., 1st sess., 5 February 1987, 70.

70. NASA, *STS 26: Flight of Discovery*, PAM-515, 6.

71. NASA, *Discovering Space for America's Economic Growth*, 6.

72. NASA, *This Is NASA*, EP-22 (Washington, D.C.: GPO, 1968), 17.

73. James M. Beggs, "The Wilbur and Orville Wright Memorial Lecture," speech to the Royal Aeronautical Society, London, England, 13 December 1984, NASA History Office, Washington, D.C., 4.

74. House Committee on Appropriations, 7 April 1964 hearing, 933.

75. NASA, *New Horizons*, EP-117 (Washington, D.C.: GPO, 1975).

76. John Noble Wilford, "Seminar Envisions U.S.-Soviet Mars Venture," *New York Times*, 17 July 1985, A9.

77. NASA, *America's Next Decades*, 78; NASA, *Space and the International Cooperation Year: A National Challenge*, by Arnold W. Frutkin, EP-30 (Washington, D.C.: GPO, 1965), 13.

78. House Committee on Appropriations, 7 April 1964 hearing, 933.

79. For example, NASA, *Most Asked Questions About Space and Aeronautics* (Washington, D.C.: GPO, 1973), 7; House Committee on Science and Astronautics, 28 February 1967 hearing, 13; and NASA, *America's Next Decades*, 84.

80. NASA, *Questions & Answers About Aeronautics and Space*, PAM-106 (Washington, D.C.: GPO, 1985), 5; Senate Committee on Aeronautical and Space Sciences, 8 March 1965 hearing, 50; and Beggs, "Wright Memorial Lecture," 4.

81. Senate Committee on Aeronautical and Space Sciences, 8 March 1965 hearing, 50.

82. NASA, *This Is NASA*, EP-22, 17.

83. NASA, *The Space Shuttle at Work*, by Howard Allaway, EP-156 (Washington, D.C.: GPO, 1979), 24.

84. Webb, "Challenge and Promise," 9.

85. NASA, *Twenty-fifth Anniversary*, NF-200, 1.

86. NASA, *Man in Space: Space in the Seventies*, by Walter Froehlich, EP-81 (Washington, D.C.: GPO, 1971), 3. See also NASA, *NASA: National Aeronautics and Space Administration* (Washington, D.C.: GPO, 1971), 1.

87. NASA, *Man in Space: Space in the Seventies*, EP-81, 3.

88. NASA, *The Journey Continues*, NP-117, 10. See also NASA, *In This Decade...*, EP-71 (Washington, D.C.: GPO, 1969), 3.

89. NASA, *Man in Space: Space in the Seventies*, EP-81, 3.

90. Beggs, "Wright Memorial Lecture," 8.

91. House Committee on Science and Astronautics, 4 February 1964 hearing, 17.

92. NASA, *This Is NASA*, EP-155, 3.

93. Senate Committee on Aeronautical and Space Sciences, 29 February 1968 hearing, 362.

94. Congress, Senate, Committee on Aeronautical and Space Sciences, *NASA Authorization for Fiscal Year 1967*, 89th Cong., 2d sess., 1 March 1966, 106.

95. Senate Committee on Commerce, Science, and Transportation, 3 February 1987 hearing, 26.

96. Congress, House, Committee on Appropriations, Subcommittee on VA, HUD, and Independent Agencies, *Departments of Veterans Affairs and Housing and Urban Development, and Independent Agencies Appropriations for 1990*, Part 6, 101st Cong., 1st sess., 25 April 1989, 45.

97. NASA, *Space: The New Frontier* (Washington, D.C.: GPO, 1963), 2; Senate Committee on Commerce, Science, and Transportation, 3 February 1987 hearing, 26; and NASA; *Leadership for the Future*, PAM-509, 1.

98. Congress, Senate, Committee on Aeronautical and Space Sciences, Subcommittee on NASA Authorization, *NASA Supplemental Authorization for Fiscal Year 1959*, 86th Cong., 1st sess., 19 February 1959, 29.

99. Senate Committee on Aeronautical and Space Sciences, *NASA Authorization for Fiscal Year 1967*, 89th Cong., 2d sess., 28 February 1966, 16.

100. Congress, Senate, Committee on Aeronautical and Space Sciences, NASA Authorization Subcommittee, *NASA Authorization for Fiscal Year 1961*, 86th Cong., 2d sess., Part 1, 28 March 1960, 18.

101. Congress, House, Committee on Science and Astronautics, *To Amend the National Aeronautics and Space Act of 1958*, 86th Cong., 2d sess., 4 April 1960, 519.

102. George M. Low, "Project Mercury Progress," speech to UPI Editors Conference, Washington, D.C., 9 September 1960, NASA History Office, Washington, D.C., 5.

103. Harold M. Schmeck, Jr., "Experts Outline U.S. Space Plans," *New York Times*, 27 May 1961, 10.

104. Robert A. Wright, "NASA Chief Seeks More Funds in '73," *New York Times*, 3 October 1971, 30.

105. Vernon Van Dyke, *Pride and Power: The Rationale of the Space Program* (Urbana: University of Illinois Press, 1964), 141.

106. Congress, House, Committee on Science and Astronautics, Subcommittee on Manned Space Flight, *1964 NASA Authorization*, 88th Cong., 1st sess., 2 April 1963, 568.

107. Senate Committee on Aeronautical and Space Sciences, 28 March 1960 hearing, 42-43.

2

The Mercury Era

The Cold War raged in the late 1950s. Soviet space achievements, most notably the 1957 launch of the Sputnik satellite, roused the United States from its somnolence of the mid-1950s, and the American people desperately wanted their nation to take action in space. NASA was created in 1958 to conduct the nation's space program, and the agency immediately began the search for political support that all government agencies must conduct.

Project Mercury, America's first manned space endeavor and NASA's first major program of any kind, ran from 1958 to 1963. NASA used nationalism as its primary image during those years because that image best fit the prevailing political conditions. The Cold War was in full swing, greatly influencing American domestic and international politics, and the prospect of the Soviet Union dominating space frightened most Americans. NASA responded to the situation with nationalism, playing up the threat from the Soviets and stressing the importance of America's space program for its national interest. NASA used all four of the major nationalist themes in its statements.

BEFORE MERCURY

In the years after World War II, Americans took their nation's leadership in technology for granted.[1] Much of the industrialized world had been crippled by the war, but the United States had emerged relatively unscathed, with its industrial might strengthened and its technological prowess enhanced. Americans were especially confident because the United States led in the development of atomic weapons and the means to deliver them.

However, the United States had not always held technological leadership. Early in the twentieth century, the United States lagged far behind many other nations in aviation research and airplane construction. With World War I on the horizon, this fact alarmed many American scientists and military officers.[2]

Congress established the National Advisory Committee for Aeronautics (NACA) in 1915 to try to remedy the situation.

Although obscure and poorly funded through most of its history, NACA managed to keep American aviation current with technological advances and even to make periodic breakthroughs.[3] NACA focused on atmospheric flight through most of its history, but after World War II it began some research on space flight at the request of the military, with which NACA had long enjoyed a friendly relationship. The Army, Navy, and Air Force were all interested in developing space programs to complement their missile research.[4]

NACA began to reassess its activities in the mid-1950s. The agency had been subjected to a series of severe budget cuts, and it believed that getting more deeply involved in space research might be a way to build political muscle. NACA was still thinking about the subject as 1957 began. In the meantime, the United States had no official overall policy for space research and development.[5]

However, America was not totally inactive in space research. In addition to the military's missile and rocket research, the nation was working on a scientific satellite. In 1954 scientists from around the world made plans to conduct an International Geophysical Year (IGY) from 1957 to 1958. The main goal was to study the sun when sunspot activity was expected to be high. The scientists had proposed launching a small scientific satellite as part of the study. America decided to develop and launch such a satellite, and placed the program to do so—named Project Vanguard—under Navy auspices. The effort made slow progress, however, because of tight budgets and rivalry among the branches of the military for control of the nation's space program.[6] Work on Vanguard dragged into 1957.

SPUTNIK AND ITS AFTERMATH

The Soviet Union had also been working on a satellite for the IGY, but made faster progress than the United States. On October 4, 1957, the Soviet Union launched into orbit the earth's first man-made satellite, named Sputnik I. Most Americans were surprised and deeply alarmed by Sputnik. The event demonstrated considerable Soviet technological and industrial skill and thus carried serious implications about Soviet military ability. Sputnik shattered Americans' long-standing certainty of their technological superiority and implied that the Soviets had acquired the missile technology to deliver nuclear warheads to American targets.[7]

The launch of a second, even more impressive Sputnik (carrying a dog named Laika) on November 3, 1957, heightened American anxieties, as did the dramatic and well-publicized December 6 explosion of an American Vanguard rocket during launch. General public awareness of the Sputnik launch was "extraordinarily high,"[8] and Americans worried about its implications.

Most believed that American national security and prestige were on the line.[9] Sputnik and the reaction to it spurred the American space effort.

The Creation of NASA

Fueled by what one historian calls a "media riot" following Sputnik, the American public's outcry over the Soviet lead in space was "lengthy, loud, and imposing."[10] A 1961 poll showed that most Americans were willing to pay for a space program: 26.5 percent said that the government should spend more money on space exploration, 28.0 percent said that current spending levels should be maintained, while only 32.1 percent wanted less money spent.[11] The public looked to the president to devise America's response to the Soviet space threat.[12]

President Dwight Eisenhower had mixed feelings about the situation. Shortly after Sputnik was launched, Eisenhower publicly asserted that the satellite "does not raise my apprehensions, not one iota," and said that Sputnik did not represent a threat to American national security because it proved little about Soviet intercontinental ballistic missile capability.[13] Privately, however, Eisenhower was surprised at the intensity of the American public's reaction to Sputnik.[14]

In general, Eisenhower saw no need to rush exploration of the universe and thought priority should be given to the military applications of space.[15] He was hesitant about establishing a separate civilian government agency to oversee the nation's space program, which he believed might emphasize satellites at the expense of missiles. Yet Congress, the public, and many scientists strongly favored such an agency, and Eisenhower acquiesced.[16]

NACA had lobbied for control of the nation's space efforts, but Eisenhower wanted an agency more subject to presidential control than NACA had been.[17] In addition, many people believed that a bold new agency was needed to tackle the challenge of space exploration. Eisenhower proposed the creation of NASA in April 1958, and Congress quickly passed the National Aeronautics and Space Act of 1958. NASA came into existence on October 1 of that year, and NACA was absorbed into the new agency.

NASA's View of Sputnik

NASA, well aware that American national pride had been damaged by Sputnik, used the event to build support for itself and the nation's incipient space program. NASA stressed Sputnik's effect on American national pride and its implications about the threat posed to America by the Soviet space program.

National Pride. NASA's first administrator, T. Keith Glennan, said about Sputnik: "The blow to our national pride in this unexpected achievement of Soviet science was tremendous."[18] The agency professed that Americans would demand a response: "Our national pride will not permit us to sidestep the challenge of space that lies before us."[19] NASA offered to accept that challenge and help America regain its pride. If America did not act, declared NASA's James Webb, "We could no longer stand large in our own image."[20]

Even though the U.S. space program lagged behind the Soviet one, NASA stressed that Americans could take pride in their space endeavors for other reasons. NASA noted that it, unlike the Soviets, would operate in the open. For example, the live televising of NASA's launches made its failures, as well as its successes, visible to all. Robert Seamans, the agency's associate administrator, remarked that NASA ran its program openly, "with pride that a free society not only *can* conduct its space activities in the open, but is determined to do so."[21] NASA also emphasized that it acted in concert with other nations. Glennan said that "as Americans, we can be proud that our country is leading" the effort to make space flight an international effort.[22]

The Soviet Threat. Sputnik raised the specter of the heavens dominated by the Soviet Union, and NASA played up the Soviet threat to win political support. NASA constantly warned that space must not be dominated by a hostile nation. The agency made it clear that the United States was in a difficult and vitally important competition with the Soviet Union in space. That competition, NASA said, set the pace of America's space efforts. Glennan told Congress, "We find ourselves in competition with another nation that is really forcing our hand to a considerable extent."[23] He also remarked that "powerful external forces are pressing this Nation in a competition for high stakes."[24]

The United States had to stay at least even with the Soviets, James Webb asserted. "If we permitted the Russians to surpass us," he said, "eventually we would almost certainly find ourselves on the receiving end of their advanced space technology, employed for military and economic aggression."[25] Losing the competition in space would be disastrous for the United States, NASA asserted. According to NASA's Hugh Dryden, "There is no doubt whatever that this Nation and the Free World would face somber consequences should another country develop and apply a superior space technology for aggressive purposes."[26]

NASA contended that Soviet space successes offered the Soviet Union the opportunity to enhance its national pride, which could have serious international ramifications. James Webb even argued that Soviet pride and self-confidence probably contributed to the building of the Berlin Wall in 1961. Webb testified to Congress in 1962, "Some people doubt very much if the Russians would have moved as aggressively with respect to Berlin if they had not had such successes in space."[27]

NASA painted a very unpleasant picture of America's competitor in space. NASA officials contended that the Soviet Union's space program was an important part of its plan to conquer the world.[28] References to the Soviets often included some form of the term "communist" or other epithet to highlight this evil intent. T. Keith Glennan spoke of the Soviet Union as "a totalitarian and determined competitor"[29] and as "the Communist dictatorship."[30] Wernher von Braun even characterized the Soviets as "the Reds" in a widely distributed article he wrote.[31]

NASA emphasized that the Soviet Union was a capable and fierce competitor. Von Braun described the opponent:

Our competitor in this cosmic contest is tough. His peacetime economy is on a wartime footing, and with great consequence and at great sacrifices in the area of badly needed consumer goods he applies his resources to efforts he deems essential in the overall national interest. . . . It would be a disaster if we underrated his ability and determination.[32]

Glennan agreed: "I am certain that we can expect no quarter in this competition."[33] Other Mercury-era statements by NASA officials noted the Soviets' "entirely pragmatic operation" and their "extreme competence in planning and in implementing" their space program.[34]

The result of all this, NASA said, was that a determined American effort would be required to keep up with the Soviets. The United States needed to formulate a plan "and then pursue it very, very diligently and very, very urgently."[35] Glennan called for the United States "to press forward with diligence on a well-planned program" of space activity because it was extremely unlikely that the Soviets would "withdraw from a race in which they hold even a slight lead."[36] Glennan also spoke to Congress of his dedication to prevail over the Soviets: "I have no doubt that they are motivated by a desire to 'beat America.' All I can say to you is, I am motivated by a desire not to be beaten."[37]

Who would eventually triumph in this decisive competition? In 1960 Glennan admitted to Congress that the Soviets were undoubtedly ahead.[38] Yet Glennan was also on record as saying, "I have faith that we will win this contest."[39] Von Braun, despite his gloomy assessment of the early situation, also expressed confidence that the United States would catch up: "I am not ready to believe that America is willing to surrender the heavens" to the Soviets.[40]

Strong Political Support for NASA

The reaction to Sputnik helped create a highly favorable political environment for NASA from 1958 to 1963. Convinced that the Soviet Union held a commanding lead in space technology, many Americans feared the Soviets would use that lead to dominate the heavens and thereby increase their power on earth. A comment by Senate Majority Leader Lyndon B. Johnson exemplified the prevailing attitude: "Control of space means control of the world."[41] The American public's fear triggered its demand that the United States take action to catch up with the Soviets. That demand, in turn, translated into potent political support for the agency designed to handle America's space program—NASA. The public, presidents, and members of Congress of the Mercury era were, for the most part, all quite supportive of NASA.

The public recognized the importance of space exploration and was fascinated with NASA's activities. President Eisenhower helped establish NASA, and President Kennedy made the space program a focal point of his administration. In addition, strong congressional backing for NASA and the space program helped the agency achieve its goals.[42] Members of Congress, like most Americans, were deeply disturbed by Sputnik and wanted America to respond quickly and vigorously.[43] In fact, the law Congress passed to establish NASA created an agency "with a broader mission and greater powers" than the Eisenhower administration had recommended.[44]

Several factors helped NASA in Congress. Lyndon B. Johnson, Senate majority leader until he became vice president in 1961, supported NASA enthusiastically, and both the House and Senate space committees wanted a strong space program.[45] In addition, NASA Administrator James Webb exercised tremendous political skill in dealing with Congress.[46] Also, NASA's great public popularity insulated the agency from much congressional criticism.[47] Finally, even if Congress had wanted to conduct strict oversight of NASA in those days, it lacked the expertise to do so.[48]

The result was that NASA in its early years got just about everything it wanted from Congress, with few hostile questions asked. In fact, Congress was so intent that the United States catch up with the Soviets in space that some members wanted to give NASA more money than the agency requested.[49] For example, in 1959 the ranking Republican on the House space committee told a NASA official he wanted America "to be firstest with the mostest in space" and asked him, "How much money do we need to do it?"[50]

It is not surprising that NASA enjoyed tremendous funding increases during the Mercury era. The agency's budget authority rose from $117 million in fiscal 1958 to $3.7 billion in fiscal 1963. The figures for the period are equally impressive when expressed in constant 1987 dollars: NASA's budget authority shot up from $551 million to $14.4 billion. (See the Appendix for more extensive data on NASA's budget.) Figure 1 illustrates the sharp rise in NASA's budget authority during the Mercury era.

Similarly, the agency easily received authorization for two major programs, Projects Mercury and Apollo, in the years from 1958 to 1963. The American people embraced both programs, and both were enthusiastically approved by Congress. In 1958 members of Congress, like most Americans, were eager for the United States to pursue manned space exploration and were therefore happy to endorse the Mercury program. In 1961 Congress approved the Apollo

Figure 1
NASA Funding in the Mercury Era: Budget Authority in Constant 1987
Dollars

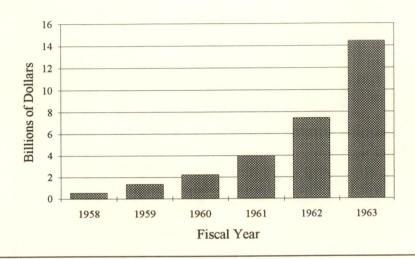

Sources: Adapted from Office of Management and Budget, *Budget of the United States Government: Fiscal Year 1995, Historical Tables* (Washington, D.C.: GPO, 1994); and Bureau of the Budget, *Budget of the United States Government* (Washington, D.C.: GPO, 1959-70).

program, the largest civilian project ever undertaken by the nation, virtually without debate.[51]

Project Mercury Announced and Justified

Having stressed the extreme importance of an American response to the Soviet lead in space, NASA had to formulate such a response quickly. In November 1958, NASA announced Project Mercury. The Mercury program was designed to study humans' ability to survive and function in space and to develop the technology and equipment needed for manned space exploration.[52] Such a program was required to learn the fundamentals of space activity and was therefore a prerequisite for later space endeavors. In addition to preparing for the technical aspects of Mercury, NASA quickly began to explain the value of Mercury and the space program generally to the public. In doing so, it relied heavily on the themes of nationalism.

National Prestige. NASA emphasized the positive effect Mercury would have on American national prestige. The agency argued that achievements in space indicated technological ability, which in turn manifested military power and national strength. Thus prestige in space meant prestige on earth. T. Keith Glennan said, "I think the world today views leadership in technological and scientific fields as evidence of real strength in any nation."[53]

James Webb concurred: "Science and technology are rightly regarded by the world's peoples today as the keys to economic progress and military strength. . . . In the minds of millions, space achievements have become to-day's symbol of tomorrow's scientific and technical supremacy."[54] As a result, according to Webb, "Today prestige is one of the most important elements of international relations."[55]

The Mercury program was vital, NASA said, because it was America's first major effort to demonstrate competence in space and thereby gain prestige. Administrator Glennan described Mercury as "an important instrument of international prestige."[56] In a statement titled "Urgency of Project Mercury," NASA explained the program's import:

One of the most significant milestones in the history of space flight will be the first successful launching, flight, and recovery of a man in space. The event will be of such importance that it cannot fail to earn worldwide acclaim for the technical skill of the nation first accomplishing the difficult task.

Project Mercury, the current manned space flight program of the NASA, represents this Nation's effort to place man in space.[57]

NASA went on to warn that American failure to be the first nation to achieve manned space flight would be a "certain psychological defeat for the United States in the eyes of the world."[58]

The space program, NASA maintained, offered the opportunity to prove to the world that the United States had the will and the ability to pursue great and complicated tasks. Glennan said that the space program tested "our belief, so often expressed, that free men can prevail in any field in which they wish to place their energy."[59]

Webb later echoed Glennan: "Essential to our prestige today is the belief of other nations that we have the capability and determination to carry out whatever we declare seriously that we intend to do."[60] Thus, meeting the challenges of space through the Mercury program would demonstrate the vigor of the nation.

In fact, NASA argued during the Mercury era, America's performance in space was nothing less than a test of its democratic system of government. A NASA official claimed that the agency played a crucial role in "demonstrating the virility and viability of our particular system of government."[61] James Webb made a similar point: "We must dispel any doubt that a people who govern themselves can measure up to the challenges of the world."[62] Webb declared that America, "the symbol of democratic government," could not accept a secondary role in space "to the leading advocate of the Communist ideology."[63]

This space-based test of America's government was critical, NASA argued, because the rest of the world would use the results to compare the relative merits of the United States and the Soviet Union. "Whether we like it or not," wrote NASA's Wernher von Braun, "we are engaged in a worldwide popularity contest with the Soviets."[64] The exploration of space was thus a competition for the respect and admiration of people all over the globe. Von Braun continued, "When the whole world sits in the audience and the heavens are the stage, pride and prestige are real issues and serve ends which are vital for our Nation's role in the world of men."[65]

T. Keith Glennan said that many people in the uncommitted areas of the world believed that "success in space research is the principal measure of the scientific and technological efforts of a nation, and hence, the real measure of the worth of a culture."[66] Von Braun believed that wooing those people, who might succumb to communism, should be a major goal of the American space program: "We are competing for allies among the many have-not nations for whose underfed multitudes the Communist formula of life has a great appeal."[67]

NASA made it quite clear who were the good guys and who were the bad guys in this extraterrestrial contest. Glennan vividly described the situation to Congress:

We are engaged in a struggle for the minds and hearts of men everywhere. The issue is simply whether our system of free government and responsible civic freedom is superior to the system of totalitarian communism and forcible direction of the lives of its captive peoples.

I believe it is becoming increasingly obvious to the world that Russia's space activities are devoted, as are most of their activities as a nation, in large part to the furthering of communism's unswerving designs upon mankind.[68]

Not only did the Soviet Union plan to use space-related prestige for evil purposes, NASA asserted, it was perfectly willing to sacrifice the lives of its citizens in order to win that prestige. NASA reported that its determination to protect the safety of American astronauts might prevent the United States from being first nation to put a man in space. The agency explained, "Other nations having less regard for human life may shortcut the development procedures that we think essential and may thereby accomplish manned space flight before we do."[69]

NASA also accused the Soviet Union of using propaganda to enhance its space reputation.[70] Glennan pointed out that although the United States and the Soviet Union were competing in many endeavors, "Space is the most glamorous, most visible area of competition—and very fruitful also for propaganda purposes."[71] NASA described the Soviets as skillful propagandists.

The prestige accrued from leadership in space would bring the United States many benefits, NASA contended. Glennan testified before Congress that with such leadership, "The Nation will regain the confidence of the entire world."[72] Thus, nations around the world would have increased respect for the United States, and uncommitted nations would be more likely to align themselves with the United States than the Soviet Union. Conversely, if America scaled back its efforts in space by reducing spending on the Mercury program, "The world will conclude that the United States is having second thoughts about facing the Communist challenge."[73]

Perceptions of American strength can be crucial in relations among nations, NASA said. After the agency had conducted several successful Mercury flights, James Webb described part of the payoff of the project: "The image of the United States is, in my view, considerably improved today as a result of what we have done in space."[74] Webb gave an example of how the nation's image, improved by the prestige generated by the space program, paid off in international affairs. He asserted that one reason President Kennedy prevailed in the Cuban missile crisis was the perception of the United States as a "can-do" nation—an image advanced through the space program generally and the Mercury program specifically.[75]

National Strength. NASA officials in the Mercury era frequently proclaimed that America's national strength largely depended on leading in space, and they vowed to attain that leadership. NASA Administrator T. Keith Glennan declared in one of his earliest appearances before Congress that NASA's fundamental mission was "to establish the United States as a leader in space research, development, and exploration."[76] Glennan also announced, "We are not about to be satisfied with being slightly behind anybody."[77]

Glennan's successor, James Webb, shared that attitude. He described NASA's primary objective as "over-all leadership, across-the-board, in the exploration of space."[78] Webb spoke of his commitment to see America "achieve mastery of space."[79] Similarly, a NASA publication stressed "the necessity that we retain unquestioned preeminence in all areas of science and technology, including the new arena of space."[80]

Webb explained that the space program "is vital to the security and well-being of the United States."[81] He wrote in a NASA pamphlet: "Our national defense requires that the United States make certain that the exploitation of space will be peaceful and open to all nations, and that none will ever be tempted to use it against us."[82] Webb believed that the nation's status in space would affect its security in another fundamental way: "My own view is that if we do not have a position of preeminence in space at the bargaining table of the nations, or in the minds of the world's leaders, the decisions that bring peace or war are not apt to be of our own making."[83] However, with leadership in space, a NASA publication argued, America would be able to "use space for whatever purpose the national interest may require."[84]

NASA affirmed that America had the capability to achieve leadership in space. Glennan testified to Congress: "The United States has the resources, the knowledge, the will—and the duty—to pioneer in the space age."[85] But, he emphasized, tremendous effort would be required to do so. The space program had to "be pursued diligently, urgently, and relentlessly,"[86] and "with a sense of dedication, with the determination to move aside mountains of redtape that might tend to slow down progress."[87]

NASA noted that Congress would have to provide the resources required to participate in the admittedly "exceedingly expensive business" of space exploration.[88] Glennan told Congress, "We must have the facilities, men and money necessary to the task. . . . We cannot win this race without all-out support from Congress."[89] In the final analysis, Glennan said, "The degree of success or failure of the U.S. space effort . . . will be gravely influenced by what Congress decides."[90]

Glennan testified to Congress that Mercury was "the highest priority project . . . primarily because of its cold war significance, and the fact that we have some competition."[91] NASA heralded the Mercury program as the means to propel America into space leadership. The agency's George Low said that America's manned space program would definitely founder in second place without the Mercury project.[92] Mercury would help advance the space program by setting a initial goal for NASA, as well as yielding vital information on human capabilities in space. T. Keith Glennan explained:

In the development of a hard-hitting space program, as in almost any difficult research and development task, it is very, very important to have particular aspects of the total program brought out as end objectives which in themselves require us to use all the ingenuity and all the genius and all the energy that we have. And in Project Mercury we have just this.[93]

Faced with the mammoth task of starting a space program, NASA said it needed a clear target to focus its activities and inspire its people, and the Mercury program provided such a preliminary goal.

NASA stressed that the information discovered and the technology developed in the space program could have vital military and national security implications. The kind of basic research done under the aegis of the space program "is required to lay the groundwork for our strength in the future," Glennan told Congress.[94] The value of such research, often not apparent at the beginning, can turn out to be tremendous. Therefore, NASA's Hugh Dryden said, "We cannot disregard the military implications [of space], even though we do not see them clearly right now."[95] He later expanded on this thought: "We pursue knowledge vigorously not alone for knowledge per se, but also because knowledge is power. We are determined that our country shall have that power."[96] Dryden also told Congress that the Mercury project was crucial because it would "advance the general technology of space at a faster rate than almost anything else I can think of."[97]

NASA pledged to cooperate closely with the military and to share any relevant information. Glennan noted that the law establishing NASA "stipulates very clearly that NASA shall make available to the armed services all discoveries that have military significance."[98] Glennan also vowed to form the "closest possible relationship" with the military.[99] Both sides profited from the relationship, Glennan explained. For example, NASA received help on the Mercury program from the military, while "just about every U.S. aircraft and missile has benefited importantly from NASA research."[100]

International Peace and Cooperation. Even though NASA's emphasis during the Mercury era was on competition in space, the agency did occasionally refer to international cooperation. NASA stressed that while the United States was watching for potential military applications of space, its foremost goal was to use space peacefully.[101] As Administrator Glennan said, "While we must recognize and concede the importance of possible use of space to accomplish military missions and objectives, the longrun objective of this Nation—indeed its primary objective—is peace."[102]

Glennan argued that the close relationships required among nations cooperating in space would foster peace on earth:

This field of space research and development may have as much to do with providing a mechanism for really getting at working relationships with the other nations in the world, developing a real climate of international good will, as almost any other process we are undertaking at the present time.[103]

Glennan also observed that cooperation in space might encourage "that common understanding and mutual trust that will break the lock step of suspicion and distrust that divides the world into separate camps today."[104]

NASA even invited America's chief rival to collaborate in space exploration. Glennan reported that America would "welcome" cooperation from the Soviet Union in space.[105] In fact, Glennan said that he was "convinced that space exploration is one of the most fruitful areas for agreement between ourselves and our principal international competitor."[106]

NASA's offer to cooperate in space was by no means limited to America's adversaries. The agency indicated during this period that it was eager to work with all nations.[107] As James Webb remarked, "The stance we have before the world is one of invitation to people all over the world to come in and participate in this tremendous effort."[108] The agency said that its major endeavor, Project Mercury, "will be an international effort carried out with the cooperation and efforts of many peoples."[109] Moreover, NASA emphasized that it would share the fruits of its efforts. The agency pledged that the information gathered in its programs "will go for the benefit of all mankind."[110] A NASA brochure depicted Project Mercury as "part of the NASA program of space research and exploration for peaceful purposes to benefit all mankind."[111] The agency clearly implied that the Soviets did not share this noble attitude. As Glennan said,

I believe, with the utmost conviction, that we have a national, . . . yes, an international responsibility to lead in the exploration of space. If all the possible benefits from space are to be made available fully, around the world, to all mankind, then it is absolutely essential that we show the way.[112]

NASA insisted that America's space efforts would benefit both itself and the other nations of the world.[113]

NASA also repeatedly promised that, unlike the Soviet program, America's space operations and results would be open to the public worldwide.[114] The agency predicted that this openness would be a boon to international affairs and a big benefit to other nations. As Glennan told Congress, "Our policy of frankness and our adherence to the traditional and well-understood policy of prompt disclosure of scientific results is building goodwill throughout the world."[115] Other nations would thus gratefully accept information from the United States and then profitably employ that knowledge at home. A NASA publication made a specific pledge concerning the agency's premier program: "The plans, the details, and the results of Project Mercury are open to all."[116]

From Eisenhower to Kennedy

President Eisenhower had seen no need to rush America's space efforts and had steadfastly rejected the notion of a "space race" between the United States and the Soviet Union.[117] Eisenhower recalled in his memoirs: "We deliberately avoided hysterically devised crash programs and propaganda stunts."[118] Furthermore, while he was pleased with the satellites NASA placed into orbit and he did authorize Project Mercury, Eisenhower seriously doubted the value of a manned mission to the moon, an idea NASA was contemplating.[119] When he asked an adviser why America should undertake such a mission, the response was that the journey could be as important as Columbus' discovery of America. Eisenhower rejoined, "I'm not about to hock my jewels" to pay for such a trip the way Queen Isabella supposedly did to finance Columbus.[120] Yet even though his approach to space was conservative, Eisenhower helped give life to NASA and provided it with solid support in its first few years.[121]

John F. Kennedy, although he had demonstrated little concern about space as a congressman, used space as a major issue in his 1960 presidential campaign against Richard Nixon. Through his vigorous attacks on the Eisenhower administration's space policy, Kennedy indirectly attacked Nixon, who was Eisenhower's vice president. According to Kennedy, Eisenhower's space policy was shortsighted and had resulted in a dangerous "space gap," or "missile gap," between the United States and the Soviet Union.[122] Such a gap, if it existed,[123] would be extremely dangerous because the missiles used to launch space vehicles could also be used to launch nuclear weapons.

As president, Kennedy followed space developments closely and was determined that the United States catch up with the Soviets. He asked NASA Administrator James Webb in 1961: "Is there any place we can catch them? Tell me how to catch up."[124] Kennedy was also enamored with the romantic and visionary aspects of space exploration. Although Kennedy's tenure in office was brief, his decisions on space policy had tremendous influence on NASA and the American space program.

THE MERCURY PROGRAM

The Mercury program quickly caught the attention of the American people. From the announcement of the first group of astronauts in 1959 to the last Mercury flight in 1963, Mercury was a highly visible and popular program.

The Original Astronauts

While public support for NASA and the Mercury program was spurred by statements from elected officials about space's role in national security, the novelty and romance of the space program also piqued public interest and generated political support. People watched with fascination as space travel, long confined to science fiction, became a reality.

The public showed particularly keen interest in the men who would travel in space, and the selection of seven Mercury astronauts in 1959 was greeted with widespread public curiosity. That interest, combined with intensive favorable media coverage, made the seven Mercury astronauts heroes almost overnight.[125] NASA was inundated with requests for information about the astronauts and the agency's activities. Many Americans, including schoolchildren around the nation, eagerly watched live televised coverage of launches. In general, the public seemed to sense that the nation was embarking on an exciting and important adventure.

NASA considered its image when selecting and publicizing the original Mercury astronauts. In keeping with its image of nationalism, the agency carefully picked "all-American" types from the ranks of military pilots, and then worked to enhance their images as exemplary citizens.[126] The seven men selected—some of whom became household names—were Scott Carpenter, Gordon Cooper, John Glenn, Virgil "Gus" Grissom, Walter Schirra, Alan Shepard, and Donald "Deke" Slayton.

In addition to its own publicity operations, NASA sanctioned a series of glowing articles in *Life* magazine that enhanced the all-American image of the Mercury astronauts. NASA largely succeeded in this image-making. According to one observer, the public worshipped the astronauts as patriotic symbols.[127]

One of the Mercury astronauts, Alan Shepard, became the first American in space with his suborbital flight on May 5, 1961. Although acclaimed in the United States, Shepard's voyage was overshadowed by the earlier orbital flight of Soviet Yuri Gagarin, who had become the first human in space on April 12, 1961. President Kennedy commended Shepard and NASA, but said that the nation should put forth "a substantially larger effort" in space.[128]

The Decision to Go to the Moon

Having promised to accelerate the nation's space program, Kennedy had to decide how to do so. His science adviser, Jerome Wiesner, urged that unmanned activity be given priority over manned spaceflight, which Wiesner condemned as risky, gimmicky, and expensive.[129] Yet Kennedy, chagrined at the repeated space firsts achieved by the Soviets and buffeted by policy and political problems (most notably fallout from the Bay of Pigs disaster), wanted a goal that America could accomplish first and that would shift attention away from his administration's failures.[130]

Kennedy soon announced his plan for America's larger effort in space. In a speech to Congress on May 25, 1961, Kennedy declared: "I believe that this nation should commit itself to achieving the goal, before this decade is out, of landing a man on the moon and returning him safely to the earth."[131] The lunar landing goal fit Kennedy's requirements for a glamorous yet technically feasible project that the United States could probably accomplish before the Soviets.[132]

His decision made, Kennedy worked to generate support for it—a fairly easy task, given the public and congressional apprehension about the Soviet lead in space. He admitted that the plan would be extremely costly, but stressed that it would be money well spent. He said in his May 25 speech to Congress: "No single space project in this period will be more impressive to mankind, or more important for the long-range exploration of space; and none will be so difficult or expensive to accomplish."[133] In addition to focusing on the competition with the Soviets, Kennedy tied the moon program to the idealism of his "New Frontier" platform. In a memorable September 1962 speech at Rice University, Kennedy proclaimed:

We choose to go to the moon in this decade and do the other things, not because they are easy, but because they are hard, because that goal will serve to organize and measure the best of our energies and skills, because that challenge is one that we are willing to accept, one we are unwilling to postpone, and one which we intend to win.[134]

The public got solidly behind the ambitious space proposals made by Kennedy.[135] A Gallup poll taken before Kennedy called for the lunar landing revealed that only 33 percent of the population supported spending the money (up to $40 billion) to finance such a trip, while 58 percent opposed it and 9 percent had no opinion.[136] Yet a poll taken in 1963, after the plan received presidential and congressional endorsement, showed that 69 percent of the public favored either maintaining or increasing the pace of the lunar program, while only 31 percent wanted to give it a lower priority.[137] Kennedy's proposal received easy approval in Congress.

NASA wanted to go to the moon but had not planned to do so in the near future, and was therefore "exhilarated but awed" by the goal and its deadline.[138] In setting that goal, Kennedy energized NASA and its political environment. Kennedy's decision to go to the moon gave NASA its clearest mandate ever.

The Conclusion of Mercury

The Mercury program continued as preparations for the lunar landing program, named Project Apollo, got under way. Both Mercury and the subsequent Gemini program served as preliminary steps to the Apollo program. Gus Grissom took the second Mercury flight, designed to duplicate the flight made by Shepard in May 1961, in July of the same year. After splashdown, however, the capsule's hatch opened prematurely. Grissom survived, but the capsule filled with water and sank. On February 20, 1962, in the third Mercury mission, John Glenn became the first American to orbit the earth. Glenn and NASA were hailed by the American public even though the Soviet Gagarin had orbited the earth nearly a year earlier.

After Glenn's triumphant voyage and tumultuous welcome back on earth, the astronaut addressed Congress. In that statement, Glenn struck the chord of national pride: "I am certainly glad to see that pride in our country and its accomplishments is not a thing of the past."[139] The clear implication was that Glenn's Mercury flight had renewed that pride in Americans.

The rest of the Mercury flights, although somewhat anticlimactic, were executed successfully. Scott Carpenter took an orbital flight in May 1962, and Walter Schirra followed suit in October 1962. In the sixth and final Mercury flight, which took place in May 1963, Gordon Cooper made twenty-two orbits around the earth.[140]

NOTES

1. Stephen E. Ambrose, *Eisenhower*, Vol. 2, *The President* (New York: Simon & Schuster, 1984), 424-26.

2. Arthur L. Levine, *The Future of the U.S. Space Program* (New York: Praeger, 1975), 10.

3. Walter A. McDougall, . . . *The Heavens and the Earth: A Political History of the Space Age* (New York: Basic Books, 1985), 75.

4. Richard Hirsch and Joseph John Trento, *The National Aeronautics and Space Administration* (New York: Praeger, 1973), 9-15; McDougall, *The Heavens and the Earth*, 164-68.

5. Levine, *Future of the U.S. Space Program*, 33-35.

6. Hirsch and Trento, *The National Aeronautics and Space Administration*, 13-14.

7. Ambrose, *Eisenhower*, 424-26; Roger E. Bilstein, *Orders of Magnitude: A History of the NACA and NASA, 1915-1990*, SP-4406 (Washington, D.C.: GPO, 1989), 44; McDougall, *The Heavens and the Earth*, Chapter 6.

8. Gabriel A. Almond, "Public Opinion and the Development of Space Technology: 1957-1960," in *Outer Space in World Politics*, ed. Joseph M. Golden (New York: Praeger, 1963), 73.

9. Vernon Van Dyke, *Pride and Power: The Rationale of the Space Program* (Urbana: University of Illinois Press, 1964), 272.

10. McDougall, *The Heavens and the Earth*, 142-145.

11. Philip E. Converse et al., *American Social Attitudes Data Sourcebook, 1947-1978* (Cambridge: Harvard University Press, 1980), 407.

12. Congress, Office of Technology Assessment, *Civilian Space Policy and Applications* (Washington, D.C.: GPO, 1982), 136.

13. Ambrose, *Eisenhower*, 429-30.

14. Dwight D. Eisenhower, *Waging Peace, 1956-1961; The White House Years* (Garden City, N.Y.: Doubleday & Co., 1965), 206; Ambrose, *Eisenhower*, 423-24.

15. Eisenhower, *Waging Peace*, 257; Ambrose, *Eisenhower*, 458.

16. Ambrose, *Eisenhower*, 458.

17. Levine, *Future of the U.S. Space Program*, 37-38.

18. Van Dyke, *Pride and Power*, 140.

19. Congress, House, Committee on Science and Astronautics, Subcommittee No. 4, *1961 NASA Authorization*, 86th Cong., 2d sess., 19 February 1960, 159.

20. NASA, *Space: The New Frontier* (Washington, D.C.: GPO, 1963), 2.

21. Robert C. Seamans, "Reliability in Space Systems—A National Objective," speech to the I.A.S. National Propulsion Meeting, Cleveland, Ohio, 8 March 1962, NASA History Office, Washington, D.C., 2-3.

22. T. Keith Glennan, "The Challenge of the Space Age," speech to Fort Worth Chamber of Commerce, 8 December 1958, NASA History Office, Washington, D.C., 5.

23. Senate Committee on Aeronautical and Space Sciences, 19 February 1959 hearing, 29.

24. Congress, Senate, Committee on Appropriations, *Supplemental National Aeronautics and Space Administration Appropriations, 1960*, 86th Cong., 2d sess., 23 February 1960, 19.

25. James E. Webb, "America's Role in Space Today," *New York Times*, 8 October 1961, sec. 12, p. 1.

26. Hugh L. Dryden, "Safety in the Space Age," speech to the National Safety Congress, Chicago, Illinois, 31 October 1962, NASA History Office, Washington, D.C., 9.

27. Van Dyke, *Pride and Power*, 129.

28. See, for example, Congress, House, Committee on Science and Astronautics, *1960 NASA Authorization*, 86th Cong., 1st sess., 20 April 1959, 3.

29. Congress, Senate, Committee on Aeronautical and Space Sciences, NASA Authorization Subcommittee, *NASA Authorization for Fiscal Year 1960*, 86th Cong., 1st sess., Part 1, 7 April 1959, 5.

30. Congress, House, Committee on Science and Astronautics, *Review of the Space Program*, 86th Cong., 2d sess., 27 January 1960, 170.

31. Wernher von Braun, "Why Should America Conquer Space?" placed in the record of this hearing: Congress, Senate, Committee on Aeronautical and Space Sciences, Subcommittee on NASA Authorization, *NASA Authorization for Fiscal Year 1961*, Part 1, 86th Cong., 2d sess., 29 March 1960, 239-41.

32. Ibid.

33. "Glennan Warns on Space Work," *New York Times*, 6 October 1959, 2.

34. T. Keith Glennan, speech at Wright Day dinner, Washington, D.C., 17 December 1958, NASA History Office, Washington, D.C., 2; Congress, House, Committee on Science and Astronautics, *1962 NASA Authorization*, Part 1, 87th Cong., 1st sess., 14 April 1961, 375.

35. Congress, House, Committee on Science and Astronautics, *Review of the Space Program*, 86th Cong., 2d sess., 29 January 1960, 284.

36. House Committee on Science and Astronautics, 20 April 1959 hearing, 4.

37. Congress, House, Committee on Science and Astronautics, *To Amend the National Aeronautics and Space Act of 1958*, 86th Cong., 2d sess., 4 April 1960, 519.

38. Congress, Senate, Committee on Aeronautical and Space Sciences, Subcommittee on NASA Authorization, *NASA Authorization for Fiscal Year 1961*, Part 1, 86th Cong., 2d sess., 28 March 1960, 16-18.

39. Van Dyke, *Pride and Power*, 141.

40. Senate Committee on Aeronautical and Space Sciences, 28 March 1960 hearing, 240.

41. *Congressional Quarterly Almanac 1958* (Washington, D.C.: Congressional Quarterly, 1958), 161.

42. Eilene Galloway, "U.S. Congress and Outer Space," in *Between Sputnik and the Shuttle*, ed. Frederick C. Durant III (San Diego: American Astronautical Society, 1981), 139-55.

43. John W. Finney, "House Unit Urges Bold Space Plan," *New York Times*, 11 January 1959, 50.

44. Levine, *Future of the U.S. Space Program*, 49-50.

45. Hirsch and Trento, *The National Aeronautics and Space Administration*, 126-29; Robert A. Divine, "LBJ and the Politics of Space," in *The Johnson Years*, Vol. 2, ed. Robert A. Divine (Lawrence: University of Kansas Press, 1987), 217-228; Levine, *Future of the U.S. Space Program*, 65-66.

46. Tom Wolfe, *The Right Stuff* (Toronto: Bantam Books, 1979), 367; "Pitchman for NASA's Trip to the Moon," *Business Week*, 27 May 1967, 71-72. See also the section on agency leadership in Chapter 8.

47. Erlend A. Kennan and Edmund H. Harvey, Jr., *Mission to the Moon: A Critical Examination of NASA and the Space Program* (New York: Morrow, 1969), 255-69; Amatai Etzioni, *The Moon-Doggle* (New York: Doubleday & Co., 1964), 174. Etzioni describes how NASA officials in the early 1960s liked to mention jokingly that none of the eight congressmen who voted against the 1962 space appropriation were re-elected.

48. Thomas P. Jahnige, "Congress and Space: The Committee System and Congressional Oversight of NASA" (Ph.D. dissertation, Claremont Graduate School, 1965), 273.

49. Van Dyke, *Pride and Power*, 22; John W. Finney, "President Gives 10-Year Program for Space Probes," *New York Times*, 3 February 1959, 1.

50. Van Dyke, *Pride and Power*, 22.

51. Ibid., 147; Eugene M. Emme, "Presidents and Space," in Durant, *Between Sputnik and the Shuttle*, 68.

52. NASA, *The Early Years—Mercury to Apollo-Soyuz* (Washington, D.C.: GPO, 1988), 1.

53. Congress, Senate, Committee on Aeronautical and Space Sciences, Subcommittee on Governmental Organization for Space Activities, *Investigation of Governmental Organization for Space Activities*, 86th Cong., 1st sess., 24 March 1959, 11.

54. NASA, *Space: The New Frontier* (Washington, D.C.: GPO, 1962), 1.

55. Van Dyke, *Pride and Power*, 126.

56. Congress, House, Committee on Science and Astronautics, Subcommittee No. 4, *1961 NASA Authorization*, 86th Cong., 2d sess., 22 February 1960, 326.

57. Congress, House, Committee on Science and Astronautics, *1960 NASA Authorization*, 86th Cong., 1st sess., 24 April 1959, 266.

58. Ibid.

59. John W. Finney, "Space Agency's Chief Says U.S. Will Shun Timetable," *New York Times*, 25 January 1959, 26.

60. Van Dyke, *Pride and Power*, 129.

61. Richard E. Horner, speech to the annual convention of the Society of Technical Writers and Editors, Chicago, Illinois, 21-22 April 1960, NASA History Office, Washington, D.C., 8.

62. NASA, *1-2-3 and the Moon* (Washington, D.C.: GPO, 1963), 29.

63. NASA, *Space: The New Frontier*, 1963, 2. See also NASA, *1-2-3 and the Moon*, 29.

64. Senate Committee on Aeronautical and Space Sciences, 29 March 1960 hearing, 240.

65. Ibid.

66. Van Dyke, *Pride and Power*, 126.

67. Senate Committee on Aeronautical and Space Sciences, 29 March 1960 hearing, 240.

68. House Committee on Science and Astronautics, 20 April 1959 hearing, 3.

69. House Committee on Science and Technology, 24 April 1959 hearing, 266. See also House Committee on Science and Astronautics, 29 January 1960 hearing, 276.

70. House Committee on Science and Astronautics, 20 April 1959 hearing, 3.

71. House Committee on Science and Astronautics, 27 January 1960 hearing, 170.

72. Senate Committee on Aeronautical and Space Sciences, 28 March 1960 hearing, 34.

73. House Committee on Science and Astronautics, 22 February 1960 hearing, 324.

74. Congress, Senate, Committee on Aeronautical and Space Sciences, *NASA Authorization for Fiscal Year 1966*, 89th Cong., 1st sess., 8 March 1965, 13.

75. Van Dyke, *Pride and Power*, 129-30; Congress, House, Committee on Appropriations, Subcommittee on Independent Offices, *Independent Offices Appropriations for 1965*, Part 2, 88th Cong., 2d sess., 7 April 1964, 956.

76. Senate Committee on Aeronautical and Space Sciences, 24 March 1959 hearing, 11.

77. House Committee on Science and Astronautics, 20 April 1959 hearing, 20. See also Congress, House, Committee on Science and Astronautics, *Full Committee Consideration of H.R. 4990 and S. 1096 with Respect to Authorizing Appropriations to the National Aeronautics and Space Administration*, 86th Cong., 1st sess., 9 March 1959, 14.

78. NASA, *Space: The New Frontier*, 1962, 1.

79. Congress, House, Committee on Science and Astronautics, *1964 NASA Authorization*, Part 1, 88th Cong., 1st sess., 4 March 1963, 5.

80. NASA, *Space: The New Frontier*, 1963, 2.

81. Webb, "America's Role in Space Today," 1.

82. NASA, *1-2-3 and the Moon*, 29.

83. House Committee on Science and Astronautics, 4 March 1963 hearing, 5.

84. NASA, *Space: The New Frontier*, 1963, 2.

85. Senate Committee on Aeronautical and Space Sciences, 7 April 1959 hearing, 5.

86. House Committee on Science and Astronautics, 27 January 1960 hearing, 169.

87. Senate Committee on Aeronautical and Space Sciences, 24 March 1959 hearing, 11.

88. Congress, House, Committee on Appropriations, Subcommittee on Independent Offices, *National Aeronautics and Space Administration Appropriations*, 86th Cong., 1st sess., 29 April 1959, 233.

89. John W. Finney, "House Space Cuts Called Crippling," *New York Times*, 5 July 1959, 25.

90. House Committee on Science and Astronautics, 22 February 1960 hearing, 323.

91. House Committee on Appropriations, 29 April 1959 hearing, 21.

92. George M. Low, "Project Mercury Progress," speech to UPI Editors Conference, Washington, D.C., 9 September 1960, NASA History Office, Washington, D.C., 5.

93. House Committee on Science and Astronautics, 29 January 1960 hearing, 272.

94. House Committee on Appropriations, 29 April 1959 hearing, 7.

95. Congress, Senate, Committee on Aeronautical and Space Sciences, Subcommittee on NASA Authorization, *NASA Supplemental Authorization for Fiscal Year 1959*, 86th Cong., 1st sess., 19 February 1959, 29.

96. Dryden, "Safety in the Space Age," 10.

97. Congress, Senate, Committee on Aeronautical and Space Sciences, Subcommittee on NASA Authorization, *NASA Supplemental Authorization for Fiscal Year 1959*, 86th Cong., 1st sess., 20 February 1959, 53.

98. House Committee on Science and Astronautics, 9 March 1959 hearing, 14.

99. Ibid.

100. House Committee on Appropriations, 29 April 1959 hearing, 3; Senate Committee on Aeronautical and Space Sciences, 7 April 1959 hearing, 6.

101. For example, House Committee on Science and Astronautics, 4 April 1960 hearing, 524; Congress, House, Committee on Science and Astronautics, *International Control of Outer Space*, 86th Cong., 1st sess., 11 March 1959, 94-95; and House Committee on Science and Astronautics, 9 March 1959 hearing, 14.

102. House Committee on Science and Astronautics, 20 April 1959 hearing, 6.

103. Senate Committee on Aeronautical and Space Sciences, 28 March 1960 hearing, 34.

104. Van Dyke, *Pride and Power*, 74.

105. Finney, "U.S. Will Shun Timetable," 26.

106. House Committee on Science and Astronautics, 4 April 1960 hearing, 516.

107. Webb, "America's Role in Space Today," 1; Glennan, speech at Wright Day dinner, 8.

108. Congress, House, Committee on Appropriations, Subcommittee on Independent Offices, *Independent Offices Appropriations for 1962*, Part 2, 87th Cong., 1st sess., 15 May 1961, 1078.

109. NASA, *Exploring Space . . . Project Mercury* (Washington, D.C.: GPO, 1961), back cover.

110. House Committee on Science and Astronautics, 4 April 1960 hearing, 524.

111. NASA, *Exploring Space: Projects Mercury and Apollo of the United States Space Program* (Washington, D.C.: GPO, 1961), 17.

112. Glennan, speech at Wright Day dinner, 10-11.

113. Ibid.; Senate Committee on Aeronautical and Space Sciences, 7 April 1959 hearing, 5.

114. See, for example, Seamans, "Reliability in Space Systems," 2; Senate Committee on Aeronautical and Space Sciences, 7 April 1959 hearing, 171.

115. House Committee on Science and Astronautics, 27 January 1960 hearing, 171.

116. NASA, *Exploring Space . . . Project Mercury*, back cover.

117. Emme, "Presidents and Space," 26; Levine, *Future of the U.S. Space Program*, 62; Loyd S. Swenson, Jr., James M. Grimwood, and Charles C. Alexander, *This New Ocean: A History of Project Mercury*, SP-4201 (Washington, D.C.: GPO, 1966), 224.

118. Eisenhower, *Waging Peace*, 260.

119. McDougall, *The Heavens and the Earth*, 228; Emme, "Presidents and Space," 26-29; Levine, *Future of the U.S. Space Program*, 62; Ambrose, *Eisenhower*, 458.

120. Hirsch and Trento, *The National Aeronautics and Space Administration*, 37.

121. McDougall, *The Heavens and the Earth*, 208; Joseph J. Trento, *Prescription for Disaster* (New York: Crown Publishers, 1987), 23.

122. McDougall, *The Heavens and the Earth*, 221-25; Robert L. Rosholt, *An Administrative History of NASA, 1958-1963*, SP-4101 (Washington, D.C.: GPO, 1966), 183.

123. Some scholars have argued that no such gap existed.

124. Howard E. McCurdy, *The Space Station Decision: Incremental Politics and Technological Choice* (Baltimore: Johns Hopkins University Press, 1990), 15. See also Wolfe, *The Right Stuff*, 227.

125. See Wolfe, *The Right Stuff*, 99-105.

126. See the section on heroism in the Chapter 3.

127. Wolfe, *The Right Stuff*, 291-92.

128. *Congressional Quarterly Almanac 1961* (Washington, D.C.: Congressional Quarterly, 1961), 69.

129. Charles Murray and Catherine Bly Cox, *Apollo: The Race to the Moon* (New York: Simon & Schuster, 1989), 67; Levine, *Future of the U.S. Space Program*, 70-71.

130. McDougall, *The Heavens and the Earth*, 315-18; Wolfe, *The Right Stuff*, 227-31.

131. U.S., President, *Public Papers of the Presidents of the United States* (Washington, D.C.: Office of the Federal Register, National Archives and Records Service, 1961), John F. Kennedy, 1961, 404.

132. For a comprehensive account of the way Kennedy reached his decision, see John M. Logsdon, *The Decision to Go to the Moon: Project Apollo and the National Interest* (Cambridge: MIT Press, 1970).

133. *Public Papers of the Presidents*, John F. Kennedy, 1961, 404.

134. *Public Papers of the Presidents*, John F. Kennedy, 1962, 669.

135. Office of Technology Assessment, *Civilian Space Policy*, 136.

136. George Horace Gallup, *The Gallup Poll: Public Opinion, 1935-1971* (New York: Random House, 1972), 1720.

137. "Attitudes Toward the Moon Race Among Opinion Leaders and the General Public," conducted for Grumman Aircraft Engineering Corporation by Fuller & Smith & Ross Inc., November 1963, NASA History Office, Washington, D.C.

138. Bilstein, *Orders of Magnitude*, SP-4406, 59.

139. Van Dyke, *Pride and Power*, 148.

140. The seventh of the original astronauts, Donald K. "Deke" Slayton, was grounded during Mercury due to a minor heart irregularity. Slayton eventually received medical clearance and flew in the 1975 Apollo-Soyuz Test Project.

3

Romanticism

"The Space Age is an era of exploration, discovery, and scientific achievement without parallel in history," declared a 1981 NASA publication. In what marks a turning point in human history, the agency observed, people are beginning to venture out from the earth. Past travelers experienced the thrill of adventure alone, but today modern communications enable people staying at home to witness the excitement. "In the Space Age," NASA said, "we are all explorers."[1]

The preceding passage typifies romanticism, an image designed to tap the romantic and adventuresome streak in human nature. Romanticism has invited the public to participate vicariously in NASA's exciting and heroic activities. It has emphasized the spectacular nature of NASA's endeavors and thus offered the public a way to escape temporarily the humdrum routine of daily life. By accenting the more intangible and personal rewards of the space program, romanticism sharply contrasts with both nationalism, which has stressed the benefits to the nation, and pragmatism, which has emphasized the practical byproducts of the space program. Romanticism has relied on the fact expressed by NASA's Richard Truly in a 1988 agency publication: "Men and women are more than economic creatures and patriots."[2]

NASA's mission has been well suited to the use of romanticism. Few if any other governmental agencies pursue activities as inherently glamorous and highly visible as those of NASA. NASA's exploration of space naturally captured people's fancy more readily than, for instance, the Department of Agriculture's inspection of meat. Highlighting the enthralling aspects of its operations lies at the center of NASA's romantic image. Although NASA has used romanticism throughout its history, the agency employed the image most heavily while pursuing the Apollo program during the 1960s.

MAJOR THEMES IN ROMANTICISM

Several distinct but related themes have emerged within romanticism. First is the idea that NASA helps fulfill the ingrained human urge, particularly strong in Americans, to explore the unknown and expand the frontier. A second theme has revolved around the heroism of the space program's most visible participants, the astronauts. Another romantic theme has stressed the emotional rewards that emanate from space exploration. Finally, NASA has portrayed its activities as a good way to satisfy humans' natural curiosity. NASA has accentuated different romantic themes at different times.

Exploration

NASA has frequently referred to exploration and its importance to the human spirit. According to this romantic theme, the yearning to explore is a fundamental and inescapable part of the human character. "The urge to explore is innate in man," declared a 1960 agency statement. NASA was still espousing this idea in 1988: "If there is one constant in human history, it is that people *will* explore."[3] NASA also asserted that "the intangible imperative of human exploration will not, in the long run, be denied."[4]

For centuries, according to NASA, this yen for exploration has prompted people to leave behind the comforts of home and set out to investigate unknown territories. However, these journeys inevitably change over time as technological advances create new means of transportation and more of the world becomes settled. "Each generation faces the perennial crisis of running out of new frontiers to explore," NASA pointed out in 1965.[5] Because of the constant search for new frontiers, "Over the past few millennia, we have succeeded in touching every corner of the planet Earth."[6] The result, said a 1960 NASA statement, is that "our globe seems to have shrunk and shriveled."[7]

Since opportunities for fresh exploration on earth have dwindled, people must look elsewhere—and space is the obvious choice. A NASA official told Congress in 1977, "Space is undoubtedly the greatest remaining frontier in terms of both its vastness and its potential for as yet unconceived discoveries."[8] Voyaging into space is also heir to a noble tradition, the agency has said. A 1965 NASA publication praised the human entry into space as "exploration in the truest and most romantic sense. It requires all of the classical ingredients: men, machines, curiosity, and determination." Therefore space naturally has become "the most recent of these 'last' frontiers" humans have tackled.[9]

Just as NASA has compared space exploration to the exploration of the earth in past times, the agency has compared its astronauts to the great explorers of history. Some of the references are general, recalling the exploits of the Spanish, the Portuguese, or the South Sea Islanders, for example.[10] Other references have named specific people. The list of explorers that NASA has alluded to in this way is long and illustrious. According to the agency, the astronauts follow in the tradition of Marco Polo, Lewis and Clark, Lindbergh, Diaz, da Gama, Cabot, Magellan, Drake, Peary, and Amundsen.[11]

The historic explorer most frequently raised in NASA statements has been, unsurprisingly, Christopher Columbus.[12] NASA also has often expressed admiration for Columbus's benefactor, Queen Isabella. In 1963 James Webb said that even though the voyage of Columbus "has pretty well disappeared from the front pages, . . . Isabella is rarely criticized for her folly in financing that expedition."[13] Twenty-five years later, Webb's successor made a similar point. In 1988 James Fletcher praised Queen Isabella for funding Columbus and hoped that Congress would follow her lead when setting NASA's budget: "She decided wisely and I expect that this Congress will decide wisely."[14]

Money alone is not enough to fuel today's voyages, NASA has indicated; modern exploration also requires modern technology. Luckily, rapid advances in technology during the past few decades have made space exploration possible. NASA announced in 1960: "With remarkable suddenness . . . a new frontier has been opened. A new domain—outer space—awaits conquest by man."[15]

Technological advances "have enabled man to escape his earthly environment" and to begin exploring space.[16] As T. Keith Glennan exclaimed in 1958, "Man always has had his eyes fixed upon the stars. Now, for the first time, he has the ability to take his first faltering steps toward those goals."[17] It is inconceivable, NASA argued, that humans will not use their new-found ability to explore space.[18] According to a 1960 agency statement, "Nothing can hold back this drive into space except the collapse of our civilization."[19]

American history, NASA has contended, demonstrates that the impulse to explore is particularly strong in the American character and helps explain why the nation pursues a space program. A NASA official told Congress in 1977, "Space exploration provides a focus for the innovative energies of Americans, whose short history is marked by the recognition of frontiers and the drive to conquer those frontiers."[20] A 1960 agency statement explaining why the United States should want to explore space said, "We yield to the urge to explore that is an American heritage."[21]

NASA has asserted that this appetite for exploration still lives in the American spirit. As James Beggs remarked in 1984, "I believe that this Nation is going to want to continue to explore indefinitely."[22] In modern times this drive means that the nation will be active in space. As a result, NASA has indicated, the United States will play a dominant role in the conquest of space. James Fletcher declared in 1986, "Space has been, and . . . will continue to be, an American frontier."[23]

NASA has highlighted its key role in the exploration of space and frequently restated its strong commitment to the endeavor.[24] In 1975, James Fletcher asserted that the agency had proven the value of space activity: "We are confident that NASA's achievements have established space exploration as a keystone in humanity's continued quest for new knowledge and better life on this planet."[25] NASA remarked in 1989 that its thirty years of exploring space had placed the agency at "the forefront of this emergence of the human species from its home planet" and that therefore "NASA stands at the edge of an American frontier."[26]

NASA has often stressed its plans to continue exploring space. NASA described its Kennedy Space Center as "the place from which our civilization will go out to other worlds."[27] A 1989 agency publication noted that NASA's position "at the edge of human technology" enables it to pursue effectively its "mission of exploring unknown realms of air and space."[28] The agency also declared that the human "imperative to explore" will fuel the ambition to visit Mars.[29] In general, Administrator Fletcher said in 1987, "NASA embodies the human spirit's desire to discover, to explore, and to understand."[30]

Frontier Images. One intriguing aspect of NASA's romantic image, especially prevalent in its references to exploration, has been the frequent use of frontier images. Several of the passages already quoted, included to illustrate other points, feature such images. NASA's heavy reliance on frontier imagery is not surprising given the importance of the frontier in American history and the romantic appeal the image seems to hold for contemporary Americans. In the early 1960s, references to the frontier also meshed nicely with President Kennedy's "New Frontier" rhetoric.

Echoes of Frederick Jackson Turner's "frontier thesis" have resounded in many of NASA's statements. Turner wrote in 1893 that the constant American movement into the frontier shaped the national character. Turner believed the "traits of the frontier" include strength, inquisitiveness, restlessness, practicality, and individuality. Even though the frontier on this continent was closed, he argued, Americans still wanted to move and "the American energy will continually demand a wider field for its exercise."[31] Turner was probably not thinking of outer space when he wrote those words, but he presaged a theme used by NASA decades after his death.

NASA apparently regards invoking the spirit of the frontier as an effective way to galvanize the American public. Looking for public support for NASA in the crucial early days of the agency, Wernher von Braun wrote in an article for a Sunday newspaper supplement, "I just don't believe the American people are ready to concede that they have lost their frontier spirit—just as we enter the struggle for man's last and limitless frontier."[32] A NASA booklet published at another key moment in the agency's history, shortly after the loss of the shuttle *Challenger* and its crew, maintained that the agency was determined "to remain undeterred by the tragedy and to continue to explore the frontiers of space."[33]

NASA has often compared the frontiers of the American West to the frontiers of space. Administrator James Webb exclaimed in 1962, "We want to give the American people something in modern terms that they can be as proud of as the heroic march of the settlers who came West over the Oregon trail."[34] In 1965 Webb lauded the ability of Americans to adjust to the space age

just as Americans adjusted to the frontiers of this Nation. We made our advance into the Western area and had to adapt the systems for development of organized society in the East to completely new conditions, such as dryland farming, the use of the six-shooter to pursue Indian raiders when a rifle would not do the job, and even the adjustment of the riparian laws to the requirements of that age.[35]

Webb employed this analogy to explain the obstacles faced by NASA: "We are on a frontier; we are facing new and difficult problems."[36]

Other examples of NASA's use of frontier images abound. Many NASA statements have included brief references to the "frontiers of space" or the "space frontier."[37] A 1966 agency publication stated, "Man has taken long steps across the frontiers of the unknown since the opening of the Space Age."[38] Frontier imagery has sometimes been employed to give a romantic flavor to subjects less romantic than space flight. For example, NASA has spoken of "the economic frontier of space,"[39] "the frontiers of knowledge,"[40] and "the frontiers of technology."[41]

Along with references to the frontier and the American West have come allusions to pioneering in general. NASA has often labeled its activities as "pioneering."[42] A 1960 agency statement said that space flight "appeals to our pioneering spirit."[43] In the early 1970s James Fletcher spoke of "our traditions as a pioneering nation."[44]

Astronauts have frequently named the chance to pioneer as a major incentive for their careers. Mercury astronaut Alan Shepard said an "urge to pioneer" led him to the space program.[45] His colleague Gus Grissom similarly credited "a spirit of pioneering and adventure" and remarked, "If I had been alive 150 years ago, I might have wanted to go out and help open up the West."[46] Scott Carpenter, another Mercury astronaut, said, "I feel that this is the greatest opportunity to pioneer that has ever been."[47]

What will be the outcome of pioneering in space? James Beggs said in 1984, "History has taught us that the process of pushing back frontiers on earth begins with exploration and discovery, which are followed by permanent settlement and economic development."[48] Space will be explored and eventually settled, NASA has argued, just as the American West was. "Compressed into one decade of activity in space," argued NASA's Harrison Schmitt, "history has seen the equivalent of two centuries of exploration of the great American West."[49] The next step will be the civilization of space; a process that is now technologically possible and that has, in fact, already begun.[50]

Differences in Modern Exploration. Despite the similarities between space exploration and the exploration of the earth, NASA has noted, there are some important differences. One is the programs' rate of progress. Five hundred years elapsed "between Leif Ericson's first visit to the New World and modern man's first settlement there." Yet today, NASA's new space station would be a "permanent outpost in space, even though our first visit took place only 30 years ago."[51]

Another major difference is the highly public nature of space exploration. "Less than 100 people witnessed Columbus' landfall in the New World," NASA said, but "half a *billion* watched on television as Armstrong and Aldrin stepped onto the Moon."[52] The chance to watch on television can also make viewers feel like participants in the exploration. As NASA explained,

In past explorations, a few hardy souls ventured out, while the rest waited for months or years to hear what they had found. In the Space Age we are all explorers. Through the miracles of modern communications we have watched together as these new worlds have been revealed.[53]

Thus, while space exploration shares many traits with earlier variations of exploration, NASA argues that it has the potential to provide an entire new range of exciting benefits. Overall, NASA said in 1981, "The exploration of space may be only the latest episode in the long human history of wondering and seeking, but the sudden explosions of travel, new sights, and scientific discovery exceed anything that preceded them."[54]

Heroism

It takes heroic people to explore unknown territories and conquer the frontier, and Americans tend to admire such people. The arrival of the space age brought a new type of hero: the astronaut. NASA has always recognized the public relations potential of the astronauts and has gone to great lengths to cultivate their images. In fact, presenting the astronauts as all-American heroes was one of the first ways NASA sought to build political support.

Numerous observers have described how NASA has manipulated the images of the astronauts, especially those of the original seven Mercury astronauts. Even before the Mercury flights began, there was tremendous press and public interest in and adulation of those first seven astronauts. This attention presented NASA with a wonderful opportunity to implement one of its images and convey the romantic image of space exploration. NASA and the press created such a fanfare around the seven men that they became, according to one critic, "hero[es]-before-the-fact."[55] Another observer, Tom Wolfe, wrote, "From a sheerly political or public relations standpoint, the astronaut was NASA's prize possession."[56]

NASA clearly emphasized the heroic and romantic aspects of the astronauts. Author Michael Smith asserts that NASA cast them in the role of the helmsman, one of the characters traditionally used in American advertising, to help sell the space program. The helmsman, says Smith, is a masculine figure "whose mastery over his environment through the products of technology provides a model for consumer aspiration."[57] Another observer makes a similar argument, noting that the early astronauts were often compared with cowboys, rugged individualists bravely working in a hostile environment.[58] The cowboy image is, of course, a natural match for NASA's talk of the frontier and pioneering.

As portrayed by NASA, the early astronauts "seemed to personify the legendary traits of an imagined earlier America," which was dominated by white, Protestant, adventurous men from a small town or rural background.[59] In fact, although the astronauts were definitely presented as heroes, they were also depicted as "typical" Americans. This was important because the astronauts represented the nation in the Cold War space contest with the Soviet Union.[60]

NASA looked for clean-cut types while screening astronaut applicants, and it encouraged the selectees to uphold that image. For instance, NASA officials frowned upon astronauts using swear words. This attitude persisted after Mercury, for officials became perturbed when Apollo 10 astronaut Gene Cernan muttered "son of a bitch" when he encountered a problem during the flight.[61] The agency's attempts to smooth the astronauts' rough edges ended up obscuring their personalities from the public. One critic contends that NASA promoted the astronauts as being nearly identical, thus eliminating most sense of character and destroying much of the public's curiosity about the astronauts.[62]

With NASA's cooperation, *Life* magazine lionized and sanitized the original Mercury astronauts in a series of exclusive articles. The articles furthered the process of turning the astronauts into bland good guys. One observer said that in the *Life* stories, the astronauts came out "deodorized, plasticized, and homogenized."[63] NASA retained the right to censor the astronauts' comments even though the articles were supposedly geared toward their personal rather than professional lives.[64]

After Mercury, the number of astronauts increased and their individual fame decreased.[65] Yet NASA still carefully tended the astronauts' images. Several former astronauts have commented on NASA's efforts to mold their images. In 1973, Edwin "Buzz" Aldrin, the second man on the moon, said that while the media attention to the Apollo astronauts probably helped NASA politically, the reporting was not wholly accurate. He said of that media coverage:

Nearly all of it had us squarely on the side of God, Country and Family. To read those accounts was to believe we were the most simon-pure guys there had ever been. This simply was not so. We all went to church when we could, but we also celebrated some pretty wild nights.[66]

Alfred Worder, who flew on Apollo 15, made a comparable statement: "We were presented as Boy Scouts, something we weren't. We were all just people, with good points and bad points."[67] Apollo 7 astronaut Walt Cunningham used a very similar phrase: "Instead of letting us be human, they wanted us to act like Boy Scouts, live in a monastery."[68] Even astronauts' spouses were not immune from NASA's efforts to cover up personal problems; Annie Glenn's stutter was kept secret.[69]

While NASA no longer exalts astronauts to the extent it once did, the agency still tries to enhance their image. To help do so, NASA has always highlighted the astronauts' bravery. Courage is a prerequisite for astronauts, the agency has maintained, because of the mysteries and risks of space exploration. T. Keith Glennan explained in 1959, "As we set out to explore the universe, we have no way of knowing what to expect, any more than the great explorers of the 15th century knew what they would find when they sailed their little ships out upon the deep Atlantic."[70] Space exploration is another example, according to NASA, of humans "defying the elements."[71] The Mercury astronauts also had to be willing to work with dangerous equipment; NASA's early rockets, tested in unmanned missions, had a disturbing tendency to blow up.[72]

Later incidents confirmed the danger of space exploration. Three astronauts died in 1967 while training in an Apollo capsule, the crew of the 1970 Apollo 13 mission barely managed to return to earth safely after an explosion in the spacecraft, and seven astronauts perished in the 1986 space shuttle *Challenger* disaster. Because of the very real danger, NASA said in 1988, astronauts "have to be brave and willing to accept the risks that accompany space exploration."[73]

The astronauts themselves have contributed to their heroic images through their words as well as their deeds. Many of them have spoken openly of the risk involved in their business and their willingness to accept that risk. John Glenn said, "Everybody is aware of the danger. . . . You feel it's important enough to take the risk."[74] John Young, commander of the first shuttle mission, said: "Riding a rocket is definitely not routine. . . . The men and women who fly these things are extremely brave."[75] Shuttle astronaut Rhea Seddon said of launches: "I think you have to be mentally prepared to die at that point in time."[76] Her colleague, George "Pinky" Nelson, commented that even though space flight is undeniably risky, "Any chance I get to fly, I jump in."[77]

Astronauts do not rely solely on their bravery, however. NASA has emphasized that they receive extensive training. In 1959, NASA asserted that the seven Mercury astronauts would "receive the most intensive course of training ever offered to a party of prospective explorers."[78] In general, NASA remarked, astronauts are "thoroughly trained to operate in space and respond correctly to emergencies."[79] Their training covers a wide range of subjects. A 1966 NASA booklet described the process undergone by the Gemini astronauts:

The astronauts are put through a rigorous course of class, laboratory, and field training. They learn the complexities not only of their spacecraft but also of launch vehicles and ground facilities. They learn such classroom subjects as upper atmosphere physics, geology, astronomy, navigation, computer technology, space medicine, meteorology, communications, and the guidance, propulsion, and aerodynamics of spacecraft.[80]

Training for other NASA programs is similar in its rigor, according to agency statements.

Emotional Rewards

Another recurring theme in romanticism has centered on the various emotional rewards space exploration can provide the exploring nation and its people. As NASA said, "There is an emotional, intangible dimension to the human presence in space."[81] That dimension of space exploration includes several emotionally rewarding aspects: challenge, inspiration, adventure, imagination, and spirituality.

Challenge. NASA has stressed that the exploration of space is one of the greatest and most difficult tasks ever undertaken by humans. T. Keith Glennan said in 1959 that the space program was "one of the most challenging assignments ever given to any generation of Americans."[82] Apollo astronaut Harrison Schmitt told Congress in 1973, "It is my personal belief that in the eyes of history man's exploration of space will be the most significant historical and humanistic activity we have ever undertaken."[83]

Part of the reason space exploration is such a great endeavor, NASA has argued, is its tremendous difficulty. In 1959 NASA said, "The challenge might seem insuperable. . . . Space will not submit readily to conquest."[84] The next year, a NASA statement added that "space is an infinitely vast region, and its conquest will place severe demands on human capabilities and resources."[85] All in all, manned space exploration "is a long road."[86]

In the 1980s NASA asserted that future space exploration would be even harder because the agency had completed the relatively "easy" tasks of reaching the moon and sending unmanned probes throughout the solar system.[87] "After 20 years of challenging and exciting activity, we have done most of the easy things and made most of the obvious discoveries," commented a 1981 agency publication.[88] The goals that remain, such as sending humans to Mars or conducting long-term sojourns on the moon, pose major challenges for NASA's future.[89]

Although exploring the space frontier presents significant difficulties, NASA has said, the United States has the proven ability to do it. NASA Associate Administrator Noel Hinners attested in 1977, "The U.S. has the capability to penetrate that frontier and has been doing so in a rather steady way." Setting goals and then implementing projects are "the essential means by which one can say 'I've done it,'" according to his statement.[90] Doing this requires "well planned, well disciplined efforts," the determined development of the necessary human resources, and significant amounts of money.[91]

Although the technological obstacles may sometimes seem insurmountable, NASA has acknowledged, perseverance will usually be rewarded. "One has only to review the technological accomplishments of mankind in the twentieth century and the 'impossible' becomes merely 'difficult,'" assured NASA in 1959.[92] Similarly, the costs of space exploration may sometimes appear prohibitive, "but mankind in its history has never let the cost of exploration deter him from the task at hand."[93] The cost of exploring space is high, NASA admitted in 1960, but it is a burden that the United States can and should bear, because space flight "poses a challenge we cannot ignore."[94]

Inspiration. According to NASA, great challenges inspire people. The individuals working on the challenging project are inspired to do their best work, which in turn prompts other people to do likewise. NASA has emphasized that the space program provides such inspiration. T. Keith Glennan said of the space program in 1958, "This is an undertaking that demands the very best effort from all of us."[95] James Webb made a similar point in 1965, saying that the space program "focuses the best of our brainpower on the mastery of this new frontier."[96]

Ventures like the space program inspire younger people especially, NASA has contended. Webb wrote in 1963, "Among the major motivations of the space program is . . . the stimulating effects of this challenging national enterprise on all segments of American society, particularly the young."[97] James Beggs concurred in 1984. He told Congress that the space program "motivates and excites our young people, which is probably the most important [reason] of all" the nation will want to continue space exploration.[98]

Unlike many challenges faced in the modern world, the challenge of space exploration does not spring from society's ills. Administrator James Fletcher explained to Congress in 1971:

With our everyday preoccupations, necessarily, with the many serious and often depressing problems we face—the war, unemployment, pollution, crime, narcotics, and so on—there is, I believe, a human hunger for positive elevating goals to work for at the same time as we do what needs to be done in all these other difficult areas.[99]

The space program, Fletcher said, provides those kind of positive challenges.

The cumulative effect of the increased efforts by an inspired citizenry can be highly beneficial to a nation. A NASA deputy assistant administrator explained in 1965, "Historically, a nation has never been dynamic unless it accepted the challenges it could accept. When it has been dynamic, it has reaped a payoff out of all proportion to the investment."[100] Thus, NASA argues, the inspiration generated by accepting the challenge of the space program produces widespread benefits for the nation as well as for individuals.

Adventure. NASA has also highlighted the adventurous side of space exploration and the excitement that it creates. Wernher von Braun's 1960 newspaper article, which he submitted to Congress as part of his testimony, provides some excellent examples of this approach. He accented adventure by writing, "Man's conquest of space is the boldest venture he has ever embarked upon."[101] Von Braun hit both the adventure theme and the frontier motif in this eloquent passage:

We have just opened the door into the limitless reaches of the universe and we can see just far enough ahead to know that man is at the threshold of a momentous area. Here is opportunity, challenge, adventure so tremendous as to exceed anything which has gone before. Here is the tomorrow which youth wants to embrace, and which we must not deny because of a waning of the frontier spirit which made America great.[102]

"Love of adventure" has always driven humans into the unknown, NASA has asserted.[103] Because of it, people have "braved the oceans, the mountains, the deserts, the skies, and finally, space."[104]

Richard Truly, writing in a 1988 NASA publication, explained the ways space exploration excites people:

People are human. They react with their heart as well as their mind. The excitement of space flight has thrilled people well before Uri Gagarin and the Mercury astronauts pioneered manned flight around the Earth. The adventure of space exploration by men and women, the purview no longer of fiction but of engineering, continues to fascinate people here in the United States and around the globe.[105]

This emotional dimension of space is undeniable and important, Truly argued.

NASA has explained that its openness allows everyone to experience the thrill of space. Speaking of the Mercury program in 1961, the agency said, "Peoples everywhere can share freely in the excitement and adventure of this peaceful research and exploration into space."[106] Largely as a result of NASA's activities, a 1965 NASA publication claimed, "Mankind has thrilled at the prospect" of space exploration.[107]

Imagination. NASA has asserted that space exploration sparks human imagination in a way few other activities can. The inherent excitement and adventure of space flight capture people's attention and ignite their imaginations. A 1959 agency publication said, "The possibility of exploring space has challenged man's imagination to the utmost."[108] In 1962, another publication stated that "no enterprise in history has so stirred the human imagination as the reaching of man into space."[109]

Stimulating human imagination is vital, NASA has argued, because imagination is the first step toward achievement. In this way, James Beggs commented in 1984, "Imagination has proved to be a powerful force in human affairs."[110] Beggs described the tremendous influence imagination has on society:

Imagination has helped to pave new paths in technology and to chart the course of science. It has nourished great art and literature and opened the way for civilizations to prosper. And, perhaps most important, it has been intimately connected with the notions of freedom and self-fulfillment that we in the democratic world hold so dear.[111]

The space program therefore is said to perform a critical function by encouraging imagination. A 1981 NASA brochure quoted Scripture to support this point: " 'Where there is no vision, the people perish,' says the Bible."[112] James Beggs advanced a similar argument: "Those nay-sayers and disbelievers who have ignored imagination and its potential to shape our destiny leave only a few, faint footprints on the sands of history."[113]

Imagination is also a crucial commodity in exploration, particularly in space ventures. Limited imaginations might cause the setting of limited objectives, and that would certainly mean limited progress. Hugh Dryden wrote in 1959, "Each age builds on the shoulders of the past. Who then dares to limit the horizons of the physical universe to be ultimately explored by man? The exploration of space has begun; who knows where it will ultimately end?"[114]

A NASA publication of the same year said,

It is presumptuous for man to think of exploring the distant reaches of the universe, but, his appetite whetted by the first ventures beyond the atmosphere, he will unquestionably continue to think about it, and thought is the forerunner of accomplishment.[115]

In this respect, the space program and imagination form a symbiotic cycle, with the space program sparking imagination, which in turn leads to advances both in the space program and in other aspects of society.

Spirituality. NASA officials have also credited space exploration with providing spiritual dividends. James Webb spoke of "the spiritual awakening which accompanies the pursuit of a new, vast and enormously challenging goal."[116] In a 1961 press release, Hugh Dryden noted both spiritual and intellectual benefits of NASA's activities:

The exploration of space can give you new interests and new motivations arising from an expansion of your intellectual and spiritual horizons as you take a longer view of man's role in time and space at this point in the history of the human race.[117]

Wernher von Braun predicted entry into space would induce a profound spiritual awakening:

We need not fear that future space explorers on their heaven-storming journeys will lose their humility. The heavens will surround them as an eternal reminder that there is a force greater than the thrust of their rocket ships, a spirit greater than the cold logic of their computers, a power greater than that of their own nation.[118]

Space exploration will certainly lead to a "revolution of human perspective," von Braun wrote.[119]

Curiosity

A final romantic theme often used by NASA has centered on curiosity, a fundamental component of the human character. People have always been interested in unfamiliar places and things, NASA has explained, and they constantly ask questions. There is, a NASA official told Congress, "a basic human need to determine what's 'out there,' how does it work, who are we, where did we come from and where are we going?"[120]

A 1981 agency publication said, "Human beings don't accept things as they find them. They ask questions, and they search for answers. What am I? Where am I? What is my past? What is my future? From earliest childhood, people want to know things."[121] A 1988 publication agreed, noting that men and women "are seekers of knowledge, inquisitive types, who are born with a desire to learn."[122]

Curiosity has focused much human attention on the heavens, which have fascinated people for centuries. According to NASA, people have long posed such questions as "Why is the sky blue? What makes the Sun shine? What is the Moon made of? What are the stars?"[123] "Man has always been curious about his environment," remarked T. Keith Glennan in 1959.[124]

Curiosity fuels the human desire to explore, NASA has contended. "Curiosity motivates human behavior," wrote NASA's Richard Truly in 1988.[125] Thus, people act on their urge to wander. According to a 1981 NASA brochure:

Curiosity drives us to explore our surroundings. We want to see the unseen and to learn what lies over the next hill. People have always been bothered by blank areas on the map or in the mind, and they have studied and worked and striven and sometimes died to fill them in.[126]

The "need to know has driven human exploration throughout the ages," NASA reiterated in 1988.[127]

Humans have long wanted to fulfill their curiosity about space by actually going there, NASA has stressed. A 1959 agency publication remarked:

For as long as he has had the intelligence to think about it, man has dreamed of penetrating the rind of atmosphere which surrounds his planet and of exploring the vastness of the universe which lie beyond. It is a magnificent dream, compounded of his inherent spirit of adventure and his insatiable thirst for knowledge.[128]

NASA restated that romantic notion in a 1963 agency pamphlet:

For centuries, man has looked to the skies and sought to break the chains which shackled him to a single planet in the vast universe. This aspiration has stemmed not only from his curiosity but also from man's fundamental thirst for knowledge and his readiness to accept a challenge.[129]

People have acted on these yearnings by developing the ability to venture into space. This too is a human characteristic, said NASA: "Man's curiosity has always driven him to search out the unknown and has led him to devise the means of exploring it."[130] Thus, as soon as humans had the chance to explore space they were sure to grab it: "As man achieved the technological advances which permitted him to reach space it was inconceivable that he should not explore it."[131] As a 1988 agency publication noted, "Curiosity led us into space."[132]

NASA has pointed out that it offers the means to satisfy some of this curiosity about space and thereby slake some of people's thirst for knowledge. "We place men and women into orbit in order to learn," according to one statement.[133] In 1989 the agency asserted that "the common thread of NASA's diverse activities is curiosity about the universe, our place and our future in it. It is a thread that extends from the agency's beginnings in 1958 to an open and unbounded future."[134]

NASA's mission is essential, the agency argued, if humans are "to answer some of our oldest and most profound questions: who are we, and what is our place in the universe?"[135] NASA's activities help fulfill humankind's "compelling urge to understand the unknown," the agency said in 1977.[136] Human space exploration "stimulates our minds" and "enables us to question further and to delve deeper."[137]

The information gained and the expertise developed in the "quest for new knowledge" have sometimes been cited as primary justifications for the space program.[138] "In the long run," a 1962 brochure stated, "the most important and valuable return from space exploration will be the vast addition to man's store of knowledge about the universe in which he lives."[139] Exploration leads to "a better understanding of our world, its mechanisms and processes, and the basic natural laws that govern them."[140]

NASA has argued that seeking to satisfy human curiosity, while a romantic activity, often pays practical dividends as well. Wernher von Braun wrote in 1960, "All our modern conveniences had their origin in research which was carried out without regard to practical application and merely because some man wanted to know the how and why of the universe."[141] Three years later, von Braun asserted, "The substance of what we call civilization . . . can all be traced back to the simple fact that at some time someone was curious about something."[142] NASA took the same line in 1981: "It is knowledge, much more than riches, that makes modern civilization possible."[143]

Curiosity will likely compel people to continue the exploration of space, NASA has argued. While the space program has answered some questions, it has raised many more. Much remains to be done in space. After all, space holds "millions of secrets."[144] NASA said in 1981,

We still have farther to reach, more questions to ask, and much more to learn. Like earlier explorers, we have painfully struggled to a high plateau from which we see new mountains and valleys beyond. The answers to our questions, the benefits from the new knowledge, still lie ahead, out of sight, but no longer out of reach.[145]

James Fletcher pledged in 1988 that NASA would continue the quest for knowledge: "For three decades NASA's guiding principle has been, as it will be in the future, the expansion of human knowledge."[146]

STYLES OF ROMANTIC APPEALS

Romanticism has exhibited some notable stylistic traits in addition to the major themes already discussed. The image has often entailed references to the future, nautical images, and the inevitability of space exploration. NASA has also demonstrated its use of romanticism through the names it has selected for some of its programs.

References to the Future

NASA has portrayed itself and its activities as strongly oriented to the future. The cutting-edge technology and long-range planning inherent in the space program make this a natural connection. A 1968 publication declared, "NASA today is a future-oriented organization."[147] James Fletcher explained to Congress in 1977 why NASA had to be that way:

I think we would be remiss if we didn't have a forward-looking agency that looked toward the future in terms of what is going to happen to this country 20 years from now and how we can anticipate and contribute to meeting national needs.[148]

In 1986, Fletcher made the same point during his second tenure as administrator. He said that NASA "is a future-oriented agency, and it is designed to be that way."[149] NASA also speaks of its "commitment to the future."[150]

NASA is a future-oriented agency largely because its activities constitute a "forward-looking program."[151] Fletcher said in 1989, "The Space Program is probably the best example this country has of its way of facing the future. I can't think of another program that's more future-oriented than our National Civil Space Program."[152]

The new space station is heavily promoted in terms of the future. NASA has called the station the "gateway to the future,"[153] "a step into the future,"[154] a "foothold on the future,"[155] and "leadership for the future."[156] All in all, "The Space Station is about the future."[157]

Nautical Images

NASA has sprinkled its romantic statements with images of the sea and sailing, and has frequently drawn analogies between the sea and space. In 1965, for example, the agency said that humans had developed the capacity "to operate in the boundless sea of space."[158] A 1981 publication spoke of America's activities in "the new ocean of space."[159] NASA called its astronauts "star sailors" in 1988.[160] This sort of imagery complements NASA's emphasis on exploration and its correlation of astronauts and previous explorers.

Wernher von Braun stressed the challenge of space in this nautical passage from 1960:

Space lies out there like a vast, unexplored ocean—accessible to all nations large or small, a challenge for anyone with sailor's blood in his veins. Now that for the first time in history man is about ready and able to build ships which can penetrate that ocean, there can be no question that some men will take up the challenge.[161]

A 1961 agency publication took a similar tack: "Just as ancient man explored the seas with ships, . . . so today's man has taken the first of many steps necessary to study and use the space beyond our earth."[162]

More recently, NASA has employed nautical images to urge continued progress in the space program. In 1988 the agency partially justified the space station this way: "By assembling a permanent habitat above Earth, America will find itself conveniently anchored off-shore, ready to sail for still longer voyages into space."[163] That same year another NASA publication sounded a similar note by asserting that "humankind must keep the spirit of exploration alive whether exploring the oceans of Earth of the oceans of space."[164]

Inevitability

Romanticism has also contended that human exploration of space, particularly by Americans, is inevitable. This is not an entirely logical argument, especially since NASA has not really explained why manned exploration is inevitable. However, the agency has tended to state this inevitability as an incontrovertible fact. This appeal recalls the notion of "Manifest Destiny," the

19th-century idea that America's obvious, and perhaps divinely inspired, destiny was to expand to the Pacific Ocean.

NASA has employed the inevitability theme throughout its history. In 1960 NASA's George Low said that "man is destined to play a vital and direct role in the exploration of the moon and of the planets."[165] That same year NASA told Congress, "Manned space flight is inevitable. . . . Space flight is part of America's future destiny."[166] In 1965 NASA remarked, "There has never been any doubt that man would challenge the dangers of space as he has challenged every other unknown."[167] It is "the certain destiny of man" to explore space, said a NASA official in 1969.[168] NASA noted in 1988 that "the fundamental purpose of the Space Station lies in the inevitable extension of human exploration into space."[169]

Program Names

Romanticism has also manifested itself in the names NASA has chosen for some of its programs. Mercury, Gemini, and Apollo are all names that conjure up romantic images. Symbolism was central to the choice of Mercury, the messenger of the gods in Roman mythology, as the name of the first manned space program.[170] One observer noted that Mercury was chosen as the name "after high level debate" because it "had a heroic ring."[171]

The second manned program, which featured two-man crews, was named Gemini, which means "twins" in Latin. The name was also symbolically suitable because the mythological Gemini twins were known as the patron gods of voyagers.[172] The lunar landing program was designated Apollo, after the Greek god known as an archer who could hit distant targets with great accuracy.[173] Apollo was also the god of the sun, who pulled the sun across the sky each day behind his golden chariot.[174]

NASA drew many of the names for its other projects and vehicles from ancient Greek and Roman mythology, which provides a wealth of romantic material. In addition to the three already discussed, the numerous NASA names originating in mythology include: Aeros, a satellite named after the Greek god of the air; Atlas, a launch vehicle referring to the Greek god who bore the world on his shoulders; Pegasus, a satellite with the same name as Greek mythology's winged flying horse; and Titan, a relatively powerful launch vehicle named for the giants of Roman mythology.[175] Yet, especially for its major programs, NASA apparently has not wanted to stray too far from the familiar in its choice of names. The Mercury program was so labeled partly because "Mercury was considered to be most familiar of the Olympians to Americans—thanks more to Detroit than to the god or the planet."[176]

The names of other, less well-known programs, such as the unmanned Magellan, Mariner, and Viking missions, have also struck a romantic chord. The earlier Magellan was a Portuguese explorer who discovered the Straits of

Magellan and the Philippine Islands. A mariner assists in the navigation of a ship and thus plays a central role in exploration. Vikings, of course, are known in part for their willingness to venture far from home. Other NASA projects with romantic names include Explorer, Pioneer, Ranger, Vanguard, Intrepid, and Odyssey.[177]

Romantic names are found even within the shuttle program, which NASA originally promoted on a very unromantic basis. The names of the shuttle orbiters to date are *Enterprise, Columbia, Challenger, Discovery, Atlantis,* and *Endeavour.* The first shuttle, which was used for training exercises and never flew in space, was named the *Enterprise* after the spacecraft in the television series "Star Trek."[178] Fans of the show waged a vigorous campaign in support of the name.[179] Captain James T. Kirk of the fictional *Enterprise* pledged "to boldly go where no man has gone before"—a romantic mission much like NASA's.

Columbia is a literary name for the United States and also recalls Christopher Columbus, one of history's most famous explorers and the man credited with discovering America. *Atlantis* refers to the mythical island that sank beneath the Atlantic Ocean, a legend that has fascinated people for hundreds of years. *Challenger, Discovery,* and *Endeavour* all carry obvious romantic connotations. In addition, the names of the space shuttles were also names of famous sea-going exploring ships.[180]

Administrator Robert Frosch told Congress that the shuttle names were selected because they would "carry a connotation of exploration . . . [and] have perhaps some other useful connotations."[181] Despite the romantic flavor of the individual shuttle names, however, NASA did not completely abandon its original pragmatic portrayal of the overall shuttle program. The program's official title, the Space Transportation System, is suitably prosaic.

CONCLUSION

Romanticism has stressed the intangible benefits of the space program. NASA has argued that the space program fulfills some fundamental human needs by answering the urge to explore, providing the opportunity for heroism, producing emotional rewards, and satisfying curiosity.

NASA has used romanticism to varying degrees throughout its history. The image was most prevalent, however, during the years 1964-72, when NASA pursued the very romantic goal of going to the moon.

NOTES

1. NASA, *A Meeting with the Universe*, ed. Bevan M. French and Stephen P. Moran, EP-177 (Washington, D.C.: NASA, 1981), iv.

2. NASA, *Space Shuttle: The Journey Continues*, by Richard Truly, NP-117 (Washington, D.C.: GPO, 1988), 10.

3. Michael D. Lemonick, "Back to the Future," *Discovery*, January 1989, 47.

4. NASA, *Space Station: A Step into the Future*, by Andrew J. Stofan, PAM-510 (Washington, D.C.: GPO, 1987), 1. See also NASA, *The Journey Continues*, NP-117, 22; and "Moonwalk," *Christian Science Monitor*, 20 July 1989, 11.

5. NASA, *Space Exploration—Why and How*, EP-25 (Washington, D.C.: GPO, 1965), 2.

6. NASA, *Space Station: A Research Laboratory in Space*, PAM-512 (Washington, D.C.: GPO, 1988), 13.

7. Congress, House, Committee on Science and Astronautics, Subcommitee No. 4, *1961 NASA Authorization*, 86th Cong., 2d sess., 19 February 1960, 159.

8. Congress, House, Committee on Science and Technology, Subcommittee on Space Science and Applications, *1978 NASA Authorization*, Part 2, 95th Cong., 1st sess., 9 February 1977, 778.

9. NASA, *Space Exploration—Why and How*, EP-25, 2.

10. For example, see NASA, *Space and the International Cooperation Year: A National Challenge*, by Arnold W. Frutkin, EP-30 (Washington, D.C.: GPO, 1965), 2; House Committee on Science and Astronautics, 19 February 1960 hearing, 159.

11. NASA, *A Meeting with the Universe*, EP-177, 3; NASA, *International Cooperation Year*, EP-30, 2; Congress, Senate, Committee on Aeronautical and Space Sciences, Subcommittee on NASA Authorization, *NASA Authorization for Fiscal Year 1961*, Part 1, 86th Cong., 2d sess., 29 March 1960, 239; and James M. Beggs, "The Wilbur and Orville Wright Memorial Lecture," speech to the Royal Aeronautical Society, London, England, 13 December 1984, NASA History Office, Washington, D.C., 2.

12. See, for example, NASA, *International Cooperation Year*, EP-30, 2; Senate Committee on Aeronautical and Space Sciences, 29 March 1960 hearing, 239; Congress, House, Committee on Science and Technology, *Future Space Programs*, 95th Cong., 2d sess., 26 January 1978, 219; NASA, *A Meeting with the Universe*, EP-177, 3; and NASA, *Space Station: The Next Logical Step*, by Walter Froehlich, EP-213 (Washington, D.C.: NASA, 1984), 48; NASA, *The Dream Is Alive*, IMAX film, 1985, National Air & Space Museum, Washington, D.C.

13. "Webb Expects Faith 7 to End Mercury Program," *New York Times*, 16 May 1963, 18.

14. Congress, House, Committee on Appropriations, Subcommittee on HUD—Independent Agencies, *Department of Housing and Urban Development—Independent Agencies Appropriations for 1989*, Part 7, 100th Cong., 2d sess., 19 April 1988, 62.

15. House Committee on Science and Astronautics, 19 February 1960 hearing, 159.

16. NASA, *International Cooperation Year*, EP-30, 2.

17. T. Keith Glennan, "The Challenge of the Space Age," speech to the Fort Worth Chamber of Commerce, 8 December 1958, NASA History Office, Washington, D.C., 2.

18. NASA, *Space: The New Frontier* (Washington, D.C.: GPO, 1962), 4.

19. House Committee on Science and Astronautics, 19 February 1960 hearing, 159.

20. Congress, House, Committee on Science and Technology, Subcommittee on Space Science and Applications, *1978 NASA Authorization*, Part 2, 95th Cong., 1st sess., 9 February 1977, 778.

21. House Committee on Science and Astronautics, 19 February 1960 hearing, 159.

22. Congress, Senate, Committee on Commerce, Science, and Transportation, Subcommittee on Science, Technology, and Space, *NASA Authorization for Fiscal Year 1985*, 98th Cong., 2d sess., 28 February 1984, 17.

23. Congress, Senate, Committee on Appropriations, Subcommittee on HUD—Independent Agencies, *Department of Housing and Urban Development—Independent Agencies Appropriations for Fiscal Year 1987*, 99th Cong., 2d sess., 15 May 1986, 921.

24. See, for example, Congress, House, Committee on Science and Astronautics, Subcommittee on Manned Space Flight, *1965 NASA Authorization*, Part 2, 88th Cong., 2d sess., 18 February 1964, 364; Congress, House, Committee on Appropriations, Subcommittee on HUD—Independent Agencies, *Department of Housing and Urban Development—Independent Agencies Appropriations for 1976*, Part 2, 94th Cong., 1st sess., 4 March 1975, 8; and NASA, *NASA Highlights 1986-1988* (Washington, D.C.: GPO, 1988), 1.

25. NASA, *New Horizons*, EP-117 (Washington, D.C.: GPO, 1975), 3.

26. NASA, *NASA*, NP-111 (Washington, D.C.: GPO, 1989), 1.

27. NASA, *Kennedy Space Center Story* (Washington, D.C.: GPO, 1973), 1.

28. NASA, NP-111, 1.

29. "NASA Plan May Put Man on Mars By 2011," *New York Times*, 21 November 1989, C13.

30. Congress, House, Committee on Science, Space, and Technology, Subcommittee on Space Science and Applications, *1988 NASA Authorization*, 100th Cong., 1st sess., 5 February 1987, 60.

31. Frederick Jackson Turner, *The Frontier in American History* (Huntington, N.Y.: Robert E. Krieger Publishing, 1976), 37.

32. Congress, Senate, Committee on Aeronautical and Space Sciences, Subcommittee on NASA Authorization, *NASA Authorization for Fiscal Year 1961: Hearing before the Subcommittee on NASA Authorization*, 86th Cong., 2d Sess., 28 March 1960, 240.

33. NASA, *A Research Laboratory in Space*, PAM-512, 1.

34. Vernon Van Dyke, *Pride and Power: The Rationale of the Space Program* (Urbana: University of Illinois Press, 1964), 148.

35. Congress, Senate, Committee on Aeronautical and Space Sciences, *NASA Authorization for Fiscal Year 1966*, 89th Cong., 1st sess., 8 March 1965, 13.

36. Ibid., 14.

37. See, for example, NASA, *A Step into the Future*, PAM-510, 1; Congress, Senate, Committee on Appropriations, Subcommittee on HUD—Independent Agencies, *Department of Housing and Urban Development—Independent Agencies Appropriations for Fiscal Year 1988*, 100th Cong., 1st sess., 9 April 1987, 1031; and NASA, *Space Shuttle: The Renewed Promise*, by Neil McAleer, PAM-521 (Washington, D.C.: GPO, 1989), 5.

38. NASA, *Space: The New Frontier* (Washington, D.C.: GPO, 1966), 4.

39. NASA, *STS 26: Flight of Discovery*, PAM-515 (Washington, D.C.: GPO, 1988), 2.

40. NASA, *Space: The New Frontier*, 1962, 49.

41. NASA, *This Is NASA*, EP-155 (Washington, D.C.: GPO, 1979), 3.

42. See, for example, Congress, Senate, Committee on Appropriations, Subcommittee on HUD—Independent Agencies, *Department of Housing and Urban Development and Certain Independent Agencies Appropriations for Fiscal Year 1983*, Part 2, 97th

Cong., 2d sess., 5 May 1982, 1032; NASA, *The Next Logical Step*, EP-213, 2, 16; "Excerpts from Shuttle Memorandum by Shuttle Chief," *New York Times*, 9 March 1986, 36; and NASA, *Discovering Space for America's Economic Growth* (Washington, D.C.: GPO, 1988), 6.

43. House Committee on Science and Astronautics, 19 February 1960 hearing, 161.

44. L. B. Taylor, Jr., *For All Mankind: America's Space Programs of the 1970s and Beyond* (New York: E. P. Dutton & Co., 1974), 29.

45. Michael L. Smith, "Selling the Moon: The U.S. Manned Space Program and the Triumph of Commodity Scientism," in *The Culture of Consumption*, ed. Richard Wightman Fox and T. J. Jackson Lears (New York: Pantheon Books, 1983), 199-200.

46. Ibid., 200.

47. Congress, House, Committee on Science and Astronautics, *Meeting with the Astronauts*, 86th Cong., 1st sess., 28 May 1959, 10.

48. Beggs, "Wright Memorial Lecture," 2.

49. Congress, Senate, Committee on Aeronautical and Space Sciences, *NASA Authorization for Fiscal Year 1974*, 93d Cong., 1st sess., 10 April 1973, 1588.

50. Ibid., 1588-89; Beggs, "Wright Memorial Lecture," 2.

51. NASA, *A Research Laboratory in Space*, PAM-512, 13.

52. NASA, *A Meeting with the Universe*, EP-177, 4.

53. Ibid., iv.

54. Ibid., 4.

55. William Hines, "NASA: The Image Misfires," *The Nation*, 24 April 1967, 519.

56. Tom Wolfe, *The Right Stuff* (Toronto: Bantam Books, 1979), 160.

57. Smith, "Selling the Moon," 184-85.

58. Kenneth Dean Cooper, "Mission Control: The Manned Space Program and the Reincarnation of the Frontier Myth" (M.A. thesis, Vanderbilt University, 1988).

59. Smith, "Selling the Moon," 199.

60. See Wolfe, *The Right Stuff*, 101-104.

61. Charles Murray and Catherine Bly Cox, *Apollo: The Race to the Moon* (New York: Simon & Schuster, 1989), 339.

62. David Bamberger, "NASA and Watergate: How the Publicists Lost the Public," *America*, 19 July 1975, 33. See also Robert Sherrod, "The Selling of the Astronauts," *Columbia Journalism Review* 12 (May/June 1973): 25.

63. Sherrod, "The Selling of the Astronauts," 17.

64. Ibid., 17-20.

65. Richard Hirsch and Joseph John Trento, *The National Aeronautics and Space Administration* (New York: Praeger, 1973), 171.

66. Col. Buzz Aldrin with Wayne Warga, "Return to Earth," *Good Housekeeping*, October 1973, 212.

67. Jeff Goldberg, "Lunar Reflections," *Omni*, July 1989, 86.

68. Sherrod, "The Selling of the Astronauts," 17.

69. Dale Carter, *The Final Frontier: The Rise and Fall of the American Rocket State* (London: Verso, 1988), 169.

70. Congress, Senate, Committee on Aeronautical and Space Sciences, NASA Authorization Subcommittee, *NASA Authorization for Fiscal Year 1960*, 86th Cong., 1st sess., Part 1, 7 April 1959, 6.

71. NASA, *Space: The New Frontier*, 1962, 28.

72. Hirsch and Trento, *The National Aeronautics and Space Administration*, 88-93.

73. NASA, *On the Wings of a Dream: The Space Shuttle*, EP-269 (Washington, D.C.: GPO, 1988), 28.

74. Bill Nelson with Jamie Buckingham, *Mission: An American Congressman's Voyage to Space* (San Diego: Harcourt Brace Jovanovich, Publishers, 1988), 15.

75. Henry S. F. Cooper, Jr., *Before Liftoff: The Making of a Space Shuttle Crew* (Baltimore: Johns Hopkins University Press, 1987), 12.

76. Rhea Seddon, interview by Al Tompkins, WSMV-TV News, Nashville, Tennessee, 27 July 1989.

77. William J. Broad, "Back Into Space," *New York Times*, 3 July 1988, sec. 6, p. 35.

78. House Committee on Science and Astronautics, 28 May 1959 hearing, 28.

79. NASA, *Most Asked Questions About Space and Aeronautics* (Washington, D.C.: GPO, 1973), 7. See also NASA, *Exploring Space: Projects Mercury and Apollo of the United States Space Program* (Washington, D.C.: GPO, 1961), 7.

80. NASA, *Project Gemini* (Washington, D.C.: GPO, 1966), 21-22.

81. NASA, *The Journey Continues*, NP-117, 7.

82. Senate Committee on Aeronautical and Space Sciences, 7 April 1959 hearing, 6.

83. Senate Committee on Aeronautical and Space Sciences, 10 April 1973 hearing, 1590.

84. NASA, *The Challenge of Space Exploration* (Washington, D.C.: GPO, 1959), 3.

85. House Committee on Science and Astronautics, 19 February 1960 hearing, 159.

86. Congress, House, Committee on Appropriations, Subcommittee on Independent Offices, *National Aeronautics and Space Administration Appropriations*, 86th Cong., 1st sess., 29 April 1959, 16.

87. NASA, NP-111, 1.

88. NASA, *A Meeting with the Universe*, EP-177, v.

89. NASA, NP-111, 1.

90. House Committee on Science and Technology, 9 February 1977 hearing, 778.

91. T. Keith Glennan, speech at the Wright Day Dinner, 17 December 1958, NASA History Office, Washington, D.C., 11; House Committee on Science, Space, and Technology, 5 February 1987 hearing, 61; and House Committee on Science and Astronautics, 19 February 1960 hearing, 159.

92. NASA, *The Challenge of Space Exploration*, 3.

93. House Committee on Science and Astronautics, 19 February 1960 hearing, 159.

94. Ibid., 161.

95. Glennan, speech at the Wright Day Dinner, 11.

96. James E. Webb, "The Challenge and Promise of the Space Age," speech at the University of Miami, 25 January 1965, NASA History Office, Washington, D.C., 2.

97. NASA, *Space: The New Frontier* (Washington, D.C.: GPO, 1963), 2.

98. Senate Committee on Commerce, Science, and Transportation, 28 February 1984 hearing, 17.

99. Congress, Senate, Committee on Appropriations, *Department of Housing and Urban Development, Space, and Science Appropriations for Fiscal Year 1972*, 92d Cong., 1st sess., 23 June 1971, 471.

100. Evert Clark, "Key Space Decision in Mid-70's Seen," *New York Times*, 14 October 1965, 8.

101. Senate Committee on Aeronautical and Space Sciences, 29 March 1960 hearing, 239.

102. Ibid., 241.

103. Congress, House, Committee on Appropriations, Subcommittee on Independent Offices, *Independent Offices Appropriations for 1966*, Part 2, 89th Cong., 1st sess., 5 April 1965, 853. See also NASA, *The Challenge of Space Exploration*, 2; and House Committee on Science and Astronautics, 19 February 1960 hearing, 159.

104. House Committee on Appropriations, 5 April 1965 hearing, 853.

105. NASA, *The Journey Continues*, NP-117, 10.

106. NASA, *Exploring Space . . . Project Mercury* (Washington, D.C.: GPO, 1961), back cover.

107. NASA, *International Cooperation Year*, EP-30, 3.

108. NASA, *The Challenge of Space Exploration*, 43.

109. NASA, *Space: The New Frontier*, 1962, 8.

110. Beggs, "Wright Memorial Lecture," 2.

111. Ibid.

112. NASA, *A Meeting with the Universe*, EP-177, v.

113. Beggs, "Wright Memorial Lecture," 2.

114. House Committee on Science and Astronautics, 28 May 1959 hearing, 29.

115. NASA, *The Challenge of Space Exploration*, 44.

116. Van Dyke, *Pride and Power*, 154-55.

117. Ibid., 89.

118. Senate Committee on Aeronautical and Space Sciences, 29 March 1960 hearing, 241.

119. Ibid., 241.

120. House Committee on Science and Technology, 9 February 1977 hearing, 779.

121. NASA, *A Meeting with the Universe*, EP-177, 3.

122. NASA, *The Journey Continues*, NP-117, 10.

123. NASA, *A Meeting with the Universe*, EP-177, 3.

124. Congress, Senate, Committee on Aeronautical and Space Sciences, Subcommittee on NASA Authorization, *NASA Supplemental Authorization for Fiscal Year 1959*, 86th Cong., 1st sess., 19 February 1959, 29.

125. NASA, *The Journey Continues*, NP-117, 10.

126. NASA, *A Meeting with the Universe*, EP-177, 3.

127. NASA, *The Journey Continues*, NP-117, 10.

128. NASA, *The Challenge of Space Exploration*, 2.

129. NASA, *1-2-3 and the Moon* (Washington, D.C.: GPO, 1963), 2.

130. NASA, *Space: The New Frontier*, 1962, 1.

131. Ibid., 4.

132. NASA, *Science in Orbit: The Shuttle & Spacelab Experience: 1981-1986*, NP-119 (Washington, D.C.: GPO, 1988), 115.

133. NASA, *The Journey Continues*, NP-117, 10.

134. NASA, NP-111, 3.

135. Ibid., 36.

136. Congress, House, Committee on Appropriations, Subcommittee on HUD—Independent Agencies, *Department of Housing and Urban Development—Independent Agencies Appropriations for 1978*, Part 5, 95th Cong., 1st sess., 29 March 1977, 13.

137. NASA, *The Journey Continues*, NP-117, 10.

138. Congress, House, Committee on Science and Astronautics, *Review of the Space Program*, 86th Cong., 2d sess., 27 January 1960, 174.

139. NASA, *Space: The New Frontier*, 1962, 1.

140. NASA, *A Meeting with the Universe*, EP-177, 3.

141. Senate Committee on Aeronautical and Space Sciences, 29 March 1960 hearing, 239.

142. Wernher von Braun, *Space Frontier* (New York: Holt, Rinehart and Winston, 1971), 250.

143. NASA, *A Meeting with the Universe*, EP-177, 3.

144. NASA, *Exploring Space*, 4.

145. NASA, *A Meeting with the Universe*, EP-177, 4.

146. NASA, *Agenda for Tomorrow* (Washington, D.C.: GPO, 1988), 1.

147. NASA, *This Is NASA*, EP-22 (Washington, D.C.: GPO, 1968), 1.

148. House Committee on Appropriations, 29 March 1977 hearing, 45.

149. Congress, House, Committee on Appropriations, Subcommittee on HUD—Independent Agencies, *Department of Housing and Urban Development—Independent Agencies Appropriations for 1987*, Part 7, 99th Cong., 2d sess., 13 May 1986, 52.

150. See, for example, Congress, Senate, Committee on Aeronautical and Space Sciences, *NASA Authorization for Fiscal Year 1974*, Part 1, 93d Cong., 1st sess., 3 March 1973, 319; and Congress, House, Committee on Science and Astronautics, Subcommittee on Manned Space Flight, *1974 NASA Authorization*, Part 2, 93d Cong., 1st sess., 27 February 1973, 10.

151. Congress, House, Committee on Appropriations, Subcommittee on HUD—Independent Agencies, *Department of Housing and Urban Development—Independent Agencies Appropriations for 1985*, Part 6, 98th Cong., 2d sess., 27 March 1984, 2.

152. Congress, House, Committee on Science, Space, and Technology, Subcommittee on Space Science and Applications, *1990 NASA Authorization*, 101st Cong., 1st sess., 2 February 1989, 35.

153. NASA, *The Next Logical Step*, EP-213, 44.

154. NASA, *A Step into the Future*, PAM-510, 1.

155. NASA, *Space Station Freedom: A Foothold on the Future*, by Leonard David, NP-107 (Washington, D.C.: GPO, 1988), 2, 40.

156. NASA, *Space Station: Leadership for the Future*, by Franklin D. Martin and Terence T. Finn, PAM-509 (Washington, D.C.: GPO, 1987), 1.

157. NASA, *A Research Laboratory in Space*, PAM-512, 11.

158. NASA, *International Cooperation Year*, EP-30, 2.

159. NASA, *A Meeting with the Universe*, EP-177, 3.

160. NASA, *On the Wings of a Dream*, EP-269, 28.

161. Senate Committee on Aeronautical and Space Sciences, 29 March 1960 hearing, 241.

162. NASA, *Exploring Space*, 1.

163. NASA, *Foothold on the Future*, NP-107, 4.

164. NASA, *On the Wings of a Dream*, EP-269, 28.

165. George M. Low, "Project Mercury Progress," speech to UPI Editors Conference, Washington, D.C., 9 September 1960, NASA History Office, Washington, D.C., 2.

166. House Committee on Science and Astronautics, 19 February 1960 hearing, 160-61.

167. House Committee on Appropriations, 5 April 1965 hearing, 853.

168. NASA, *Man in Space*, by David A. Anderton, EP-57, (Washington, D.C.: GPO, 1969), introduction.

169. NASA, *A Research Laboratory in Space*, PAM-512, 13.

170. Helen T. Wells, Susan H. Whiteley, and Carrie E. Karegeannes, *Origins of NASA Names*, SP-4402 (Washington, D.C.: GPO, 1976), 106.

171. John Noble Wilford, *We Reach the Moon* (New York: Bantam Books, 1969), 14.

172. Wells et al., *Origins of NASA Names*, SP-4402, 104.

173. Wilford, *We Reach the Moon*, 14.

174. Wells et al., *Origins of NASA Names*, SP-4402, 99.

175. Ibid., 33, 9, 66, 25.

176. Wilford, *We Reach the Moon*, 14.

177. Wells et al., *Origins of NASA Names*, SP-4402.

178. Congress, Senate, Committee on Commerce, Science, and Transportation, *NASA Authorization for Fiscal Year 1980*, 96th Cong., 1st sess., 21 February 1979, 908.

179. Andrew Wilson, *Space Shuttle Story* (London: Hamlyn Publishing, 1986), 18.

180. Senate Committee on Commerce, Science, and Transportation, 21 February 1979 hearing, 908.

181. Congress, Senate, Committee on Commerce, Science, and Transportation, Subcommittee on Science, Technology, and Space, *U.S. Civilian Space Policy*, 96th Cong., 1st sess., 25 January 1979, 24.

4

The Apollo Era

NASA was on the move in the 1960s. The agency had been given an ambitious goal—to land men on the moon and return them safely to earth, and to do so by the end of the decade—and it worked strenuously to reach that goal. The Apollo project, consisting of eleven manned missions between 1968 and 1972, was NASA's program to achieve that lunar goal. Work on Apollo began soon after President John F. Kennedy announced the objective in 1961 and intensified after the Mercury program concluded in 1963. As discussed here, the Apollo era stretched from 1964 to 1972, the period between the end of the Mercury program and the last Apollo mission in December 1972.[1]

NASA continued to use nationalism as its primary image during the Apollo era. Apollo was conceived, sold, and carried out during the Cold War, and competition with the Soviet Union—a nationalist theme—played a crucial role in generating support for the program. NASA emphasized the important role Apollo would play in protecting America's national interests. Yet NASA also frequently used romanticism to sell the Apollo program. In fact, while NASA has employed romanticism to varying degrees throughout its history, it used the image most extensively during the Apollo years. Therefore the Apollo era makes a good case study of romanticism.

Kennedy helped set the stage for NASA's use of romanticism by urging America to do great things. For example, Kennedy's September 12, 1962, speech on space struck a clearly romantic theme: "We choose to go to the moon in this decade, and do the other things, not because they are easy but because they are hard."[2] In addition, events later in the 1960s made romanticism seem more appealing than nationalism. As the United States eroded the Soviet Union's lead in space, Americans felt less threatened by the Soviet space program and found nationalism less compelling.

Furthermore, for many Americans, the nation's involvement in Vietnam provoked distrust of the government and skepticism about nationalist claims. Romanticism also matched well the inherently romantic Apollo program.

NASA employed all four of the major romantic themes in its statements on Apollo.

PREPARING FOR APOLLO

NASA had been contemplating a manned mission to the moon even before Kennedy made such a trip a definite NASA goal. Although thrilled with Kennedy's 1961 mandate, the agency had not expected to conduct the lunar landing program until the 1970s or later. The end-of-the-1960s deadline therefore forced a radical acceleration in planning and development.

Preliminary Steps

Because a manned landing on the moon involved many technical issues the agency had never resolved, NASA had to take some preliminary steps before beginning Apollo operations. The agency's first two manned space projects, the Mercury and Gemini programs, served as stepping stones for Apollo. Although already under way when Apollo was announced, the six Mercury flights between 1958 and 1963 provided the basic information about human and mechanical capabilities in space needed for more advanced space activities. NASA described Mercury as "a necessary prelude to more extensive manned space flights."[3]

While the Mercury flights were taking place, other work on Apollo proceeded. The most fundamental technical difficulty was creating a spacecraft capable of traveling to the moon and back, yet light enough to escape the earth's atmosphere during lift-off. NASA was developing a powerful booster, the Saturn V, but the engineering challenge was still daunting because of the distances involved and the need for additional rocket power to land on and ascend from the moon's surface.

NASA's solution—lunar orbit rendezvous (LOR)—was ingenious. Landing the entire spacecraft on the moon's surface and then blasting off would have required a heavy vehicle with tremendous thrust, so NASA designed a system in which only one component of the spacecraft, the lunar excursion module (LEM), would descend to the moon's surface, carrying two of the crew's three astronauts. The mother ship, piloted by the third astronaut, would stay in lunar orbit. After the two astronauts' stay on the moon, the LEM would take off, rendezvous with the mother ship, and return to earth. NASA chose LOR as "the basic plan for Apollo" because it offered "advantages of cost, schedule, simplicity, and minimal additional [technological] developments."[4]

Yet NASA still had some work to do before Apollo could be undertaken. Project Gemini, which involved ten flights during 1965 and 1966, was designed especially "to bridge the gap in technology and operational know-how between Mercury and Apollo."[5] The Gemini spacecraft was larger and more sophisticated than its Mercury predecessor, and enabled NASA to practice the procedures astronauts would have to perform in the Apollo program. Those included maneuvering and docking two vehicles in space, working outside the spacecraft (spacewalks), and staying in space for days at a time.[6] Gemini also tested some of the equipment required for the Apollo program.

NASA embarked on a massive building program in the 1960s to construct the ground facilities needed to support the Apollo program. In Houston, NASA built the Manned Spacecraft Center (later renamed the Johnson Space Center in honor of Lyndon Johnson), and the agency made significant improvements at the Marshall Space Flight Center in Alabama and at the Kennedy Space Center in Florida. NASA also enhanced its network for tracking the progress of space flights and added new tracking stations around the world.[7]

Early Political Support

NASA enjoyed strong political backing in the early years of the Apollo era. Americans still felt threatened by the Soviet space program, and competition was still a major theme of the American space program. Many Americans regarded Apollo as the nation's entry in the race to the moon with the Soviets.

Survey results from the period indicate that public support for space exploration, particularly the Apollo program, was high early in the period. A 1964 poll conducted by Trendex found that most Americans supported the lunar landing goal.[8] Similarly, a 1965 Gallup Poll showed that 58 percent of those surveyed wanted to increase or maintain spending on space, while only 33 percent wanted to cut it.[9] A Harris poll taken the same year found that Americans, by a margin of 45 percent to 42 percent, thought Apollo was worth the billions of dollars it would cost.[10]

President Lyndon Johnson was, if anything, more enthusiastic about the space program than Kennedy had been. Johnson had been a vigorous proponent of the space program as a senator and as Kennedy's vice president.[11] Recognizing Johnson's interest in space, Kennedy appointed him chairman of the National Aeronautics and Space Council, the president's advisory board on space issues, and told him that space would be Johnson's major responsibility as vice president.[12]

Vice President Johnson demonstrated his support for the space program in his 1963 defense of the cost of Apollo: "I, for one, don't want to go to bed by the light of a Communist moon."[13] Johnson continued his advocacy of the space program as president. He also retained his Cold War rhetoric on space, as reflected in this statement he made as president: "We cannot be second in space and first in the world."[14]

NASA's congressional relations were also smooth, certainly easier than those of most government agencies.[15] The political momentum that had built up behind NASA made it hard for Congress to exert much control over the agency, as did the technical complexity of NASA's programs. Congress simply did not have the expertise to challenge the agency on most technical matters. As one ranking member of the House, befuddled by the details of NASA's activities, commented in 1965, "In general, our dealings with NASA are one grand 'act of faith.' "[16] NASA also benefited from the overrepresentation on the space committees of members from districts with strong interests in the space program.[17]

NASA had a number of staunch supporters in Congress in the 1960s, including some who held key committee positions. Rep. Olin "Tiger" Teague, chairman of the Manned Space Flight Subcommittee of the House Committee on Science and Astronautics, and Rep. George P. Miller, chairman of the full committee, both unstintingly backed the agency.[18] Rep. Albert Thomas, who headed the House appropriations subcommittee over NASA, was also a strong ally. Other agency friends in Congress included House Speaker John McCormack, House Majority Leader Carl Albert, House Minority Leader Gerald Ford, and Senators Clinton Anderson, Margaret Chase Smith, and John Pastore.[19]

Support from Congress was instrumental in Apollo's success. Congress provided NASA with generous funding even in the face of other serious national problems. As a NASA publication put it, "Congressional support paved the way to the moon."[20]

Justifying Apollo with Romanticism

Just as NASA worked during the 1960s on the technical aspects of going to the moon, it also labored to maintain the political support required for the endeavor. Romanticism, including the themes of exploration, heroism, emotional rewards, and curiosity, played a large part in the agency's search for political support in the era.

Exploration. In discussing the Apollo program, NASA made numerous references to the innate human urge to explore. Speaking to Congress upon return from his Apollo 8 flight, astronaut Frank Borman said, "Exploration really is the essence of the human spirit, and to pause, to falter, to turn our back on the quest for knowledge, is to perish."[21] Neil Armstrong, Apollo 11 astronaut and the first man on the moon, remarked after his historic trip:

Man has always been an explorer. There's a fascination in thrusting out and going to new places. It is like going through a door because you find the door in front of you. I think that man loses something if he has the option to go to the moon and does not take it.[22]

A NASA statement agreed: "Mankind is deeply motivated toward exploration of the unknown for its own sake without regard to immediate or specific benefits."[23]

Armstrong's crewmate Mike Collins stressed that the yen to explore is an especially important part of the American character: "We're a nation of explorers. . . . We started on the east coast, we went to the west coast, and then vertically. . . . It's in our tradition, it's in our culture."[24] Collins summed up this outlook: "Man has always gone where he has been able to go. It's that simple."[25]

NASA compared Apollo to earlier explorations of unknown territories. According to a NASA statement,

In the 14th and 15th centuries, when he first developed the technical ability to sail the oceans with reasonable likelihood of survival, man entered a period of far-reaching discovery that is an excellent analogue of our circumstance in the final third of the 20th century.[26]

An agency publication said that Apollo was "akin to the early voyages of discovery" and had the goal of seeing "a man stepping onto the lunar surface, like Columbus stepping onto the beach of the new world."[27]

Apollo was only possible, NASA acknowledged, because of major technological strides in the preceding years. "Just in the last 10 years has technology advanced to open space beyond the atmosphere for exploration by men," the agency remarked. That newfound ability brought the opportunity to do what man had longed to do for centuries: "Escape from the confines of the Earth where he has been a prisoner since his creation."[28] "New horizons," NASA said, "have now been opened to mankind."[29]

A NASA statement to Congress said that the Apollo program would use advanced technology "to land American explorers on the moon and bring them safely back to earth."[30] A NASA publication predicted that Apollo would be "the greatest voyage of exploration ever undertaken by man."[31] Another agency document argued, "It is likely that the greatest value of all in the space program will be the introduction of a new era of exploration, in which the solar system will be opened to mankind."[32]

The frontier motif, which NASA has often used in references to exploration, appeared frequently in its Apollo era statements. A NASA official told Congress that the space program "is on the frontier of our knowledge, . . . the frontier of our understanding."[33] Administrator Thomas Paine declared that the United States "must be a country that continues to look to frontiers of science, frontiers of technology, frontiers of mankind."[34] Apollo 11 astronaut Michael Collins told Congress after his triumphant flight that man "will continue pushing back his frontier, no matter how far it may carry him from his homeland."[35] Speaking of the space program generally and Apollo specifically, Hugh Dryden said, "That is where the frontier is today."[36]

The pioneering image also appeared frequently. Administrator Thomas Paine said, "Apollo 8's pioneering flight into lunar orbit demonstrated to men everywhere the existence of a challenging new frontier for mankind in the vastness of extraterrestrial space."[37] Paine told Congress that "the space program can stand up as an example of America's pioneering spirit," while a NASA brochure called Apollo a "pioneering scientific program."[38]

Just as Americans pioneered the West in the nineteenth century, NASA said, they pioneered in space during the twentieth. Astronaut Tom Stafford compared the Apollo program to "the conquering of the West, the epitome of the great American spirit."[39] Apollo would pierce the frontier and blaze the trail for the next wave of explorers. NASA proclaimed after the first lunar landing, "The endless frontier now lies open."[40]

Heroism. Although NASA still tried to capitalize on the public relations value of the astronauts, the heroism of astronauts was a somewhat less conspicuous theme during Apollo than in the Mercury days. NASA also seemed to spend less effort crafting the images of individual astronauts. The dramatic increase in the number of astronauts may be one reason for this. In the Mercury program, there were only seven astronauts to share the spotlight, but when Apollo operations began in 1967 there were about fifty active astronauts to vie for public attention.[41] In addition, the public's interest in individual astronauts, although still extremely high at certain times, had cooled somewhat by the time Apollo arrived.

NASA certainly did not ignore the Apollo astronauts, however. The agency highlighted their extensive training. A NASA brochure remarked, "Their training is rigorous, exacting and long."[42] Physical fitness regimes, academic work, and flight training were all part of the astronauts' schooling, NASA explained. The agency noted that the Apollo astronauts received the same "basic space training" given the Mercury and Gemini astronauts in addition to simulated "moon trips" to practice descent and ascent from the lunar surface, runs through a "lunar obstacle course" to rehearse working on the moon, and "space suit workouts" to thoroughly familiarize the men with their equipment.[43]

NASA did make numerous statements about the dangers of spaceflight and the heroism of the Apollo astronauts. NASA noted that bravery and a taste for adventure were prerequisites for the astronauts. According to an agency publication,

Many persons have asked why men volunteer for such assignments. There is no simple answer to this question, for each astronaut has strong individual characteristics. Perhaps the one characteristic found in each of them is a spirit of adventure—a desire to explore the unknown.[44]

Astronauts faced a variety of dangers, said NASA, including the perils of reentry into the earth's atmosphere:

No matter how much experience is available, how many rehearsals, each re-entry is new. The exact angle is critical; too shallow, and the spacecraft caroms off into space like a skipping stone over water; too steep, and the heat of reentry builds too rapidly for survival.[45]

NASA described the space program as "a story of faith, dedication and perseverance, of heroic efforts."[46]

The Apollo astronauts were matter-of-fact about the risks they faced. Just days before he died in the 1967 Apollo fire, Gus Grissom said: "We recognize that we can get killed flying spacecraft but . . . it's worth the risk."[47] Grissom hoped the American public would understand the risk too. He remarked: "If we die, we want people to accept it. . . . The conquest of space is worth the risk of life."[48] Neil Armstrong remarked that he did not plan what he would say upon first stepping on the moon's surface before he landed there because he did not think there was much of a chance of arriving safely.[49]

In general, NASA stressed that Apollo was a very difficult and risky enterprise. While it certainly conveyed the belief that the program could be accomplished, NASA also warned that disasters were quite possible. NASA repeatedly emphasized that Apollo was the "biggest and most complex project in the manned space flight program."[50] As a NASA official told Congress, "This lunar landing program . . . is a very difficult mission."[51]

NASA explained that the immense difficulty and complexity sprang from Apollo's technical sophistication, the long duration of the missions, the distance traveled from earth, the use of new and untested launch vehicles, and the large number of contractors involved in building the system.[52] NASA's Robert Seamans wrote: "The systems and the missions are extremely complex, involving long periods of operation in space and a return launch from the moon without the help, needless to say, of a lunar Cape Canaveral."[53] These problems were in addition to the inherent risks of exploring space. As James Webb said of the space program, "This is a risky business we are in."[54] All in all, NASA said of Apollo, "It is indeed a challenging mission."[55]

NASA stressed that it was striving to minimize Apollo's risk. Doing so was crucial to optimizing the chance of mission success and the safety of the crew, the two factors NASA labeled its top priorities in Apollo.[56] In fact, NASA reported early in the program's planning that "Apollo will have even more safety devices to protect the crew than has Mercury."[57] The tremendous expense of the Apollo vehicles and the prestige of the United States were other reasons NASA gave to explain the importance of minimizing the risk of Apollo.[58]

A NASA official reported to Congress, "Extremely high standards of reliability are essential to the success of our manned space flight program." The official went on to say, however, that achieving those high standards would be "very difficult."[59] Thus while NASA expressed optimism that Apollo would succeed, the agency tempered its confidence with caution.

Emotional Rewards. NASA highlighted a variety of emotional rewards the Apollo program would provide. The agency spoke frequently of the challenge the endeavor represented. James Webb said of Apollo, "These are tremendous undertakings. Nothing like them has ever been attempted."[60] Webb also called Apollo the "greatest and most challenging enterprise in this history of mankind."[61] Similarly, a NASA report to Congress called Apollo "the greatest scientific and technical endeavor ever attempted."[62] In a statement to Congress, Wernher von Braun also emphasized the challenge of the program: "I think the essential objective in landing a man on the moon is not the fact that a man will set his foot on the moon and be able to recover some samples from the moon, but it lies in the fact that the challenge is so great."[63] A NASA publication asserted that Apollo "will stand as the greatest and most far-reaching achievement of our time."[64]

NASA also stressed the adventure and excitement offered by the lunar program. NASA claimed that, through Apollo, people everywhere could "share vicariously the excitement of opening this great new frontier" of space.[65] An agency publication describing the 1968 flight of Apollo 8 declared that "never, indeed, had adventure ever borne all mankind so daringly near the boundaries of its aspirations."[66] NASA also referred to the space program as a "high human adventure," as well as "man's greatest adventure."[67]

Apollo would serve as a powerful inspiration to all kinds of people, NASA argued. Setting high goals motivates people and extracts their best efforts, according to the agency. NASA said that the space program "demands the very best we can do simply to achieve success."[68] A NASA official described to Congress the inspirational importance of the Apollo program:

In taking on this mission—a very difficult mission—you are setting for the country long-range goals on an accelerated basis that will require all of us, everyone participating, to essentially perform at the top level of his performance. Not a level below the top, but at the top.[69]

As Apollo approached culmination, NASA noted with pride that program participants had "built a powerful capability, a national resource, based on a whole new technology of manned space flight."[70]

Apollo would undoubtedly exert a strong influence on human imagination, NASA said. The tremendous effort required to make Apollo work would "extend everyone to make him think and make him imagine the kind of things this Nation can accomplish."[71] The "awesome dimensions" of the space program spark the imagination and cause people to dream of further space exploration. This can be worthwhile, NASA continued, for "who would say these dreams will not some day be realized."[72] Administrator Thomas Paine said that Apollo continued the tradition of great explorations that "have always opened up new vistas of the possible" and because of which "the sights of all men have been raised and their hearts inspired."[73]

Finally, NASA occasionally mentioned the spiritual effects of space exploration during the Apollo era. According to one agency statement:

In assuming some of the aspects of what used to be called natural philosophy, space research and exploration can engage the attention and interest of the man in the street, and can play an important role in shaping his own concept of the world and his place in the scheme of things. . . . Thus in a very real sense the space program touches virtually everyone.[74]

In general, the space program results in "the lifting of the human spirit," NASA contended.[75] While in lunar orbit, the crew of Apollo 8 read from the Bible in a transmission to the people on earth.

Curiosity. NASA noted that satisfying some of the intense human curiosity about the universe and humankind's place in it would be another benefit of Apollo. A NASA official told Congress that curiosity was a "real and powerful" reason to have a space program.[76] Apollo, of course, would slake much of people's inquisitiveness about the moon. For centuries, earthlings had gazed in wonder at the moon, curious about what that body was like. The intrinsic human urge to explore made it natural that people would want to go to the moon. Apollo was a milestone because it would fulfill that desire and, in the process, provide first-hand scientific information about the moon and the earth.

NASA emphasized that human curiosity required that people go to the moon themselves rather than relying solely on unmanned probes. As Apollo astronaut Mike Collins explained: "It's a fundamental thing to want to go to touch, to see, to smell, to learn."[77] Shortly before his death in 1967, astronaut Gus Grissom spoke of the same issue. He said of the moon, "Our God-given curiosity will force us to go there ourselves because in the final analysis only man can fully evaluate the moon in terms understandable to other men."[78]

In addition to the acquisition of valuable information about the moon and the satisfaction of seeing humans on its surface, NASA maintained that Apollo would provide some answers to other questions that people have long pondered. The geology of the moon possibly held the key to a better understanding of the earth. NASA explained:

Nature may have hidden coded messages into Moon rocks about the evolution of that neighborhood of the universe of which the Earth is a part. From rocks on the Moon, man may be assisted in learning about his origin and his destiny. He may discover clues for answers to his questions, "Where did I come from?" and "Why am I here?"[79]

Such information would be priceless. As NASA said, "The matchless treasure to be retrieved from the Moon in the 1970s is knowledge."[80]

TROUBLES FOR NASA

For the most part, NASA enjoyed smooth sailing from its creation in 1958 until the mid-1960s. The agency received strong political support and was granted ever-larger budgets. Although NASA suffered some technical problems, including the explosion of several unmanned rockets, such failures were to be expected in a new and difficult endeavor like space exploration. Furthermore, the agency's first major program, Project Mercury, was a definite overall success. In the mid-1960s, however, NASA's luck took a marked turn for the worse as the agency ran into some serious technical and political problems.

The Apollo Fire

By early 1967 NASA was preparing for the first manned Apollo flight. Tragedy struck on January 27, 1967, when three astronauts—Gus Grissom, Edward White, and Roger Chaffee—were inside a sealed Apollo spacecraft conducting preflight tests. An electrical fire started, and all three astronauts died from asphyxiation before the capsule could be opened.[81] The shock of the first fatalities in the American space program was compounded by surprise that they happened on the ground rather than in space.

NASA and the nation were stunned by the fire. The review board NASA appointed to investigate the incident reported that both NASA and its major contractor, North American Aviation, had been lax about safety. The report said that the Apollo spacecraft, as configured for the ill-fated test, was a "death trap."[82] NASA's credibility was further damaged when Congress discovered that the director of the Apollo program, Samuel C. Phillips, had sent a report to NASA management in 1965 harshly criticizing North American Aviation's performance. Congress was incensed that before the fire NASA had neither acted on nor transmitted to Congress the Phillips report.[83]

The Apollo fire raised some serious doubts in the public mind about NASA and space exploration.[84] NASA's image of managerial and technical prowess was badly tarnished, and its relationship with Congress was shaken. NASA quickly set out to restore its good name and mend its political fences.

NASA's Response to the Fire

One way NASA reacted to the Apollo fire was to make some management changes. Administrator James Webb increased the monitoring of contractors, established new safety guidelines, and made sure Congress was kept informed of all important NASA actions.[85] These reforms helped blunt some of the criticism directed at the agency.

NASA also responded to the Apollo fire in its public statements, many of which had a romantic flavor because that image best admitted and justified the riskiness of the space program. NASA pointed out that it had always acknowledged the risks of Apollo, and indicated that anyone who had been listening to NASA in previous years should not have been too surprised at the tragedy. A few months after the fire, NASA's Robert Seamans testified to Congress:

When we stressed the difficulties, the thin margins, and the risks in the program, we were frequently charged with being unduly pessimistic and with underrating our own achievements. The accident has made painfully clear to all what every responsible leader in the space program has known and said all along: we are in a business that is both hazardous and highly experimental.[86]

The agency's post-fire attitude was almost one of "I told you so."

While NASA characterized the tragedy as part of doing business in space, it did not dismiss the event lightly. The agency pledged to discover the cause of the accident and take the necessary measures to remedy the underlying problems. Seamans said after the Apollo fire:

We are making a sober and careful examination of our failures and will not attempt to evade in any way our just responsibility for them. . . . We will spare no effort to learn every lesson we can from these events when they occur and act decisively on the technical, procedural, or management problems they disclose.[87]

NASA made clear its unhappiness that the accident occurred and promised to work to prevent a recurrence.

In 1967 and after, NASA continued to aver its past, present, and future commitment to safety. Robert Seamans emphasized that NASA's testing program was made even more rigorous for Apollo.[88] He avowed to Congress in April 1967: "First let me say that we have never proceeded and never will proceed on blind faith."[89] That same year, James Webb told Congress that although NASA's job forced it to take risks, the agency never abandoned its priority on safety. Webb remarked, "In our specifications, tradeoff studies, test criteria, or mission plans, we have taken no risks to the lives or safety of the astronauts that we could find a way to avoid."[90] Yet even with NASA's efforts at safety, Seamans said, "We know we are not infallible."[91]

In the years following the fire, NASA continued to emphasize the inherent risks of the Apollo program. Apollo was, NASA asserted, "the most ambitious and demanding engineering development ever undertaken by man."[92] NASA reiterated that Apollo was much more complex than Mercury or Gemini. The agency said, "The complexity of the lunar mission far exceeds any space mission ever attempted."[93] NASA's associate administrator spoke to Congress about Apollo: "The road leading to success is narrow indeed, and it is bounded on both sides by potential problems, frustrations, and occasionally the possibility of catastrophe."[94] Just prior to Apollo 11, Administrator Thomas Paine said that it was "quite possible" the mission would fail because "the demands we are making of our astronauts and the equipment are very high."[95]

NASA again noted that it was doing what it could to control the inherent risks in its program. James Webb told Congress in 1967:

The plain fact is that we are in a business that is both hazardous and highly experimental. We have to do, and to the best of our human, and therefore limited, ability are doing, everything we can to reduce the hazards, particularly to human life.[96]

Despite these efforts, Webb stressed, "We are going to have failures."[97] A NASA official reminded Congress that despite the overall success of the two programs, "There never was a completely successful Mercury or Gemini flight."[98]

NASA stressed that errors are unavoidable in any activity conducted by humans. The success of no mission can be guaranteed, NASA explained: "Even with unlimited availability of resources and time, a pre-launch certainty of 100% cannot be assured because fallible human beings operate this program; planning and its execution are always subject to the risk of human error."[99] In addition, the advanced technology required by space flight entails many more possibilities for problems. There are definite risks in advanced aviation and space programs, NASA said, and this fact must be accepted.[100] NASA reported to Congress in 1967: "Uncertainty, and therefore risk, is a quality that cannot be eliminated entirely from projects that seek to advance technology and explore the frontiers of science."[101]

When these inevitable failures occur, NASA argued, the nation's will to explore space should not flag. There is no reason to be totally demoralized in the wake of an accident because they are bound to happen. The proper attitude, NASA said, is to fix the problem and move forward. Webb said to Congress a month after the Apollo fire: "I think the important element here is that we have to fly again as soon as we are sure that the risks are within proper limits."[102]

Declining Political Support

NASA's political environment began to deteriorate in the mid-1960s. America's deepening involvement in Vietnam, its economic problems, and domestic unrest detracted from NASA's political support by absorbing ever-increasing amounts of public attention and money.[103] Space exploration no longer seemed like a top priority. Americans began to wonder, especially after it became clear that the U.S. space program was catching up to the Soviet program, if being the first nation on the moon really mattered. In addition, the Apollo fire exacerbated the agency's political problems by making NASA look incompetent. Even as NASA triumphed with Apollo 11 in 1969, there were clear signs of political trouble ahead for the agency.

NASA encountered significant public opposition for the first time in the mid-1960s. The large amounts of money and attention given to NASA in the era made it a natural target for criticism.[104] Two Trendex polls taken in 1966 showed public support for NASA but also indicated a downward trend. According to a July poll, 71.4 percent of Americans were satisfied with the Apollo program—up 10.4 percentage points from 1963—while a November poll indicated that 69 percent supported the program.[105] The July poll revealed that 58 percent believed the nation was either spending enough or too little on space, while only 37 percent thought too much was spent on space. In the November survey, the margin on the same question narrowed to 53 percent to 42 percent.

Two 1967 Harris polls also expressed slipping public support for the space program. An April poll revealed that 42 percent believed the space program should be cut, 38 percent thought it should stay at the same level, and only 13 percent wanted to expand it.[106] More people wanted to cut the space program than any other federal program mentioned. A July 1967 poll disclosed that, by a margin of 54 percent to 34 percent, Americans did not believe the Apollo program was worth its cost.[107]

Although public support for space revived moderately just prior to and after the Apollo 11 mission,[108] 1969 poll results generally confirmed the decline in support for space. A February 1969 Harris poll showed that, by a margin of 49 percent to 39 percent, Americans opposed the lunar program, and 55 percent said that space exploration was not worth the $4 billion spent on it annually.[109] Another Harris poll indicated that more people, 39 percent, would cut the space program before they cut any other of the ten federal programs listed.[110]

President Johnson maintained his strong interest in and support for NASA and the space program throughout his presidency, but his ability to back NASA politically waned somewhat in his second term as he devoted more time, effort, and political capital to his Great Society programs and to the Vietnam War, economic troubles, and domestic disturbances.[111] He fought hard to ensure that NASA received the resources needed to reach the moon but realized that the political climate did not favor ambitious post-Apollo ventures.[112]

Like public opinion and presidential backing, congressional support for the space program began to slip in the 1960s. The same problems that diverted President Johnson's attention from space in the middle and late 1960s also distracted Congress. The Apollo fire also cooled relations between NASA and Congress.[113] Some in Congress charged that the fire could and should have been prevented by NASA. In 1967, Sen. William J. Fulbright called for a "full reappraisal of the space program."[114] Sen. Walter Mondale was also a vocal opponent of NASA, as was Sen. William Proxmire.[115] House critics of NASA included Representatives Edward Koch, James G. Fulton, and H.R. Gross.[116] While some of these legislators were critical of NASA before the fire, the blaze did lasting damage to NASA's congressional relations.[117] As one congressman said, NASA would "no longer be taken at face value" by the members.[118]

FULFILLMENT OF THE LUNAR GOAL

The investigation of the Apollo fire and subsequent design modifications delayed manned Apollo flights eighteen months, raising some doubt about whether NASA would be able meet its deadline. Yet, at least on Apollo's technical aspects, NASA recovered fairly rapidly from the fire, and the race to the moon resumed its rapid pace.

The Buildup to the Landing

In late 1967 and early 1968, NASA conducted three unmanned flights to test the Apollo spacecraft and the Saturn launch vehicle. The first manned Apollo flight, Apollo 7, performed tests in earth orbit in October 1968. NASA was pleased enough with the results to take the next step: sending a spacecraft into lunar orbit. On December 21, 1968, Apollo 8 began its flight to the moon.

The mission of Apollo 8 demonstrated how powerful the notion of the spirituality of space could be. On the way to the moon, the three crew members were the first humans to see the spectacular sight of the whole earth from thousands of miles away, as well as the first to see personally the surface of the moon so closely. Orbiting the moon on Christmas Eve, the crew took turns reading from Genesis. As the spacecraft beamed back to earth spectacular pictures of the moon's surface, Commander Frank Borman concluded:

"And God said, Let the waters under the Heaven be gathered together unto one place, and let the dry land appear, and it was so. And God called the dry land Earth, and the gathering together of the waters He called Seas, and God saw that it was good." And from the crew of Apollo 8, we close with goodnight, good luck, a Merry Christmas, and God bless all of you—all of you on the good earth.[119]

The effect was powerful on the millions of people watching on earth and revealed the impact that romantic appeals sometimes had.[120]

After two more test missions, Apollos 9 and 10, NASA was ready to fulfill the goal set by John F. Kennedy in 1961. On July 16, 1969, Apollo 11 lifted off, carrying astronauts Neil Armstrong, Edwin "Buzz" Aldrin, and Michael Collins toward the moon. Four days later, Armstrong and Aldrin descended to the moon's surface in the lunar excursion module, which was named the *Eagle*. On touchdown, Armstrong calmly radioed to earth: "Houston, Tranquility base here. The *Eagle* has landed."

A few hours after landing, as much of the world watched televised coverage in awe, Neil Armstrong became the first human to set foot on the moon.[121] Armstrong exited the *Eagle* and slowly climbed down the ladder on its side. Standing on the last step, he described what the moon's surface looked like and then announced that he was going to step down. Armstrong stepped, paused, and then spoke his immortal—and highly romantic—line: "That's one small step for a man, one giant leap for mankind."[122]

Aldrin soon joined Armstrong on the surface, where they spent over two and a half hours taking photographs, collecting lunar samples, and setting up scientific experiments. Twenty-one hours after it landed, the *Eagle* blasted off from the moon and headed for its rendezvous with its mother ship, *Columbia*. After a smooth docking and journey home, the crew of Apollo 11 returned safely to earth on July 24, capping one of the greatest voyages in history.[123]

Ironically, Richard Nixon was president when men first landed on the moon—the fulfillment of an objective established by his political nemesis, John F. Kennedy.[124] Nixon traveled to the U.S.S. *Hornet* to greet the astronauts immediately after their splashdown in the Pacific. Speaking to the astronauts through the window of their quarantine trailer, Nixon described the voyage of Apollo 11 as "the greatest week in the history of the world since the Creation."[125]

NASA's References to Apollo 11

NASA tried to parlay its lunar success into political support. The agency hailed Apollo as a magnificent achievement. A NASA report to Congress called Apollo "the most extensive technological endeavor ever undertaken by mankind."[126] An agency brochure discussed Apollo's part in satisfying the human imperative to explore: "These first travels beyond the immediate vicinity of the Earth fulfilled an old dream. They culminated a primordial human aspiration, and started a movement that will never stop."[127] Apollo "not only opened up vast reaches of space to man's machines, but made them accessible to man himself."[128]

NASA maintained that the Apollo program could have vital long-reaching consequences for human's place in the universe. The agency explained:

The bridge men built to the Moon in the 1960's is only the first step into the infinite universe. Because of that bridge, neither the Moon nor man will ever be the same again. . . . For man, that bridge is his first possible escape from the confines of the Earth where he has been a prisoner since his creation. For the first time in his long history, man has the tools to leave Earth to explore companion worlds. . . . From a mere spectator he is maturing into a participant in the universe.[129]

In a similar vein, Thomas Paine declared that Apollo represented an "enormous new phase of evolution" that might be "as significant as when the first amphibian came from the sea up onto the land and began to conquer a new domain for life."[130]

In 1971, NASA's new administrator, James Fletcher, testified to Congress about the lunar program: "The first Apollo landing was tremendous; it was spectacular, and the whole world was impressed at that achievement—maybe the biggest achievement in the century."[131] As great as the achievement was, Fletcher said, NASA could go on to other projects of equal or even greater value. However, the agency would need continued political support to do so.

Later Apollo Flights

In November 1969, to much less public interest than accompanied Apollo 11, Apollo 12 made the second landing on the moon. Sending men to the moon looked easy until the flight of Apollo 13 in April 1970.[132] On the way to the moon, one of the craft's oxygen tanks exploded, leaving serious doubt as to whether the crew would make it back alive. The nation and much of the world waited and watched for several days as NASA struggled to return the crew safely. Some ingenious work by NASA engineers and managers as well as the astronauts did bring Apollo 13 back with the crew alive. Public interest was rekindled by Apollo 13, and the flight received much more attention than any Apollo flight other than the first moon landing.[133]

NASA's public response to Apollo 13 was quite similar to its reaction to the Apollo fire; it stressed that accidents were unavoidable. As one agency document said, "The Apollo 13 accident, which aborted man's third mission to explore the surface of the Moon, is a harsh reminder of the immense difficulty of this undertaking."[134] NASA also again emphasized its determination to continue. Administrator Thomas Paine said: "There will be those . . . who will seize upon this accident as an opportunity to call for a slowdown or turning back. But . . . we are not that kind of people. We're not going to be diverted by adversity or setback."[135]

In a clever argument, NASA used the Apollo 13 episode to boast of its competence. The agency contended that for an Apollo mission to succeed, all parts of the system had to work to near perfection. Therefore, NASA argued, the overall Apollo performance was quite impressive: "That this system has already resulted in two successful lunar surface explorations is a tribute to those men and women who conceived, designed, built, and flew it." The agency went on to stress that the "outstanding performance" of the crew and ground control prevented any loss of life during Apollo 13.[136] Thus NASA argued that the failed Apollo 13 mission actually demonstrated its prowess rather than its incompetence.

Four more missions to the moon—Apollos 14, 15, 16, and 17—were successfully completed. The missions had scientific value, but the public showed little interest. Drastically smaller NASA budgets and increased debate over the value of the Apollo project forced the cancellation of two planned flights to the moon, and the lunar program ended with the return of Apollo 17 in December 1972.[137]

PLANNING FOR THE FUTURE

As the Apollo program came to an end, NASA's future was under debate. Having achieved the goal that had driven it for the past decade, the agency needed a new mission. NASA had some bold ideas, but, as the agency quickly discovered, its political environment was not conducive to getting bold ideas approved.

NASA's Political Environment

As the 1970s opened, NASA faced a political situation that had deteriorated drastically over the preceding years. The decline in support that began in the mid-1960s continued unabated in the late 1960s and early 1970s. The public, the president, and Congress were all much less supportive of NASA than they had been earlier in the agency's history.

The public disillusionment with space exploration that began to surface even before Apollo 11 continued into the early 1970s.[138] Observers have advanced several explanations for this drop in public support: increased cynicism about big government projects, NASA's lack of a clear post-Apollo goal, heightened awareness of societal problems that needed funds, the emergence of detente, and the rise of pressing issues such as Vietnam, economic distress, and domestic strife.[139] James Fletcher provided an additional explanation by saying that support for NASA dropped simply "because we'd finished the mission" assigned by Kennedy.[140] Fletcher also said the public's mistaken notion that NASA was spending the same kind of money it spent on Apollo cost the agency some support.

Opinion polls reflected NASA's bleak situation. An April 1970 Harris poll revealed that, by a margin of 56 percent to 39 percent, Americans did not think going to the moon had been worth the cost. The same poll showed even greater opposition, 64 percent to 30 percent, to spending money at the rate spent in the 1960s ($4 billion annually) on future space exploration.[141] Numerous polls indicated that most Americans of the era considered the space program a low priority compared with other federal government activities.[142]

Things were not much better for NASA on the presidential front. Although Richard Nixon frequently associated himself with space exploration to reap political benefits, he demonstrated little interest in the specifics of the space program and was not a tremendous booster of NASA.[143] Nixon summarized his attitude toward space in this pronouncement: "Space expenditures must take their proper place within a rigorous system of national priorities."[144] Nixon's primary criterion for NASA's post-Apollo program seemed to have been the size of its budget.[145]

NASA's long honeymoon with Congress was also definitely over. Lingering resentment over NASA's behavior at the time of the Apollo fire along with the array of pressing new national problems made Congress less inclined to grant NASA as much money and authority as it had.

This political shift dramatically affected NASA's budgets. Funding for NASA peaked in fiscal 1965, early in the Apollo period, and then began a steep decline. In current dollars, NASA's budget authority of $5.3 billion in fiscal 1965 dropped to $3.3 billion in fiscal 1972. The figures expressed in constant 1987 dollars tell the story even more starkly: The agency's budget authority plummeted from $19.8 billion to $8.8 billion in that seven-year period. (See the Appendix for more extensive data on NASA's budget.) Figure 2 illustrates the sharp decline in NASA's budget authority during the Apollo era.

The Shuttle Program

Accustomed to having most of their requests met, NASA officials made some extremely ambitious proposals for space exploration in the 1970s.[146] NASA Administrator Thomas Paine pushed for a manned lunar base, a large orbiting space station and a new space transportation system to service it, and a manned mission to Mars.[147] Nixon balked at Paine's plan, however, and instead appointed a task force to outline the nation's alternatives in space.

The task force endorsed continued manned space exploration and outlined three options to pursue such a program, all of which Nixon considered too expensive.[148] One of the options called for developing a reusable "space shuttle" that would provide easy and economical access to earth orbit and to the space station that would eventually be built there. Paine's successor, James Fletcher, became convinced that a scaled-down version of the shuttle was "the only meaningful new manned space program" that could fit the president's stringent budget guidelines.[149] Fletcher recalled, "There weren't a heck of a lot of alternatives [to the shuttle] because . . . the president said, 'No, we're not going to do any of those.' "[150]

NASA was not happy with the situation, but had little choice but to push for approval of the shuttle. As Fletcher explained, "We had to do something with the manned space program. The strategy there . . . was to undertake a much less expensive transportation mode."[151] Some in NASA also believed that once the shuttle was operational, the stage would be set for selling the space station, which was the agency's first programmatic choice.[152]

In the meantime, NASA searched for ways to strengthen its political position and get the shuttle approved.[153] NASA's solution included changing the

Figure 2
NASA Funding in the Apollo Era: Budget Authority in Constant 1987 Dollars

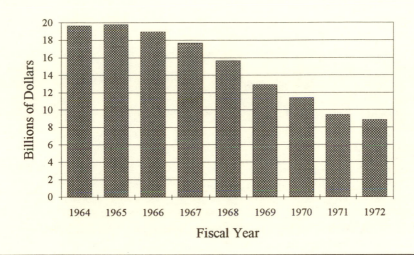

Sources: Adapted from Office of Management and Budget, *Budget of the United States Government: Fiscal Year 1995, Historical Tables* (Washington, D.C.: GPO, 1994); Bureau of the Budget, *Budget of the United States Government* (Washington, D.C.: GPO, 1959-70); and Office of Management and Budget, *Budget of the United States Government* (Washington, D.C.: GPO, 1971-77).

shuttle's design to reduce development costs, promising to stay within certain budget limits, forging an alliance with the military, and making extremely optimistic predictions about the cost-effectiveness of the program.[154] These tactics would come back to haunt the agency. The budget restrictions led to development problems, the deal with the military forced NASA to make concessions on the shuttle's design and operation, thus sacrificing some autonomy, while the overselling of the shuttle meant NASA would be pressured to meet unrealistic standards.

Yet NASA's approach helped it achieve its immediate goal—presidential approval of the shuttle. On January 5, 1972, Nixon announced his endorsement of the program, saying it would "take the astronomical costs out of astronautics."[155] Thus, through a process one scholar described as "bargaining, compromise, and coalition-building," the space shuttle was born.[156]

Nixon authorized the shuttle because of its promised cost-effectiveness, its military potential, and its salutary effect on aerospace jobs.[157] His approval of the shuttle kept NASA in the manned space business, but just barely. The budgetary restrictions he instituted hampered the agency and delayed development of the shuttle.

NOTES

1. NASA statements made before 1964 specifically about the Apollo program are included in this discussion.

2. Thomas R. McDonough, *Space: The Next 25 Years* (New York: John Wiley & Sons, 1987), 26.

3. NASA, *Man in Space*, by David A. Anderton, EP-57, (Washington, D.C.: GPO, 1969), 4.

4. Ibid.

5. Ibid., 5.

6. Joseph J. Trento, *Prescription for Disaster* (New York: Crown Publishers, 1987), 51-52; Virgil I. Grissom, *Gemini: A Personal Account of Man's Venture into Space* (New York: Macmillan, 1968), 7-8; NASA, *Thirteenth Semiannual Report to Congress, January 1-June 30, 1965* (Washington, D.C.: GPO, 1966), 13.

7. NASA, *In This Decade . . .*, EP-71 (Washington, D.C.: GPO, 1969), 12.

8. Evert Clark, "Moon Plan Given Backing in Polls," *New York Times*, 15 November 1964, 4.

9. George Horace Gallup, *The Gallup Poll: Public Opinion, 1935-1971* (New York: Random House, 1972), 1952. Specifically, 16 percent of respondents wanted an increase in spending while 42 percent wanted to maintain current levels.

10. Louis Harris, "Public Has Doubts About Space Program," *Washington Post*, 1 November 1965. The poll also revealed that, if not for the Soviet achievements in space, the public would have opposed the current spending on space by a 50 percent to 38 percent margin.

11. Eugene M. Emme, "Presidents and Space," in *Between Sputnik and the Shuttle*, ed. Frederick C. Durant III (San Diego: American Astronautical Society, 1981), 85; Robert A. Divine, "LBJ and the Politics of Space," in *The Johnson Years*, Vol. 2, ed. Robert A. Divine (Lawrence: University of Kansas Press, 1987), 247.

12. Richard Hirsch and Joseph John Trento, *The National Aeronautics and Space Administration* (New York: Praeger, 1973), 137-39.

13. Tom Wolfe, *The Right Stuff* (Toronto: Bantam Books, 1979), 336.

14. *Congressional Quarterly Almanac 1964* (Washington, D.C.: Congressional Quarterly, 1965), 453.

15. Thomas P. Jahnige, "Congress and Space: The Committee System and Congressional Oversight of NASA" (Ph.D. dissertation, Claremont Graduate School, 1965); William Hines, "NASA: The Image Misfires," *The Nation*, 24 April 1967, 518.

16. Jahnige, "Congress and Space," 275.

17. Ibid., 283.

18. Ken Hechler, *The Endless Space Frontier: A History of the House Committee on Science and Astronautics, 1959-1978* (San Diego: American Astronautical Society, 1982), 155-66, 388-89.

19. Arthur L. Levine, *The Future of the U.S. Space Program* (New York: Praeger, 1975), 89. NASA's Manned Spacecraft Center was built in Rep. Thomas' district.

20. Charles D. Benson and William Barnaby Faherty, *Moonport: A History of Apollo Launch Facilities and Operations*, SP-4204 (Washington, D.C.: GPO, 1978), 528.

21. L. B. Taylor, Jr., *For All Mankind* (New York: E. P. Dutton, 1974), 137.

22. Laurence J. Peter, *The Peter Pyramid: Or Will We Ever Get the Point?* (New York: William Morrow, 1986), 119.

23. Congress, Senate, Committee on Aeronautical and Space Sciences, *NASA Authorization for Fiscal Year 1972*, 92d Cong., 1st sess., 30 March 1971, 17.

24. "The Moon Above, the Earth Below," CBS-TV, 13 July 1989.

25. "Transcript of Astronauts' Addresses to Congress," *New York Times*, 17 September 1969, 30.

26. Congress, Senate, Committee on Aeronautical and Space Sciences, *NASA Authorization for Fiscal Year 1969*, 90th Cong., 2d sess., 29 February 1968, 361.

27. NASA, *Man in Space*, EP-57, 3.

28. NASA, *Man in Space: Space in the Seventies*, by Walter Froehlich, EP-81 (Washington, D.C.: GPO, 1971), 17.

29. Congress, House, Committee on Science and Astronautics, Subcommittee on Manned Space Flight, *1972 NASA Authorization*, Part 2, 92d Cong., 1st sess., 4 March 1971, 59.

30. Congress, House, Committee on Appropriations, Subcommittee on Independent Offices, *Independent Offices Appropriations for 1966*, Part 2, 89th Cong., 1st sess., 5 April 1965, 856.

31. NASA, *Man in Space*, EP-57, introduction.

32. NASA, *America's Next Decades in Space* (Washington, D.C.: GPO, 1969), 73.

33. Congress, Senate, Committee on Aeronautical and Space Sciences, *NASA Authorization for Fiscal Year 1968*, 90th Cong., 1st sess., 19 April 1967, 134.

34. William K. Stevens, "Space Official Talks About Problems on Earth," *New York Times*, 19 May 1969, 31.

35. "Transcript of Astronauts' Addresses to Congress," 30.

36. Congress, House, Committee on Science and Astronautics, *1962 NASA Authorization*, Part 3, 87th Cong., 1st sess., 11 July 1961, 1053.

37. NASA, *Apollo: Man Around the Moon* (Washington, D.C.: GPO, 1968), 1.

38. Congress, Senate, Committee on Aeronautical and Space Sciences, *Future NASA Space Programs*, 91st Cong., 1st sess., 5 August 1969, 48; NASA, *Man in Space*, EP-57, 3.

39. Paul Hoversten, "World Saw 'Eagle' Land in 1969," *Sunday (Nashville) Tennessean*, 16 July 1989, 3G.

40. NASA, *Space in the Seventies*, EP-81, v.

41. NASA, *In This Decade . . .*, EP-71, 22.

42. Ibid.

43. NASA, *Manned Space Flight: Apollo*, NF-23 (Washington, D.C.: GPO, 1969), 10.

44. NASA, *NASA Astronauts*, EP-34 (Washington, D.C.: GPO, 1967), 2.

45. NASA, *In This Decade . . .*, EP-71, 42.

46. NASA, *Man in Space*, EP-57, introduction.

47. "Man in Space," ABC-TV, 9 July 1989.

48. Erlend A. Kennan and Edmund H. Harvey, Jr., *Mission to the Moon: A Critical Examination of NASA and the Space Program* (New York: Morrow, 1969), 19.

49. "Man in Space," ABC-TV.

50. Congress, Senate, Committee on Aeronautical and Space Sciences, *NASA Authorization for Fiscal Year 1963*, 87th Cong., 2d sess., 14 June 1962, 433. See also House Committee on Appropriations, 5 April 1965 hearing, 856; and Congress, House, Committee on Science and Astronautics, Subcommittee on Manned Space Flight, *1964 NASA Authorization*, 88th Cong., 1st sess., 6 June 1963, 1215.

51. Congress, House, Committee on Science and Astronautics, *1962 NASA Authorization*, Part 3, 87th Cong., 1st sess., 12 July 1961, 1064.

52. Congress, House, Committee on Science and Astronautics, Subcommittee on Manned Space Flight, *1964 NASA Authorization*, 88th Cong., 1st sess., 7 March 1963, 210; Senate Committee on Aeronautical and Space Sciences, 14 June 1962 hearing, 433; Robert C. Seamans, "Reliability in Space Systems—A National Objective," speech to the I.A.S. National Propulsion Meeting, Cleveland, Ohio, 8 March 1962, NASA History Office, Washington, D.C., 8.

53. Seamans, "Reliability in Space Systems," 8.

54. Congress, House, Committee on Appropriations, Subcommittee on Independent Offices, *Independent Offices Appropriations for 1965*, Part 2, 88th Cong., 2d sess., 7 April 1964, 976.

55. Senate Committee on Aeronautical and Space Sciences, 14 June 1962 hearing, 433.

56. Congress, House, Committee on Science and Astronautics, Subcommittee on Manned Space Flight, *1964 NASA Authorization*, 88th Cong., 1st sess., 8 May 1963, 1079.

57. NASA, *Exploring Space: Projects Mercury and Apollo of the United States Space Program* (Washington, D.C.: GPO, 1961), 16.

58. House Committee on Science and Astronautics, 7 March 1963 hearing, 215.

59. Ibid.

60. Congress, Senate, Subcommittee of Committee on Appropriations, *Independent Offices Appropriations, 1963*, 87th Cong., 2d sess., 10 August 1962, 870.

61. Congress, House, Committee on Science and Astronautics, Subcommittee on Manned Space Flight, *1965 NASA Authorization*, Part 1, 88th Cong., 2d sess., 4 February 1964, 8.

62. NASA, *Ninth Semiannual Report to Congress, January 1-June 30, 1963* (Washington, D.C.: GPO, 1964), 26.

63. Congress, House, Committee on Appropriations, Subcommittee on Independent Offices and the Department of Housing and Urban Development, *Independent Offices and Department of Housing and Urban Development Appropriations for 1969*, Part 2, 90th Cong., 2d sess., 11 March 1968, 1035-36.

64. NASA, *Decades*, 3.

65. Congress, Senate, Committee on Aeronautical and Space Sciences, *NASA Authorization for Fiscal Year 1968*, 90th Cong., 1st sess., 19 April 1967, 437.

66. NASA, *Apollo: Man Around the Moon*, 1.

67. NASA, *Decades*, 73; NASA, *In This Decade . . .*, EP-71, 3; Senate Committee on Aeronautical and Space Sciences, 30 March 1971 hearing, 141.

68. Senate Committee on Aeronautical and Space Sciences, 19 April 1967 hearing, 439.

69. House Committee on Science and Astronautics, 12 July 1961 hearing, 1081.

70. NASA, *In This Decade . . .*, 3.

71. House Committee on Science and Astronautics, 12 July 1961 hearing, 1081.

72. NASA, *Space: The New Frontier*, EP-6 (Washington, D.C.: GPO, 1967), 6.

73. NASA, *Space in the Seventies*, EP-81, 17.

74. Senate Committee on Aeronautical and Space Sciences, 19 April 1967 hearing, 437.

75. Senate Committee on Aeronautical and Space Sciences, 30 March 1971 hearing, 17.

76. Senate Committee on Aeronautical and Space Sciences, 29 February 1968 hearing, 362.

77. "The Moon Above, the Earth Below," CBS-TV.

78. Courtney G. Brooks, James M. Grimwood, and Loyd S. Swenson, Jr., *Chariots for Apollo*, SP-4205 (Washington, D.C.: GPO, 1979), 220.

79. NASA, *Space in the Seventies*, EP-81, 5.

80. Ibid.

81. Roger E. Bilstein, *Orders of Magnitude: A History of the NACA and NASA, 1915-1990*, SP-4406 (Washington, D.C.: GPO, 1989), 80.

82. Hirsch and Trento, *The National Aeronautics and Space Administration*, 113.

83. Ibid., 112-14; Levine, *Future of the U.S. Space Program*, 96-97.

84. Benson and Faherty, *Moonport*, SP-4204, 394; Divine, "LBJ and the Politics of Space," 243.

85. Levine, *Future of the U.S. Space Program*, 97-98.

86. Congress, House, Committee on Appropriations, Subcommittee on Independent Offices and the Department of Housing and Urban Development, *Independent Offices and Department of Housing and Urban Development Appropriations for 1969*, Part 3, 90th Cong., 1st sess., 12 April 1967, 678.

87. Ibid., 679.

88. One result of the enhanced testing program was that failures in the Apollo system, unlike those in Mercury, were usually discovered at a fairly early stage in the program.

89. House Committee on Appropriations, 12 April 1967 hearing, 696.

90. Congress, House, Committee on Science and Astronautics, *1968 NASA Authorization*, Part 1, 90th Cong., 1st sess., 28 February 1967, 14.

91. House Committee on Appropriations, April 1967 hearing, 696.

92. Congress, House, Committee on Science and Astronautics, *The Apollo 13 Accident*, 91st Cong., 2d sess., 16 June 1970, 85.

93. NASA, *This Is NASA*, EP-22 (Washington, D.C.: GPO, 1968), 5. See also NASA, *Manned Space Flight: Apollo*, NF-23, 1, 15; and NASA, *Space Station: Key to the Future*, EP-75 (Washington, D.C.: GPO, 1970), 1.

94. Congress, House, Committee on Science and Astronautics, *1970 NASA Authorization*, Part 1, 91st Cong., 1st sess., 4 March 1969, 14.

95. "Space Agency Head Warns Moon Mission Might Fail," *New York Times*, 30 June 1969, 16.

96. House Committee on Science and Astronautics, 28 February 1967 hearing, 6-7.

97. Congress, Senate, Committee on Aeronautical and Space Sciences, *Apollo Accident*, Part 4, 90th Cong., 1st sess., 13, 17 April 1967, 348.

98. Evert Clark, "Six Months After the Tragedy, the Apollo Program Finds Itself Gaining but 'Still in a Time of Testing,' " *New York Times*, 2 July 1967, 21.

99. NASA, *Report to the House Authorization Committee*, as per the Request of Rep. Karth, 21 March 1967, 4.

100. House Committee on Science and Astronautics, 28 February 1967 hearing, 6, 18.

101. NASA, *Report to the House Authorization Committee*, 21 March 1967, 1.

102. House Committee on Science and Astronautics, 28 February 1967 hearing, 25.

103. Michael A. G. Michaud, *Reaching for the High Frontier: The American Pro-Space Movement, 1972-84* (New York: Praeger, 1986), 14; Levine, *Future of the U.S. Space Program*, 90.

104. Eli Ginzberg et al., *Economic Impact of Large Public Programs: NASA Experience* (Salt Lake City: Olympus Publishing Co., 1976), 147.

105. "Poll Shows Growing Space Complacency," *Space Business Daily*, 29 July 1966, 153; "Poll Shows 69 Percent Support of Project Apollo," *Space Business Daily*, 30 November 1966, 143.

106. Louis Harris, "Most OK Great Society," *Philadelphia Inquirer*, 3 April 1967.

107. Louis Harris, "Space Programs Losing Support," *Washington Post*, 31 July 1967.

108. Louis Harris, "Public, in Reversal, Now Backs Landing on Moon, 51 to 41 Pct.," *Washington Post*, 14 July 1969.

109. Louis Harris, "49% Oppose Moon Project," *Philadelphia Inquirer*, 17 February 1969.

110. Louis Harris, "Public Would Cut Funds For Space," *New York Post*, 18 February 1969. See also Gallup, *The Gallup Poll: Public Opinion, 1935-1971*, 2184.

111. Levine, *Future of the U.S. Space Program*, 90-91; Divine, "LBJ and the Politics of Space," 233-47.

112. Divine, "LBJ and the Politics of Space," 237, 242-43.

113. Levine, *Future of the U.S. Space Program*, 98.

114. Benson and Faherty, *Moonport*, SP-4204, 394.

115. In a private meeting with NASA officials after the Apollo fire, Mondale supposedly told NASA Administrator James Webb, "I intend to ride this for every nickel's worth of political power I can get out of it. I don't give a hoot in hell about the space program or about your future." See Trento, *Prescription for Disaster*, 69.

116. *Congressional Quarterly Almanac 1969* (Washington, D.C.: Congressional Quarterly, 1970), 300-305.

117. Levine, *Future of the U.S. Space Program*, 98; Arnold S. Levine, *Managing NASA in the Apollo Era*, SP-4102 (Washington, D.C.: GPO, 1982), 209.

118. Levine, *Future of the U.S. Space Program*, 98. See also similar comments by Rep. Ken Hechler, *Congressional Quarterly Almanac 1967* (Washington, D.C.: Congressional Quarterly, 1968), 427.

119. Charles Murray and Catherine Bly Cox, *Apollo: The Race to the Moon* (New York: Simon & Schuster, 1989), 330-31.

120. Ibid., 82-83.

121. It is estimated that at least one billion people either watched the Apollo 11 landing on television or heard it on radio. See Robert C. Seamans, Jr. and Frederick I. Ordway III, "Lessons of Apollo for Large-Scale Technology," in *Between Sputnik and*

the Shuttle, ed. Frederick C. Durant III (San Diego: American Astronautical Society, 1981), 252.

122. That is what Armstrong meant to say, in any case. The sentence heard on earth was, "That's one small step for man, one giant leap for mankind." Armstrong was disappointed when he returned and discovered how his words had been heard. As he noted, the sentence does not make much sense without the "a" before "man." Either he forgot to say "a" or the word was lost through a momentary communications glitch between the moon and earth. See Murray and Cox, *Apollo: The Race to the Moon*, 356.

123. Murray and Cox, *Apollo: The Race to the Moon*, 356-69.

124. Plans for the U.S.S. *John F. Kennedy* to recover the Apollo 11 astronauts after splashdown were vetoed by the Nixon administration. See Trento, *Prescription for Disaster*, 86; "The Moon Above, the Earth Below."

125. Emme, "Presidents and Space," 101; Larry Light, "One Decade After the Moon Landing, Space Program Gets Little Attention or Interest," *Congressional Quarterly Weekly Report*, 28 April 1979, 780.

126. NASA, *Twenty-first Semiannual Report to Congress, January 1-June 30, 1969* (Washington, D.C.: GPO, 1970), 1.

127. NASA, *Space in the Seventies*, EP-81, v.

128. NASA, *Decades*, 3.

129. NASA, *Space in the Seventies*, EP-81, 17-18.

130. NASA, *In This Decade . . .*, EP-71, 46.

131. Congress, Senate, Subcommittee of Committee on Appropriations, *Department of Housing and Urban Development, Space, and Science Appropriations for Fiscal Year 1972*, 92d Cong., 1st sess., 23 June 1971, 455.

132. Superstitious persons might argue that the mission was doomed from the start because it was flight number thirteen, launched in the thirteenth minute of the thirteenth hour of the day, Houston time. The explosion occurred on April 13. See Murray and Cox, *Apollo: The Race to the Moon*, 387.

133. Murray and Cox, *Apollo: The Race to the Moon*, 420-21.

134. House Committee on Science and Astronautics, 16 June 1970 hearing, 85.

135. John Noble Wilford, "Nixon Restates His Support of Space Effort," *New York Times*, 20 April 1970, 1.

136. House Committee on Science and Astronautics, 16 June 1970 hearing, 85.

137. Murray and Cox, *Apollo: The Race to the Moon*, 449; NASA, *The Early Years—Mercury to Apollo-Soyuz* (Washington, D.C.: GPO, 1988), 13.

138. McDonough, *Space: The Next Twenty-five Years*, 27; Richard S. Lewis, *The Voyages of Apollo: The Exploration of the Moon* (New York: Quadrangle, 1974), 170; Michaud, *Reaching for the High Frontier*, 14; Trento, *Prescription for Disaster*, 86; Hechler, *The Endless Space Frontier*, 254.

139. Lewis, *The Voyages of Apollo*, 169-70; Sherry Rae McNeal, "Public Awareness and Attitude Toward the Space Program," in *Remember the Future: The Apollo Legacy*, ed. Stan Kent (San Diego: American Astronautical Society, 1980), 130; Tom Bethell, "NASA (That's Right, NASA) Is a Good Thing," *Washington Monthly*, November 1975, 11; Richard S. Lewis, "End of Apollo: The Ambiguous Epic," *Bulletin of the Atomic Scientists* 28 (December 1972): 39.

140. Dr. James C. Fletcher, interview by author, Washington, D.C., 5 October 1990.

141. *Harris Survey Yearbook of Public Opinion, 1970* (New York: Louis Harris & Associates, 1971), 83-84.

142. Congress, Office of Technology Assessment, *Civilian Space Policy and Applications* (Washington, D.C.: GPO, 1982), 137-38.

143. Regarding Nixon's political use of space, see Emme, "Presidents and Space," 100-102; Robert Lee Hotz, "Lunar Rocks Open Window to Solar System's Birth," *Atlanta Journal & Constitution*, 16 July 1989, B5. Regarding his interest in space, see Alex Roland, "The Shuttle: Triumph or Turkey?" *Discover*, November 1985, 31; Trento, *Prescription for Disaster*, 84, 99; "The Future of NASA," *Time*, 10 August 1970, 45. The *Time* article describes how, after the Apollo 12 astronauts visited Nixon following their flight, they "recalled bitterly that Nixon seemed more inclined to talk about football than the moon trip."

144. Levine, *Future of the U.S. Space Program*, 129.

145. Emme, "Presidents and Space," 105.

146. Jerry Grey, *Beachheads in Space* (New York: Macmillan Publishing Co., 1983), 16-17; Levine, *Managing NASA in the Apollo Era*, 258.

147. Alex Roland, "Priorities in Space for USA," *Space Policy*, May 1987, 105; Levine, *Future of the U.S. Space Program*, 108, 115.

148. Levine, *Future of the U.S. Space Program*, 128-29; Fletcher interview.

149. "Space Shuttle NASA Versus Domestic Priorities," *Congressional Quarterly Weekly Report*, 26 February 1972, 435; Fletcher interview; *Congressional Quarterly Almanac 1972*, (Washington, D.C.: Congressional Quarterly, 1972), 171; Bilstein, *Orders of Magnitude*, 108-109.

150. Fletcher interview.

151. Ibid.

152. Hans Mark, *The Space Station: A Personal Journey* (Durham, N.C.: Duke University Press, 1987), 41; John M. Logsdon, "A Response to Alex Roland," *Space Policy*, May 1987, 113.

153. Barbara S. Romzek and Melvin J. Dubnick, "Accountability in the Public Sector: Lessons from the Challenger Tragedy," *Public Administration Review* 47 (May/June 1987): 231-32.

154. John M. Logsdon, "The Space Shuttle Program: A Policy Failure?," *Science*, 30 May 1986, 1100-104; Fletcher interview; Trento, *Prescription for Disaster*, 105-12; Office of Technology Assessment, *Civilian Space Policy*, 99-100; Romzek and Dubnick, "Accountability in the Public Sector," 231-32; Ruth A. Lewis and John S. Lewis, "Getting Back on Track in Space," *Technology Review* 89 (August/September 1986): 34; Roland, "The Shuttle: Triumph or Turkey?," 35.

155. "Space Shuttle NASA Versus Domestic Priorities," 435.

156. Logsdon, "A Policy Failure?," 1099.

157. Ibid., 1101.

5

Pragmatism

In 1972, NASA Administrator James C. Fletcher declared: "We now look ahead to several decades of a highly rational use of space. . . . We have turned from a period of space exploration to a period of space exploitation for practical purposes." He gave examples of some space-based practical activities, including remote sensing of the earth, satellite communications, and manufacturing in space. Fletcher concluded: "By learning more about our planetary environment, we will be better able to apply the knowledge we gain in practical ways to the enrichment of life on earth."[1]

Fletcher's remarks epitomize pragmatism, NASA's image that emphasizes the tangible benefits created for all people by the space program. The central tenet of pragmatism has been that activity in space improves the quality of life on earth in practical ways. As a 1969 NASA publication said, "Space systems can provide unique, direct benefits to man, benefits not before possible or economically feasible."[2]

NASA has argued that space exploration generates new knowledge, which in turn leads to practical dividends. In discussing its goals for the space program, the agency told Congress in 1960: "We seek knowledge. We seek the benefits of knowledge. We seek the practical applications of the new technology that will develop."[3]

NASA Administrator Thomas Paine made the same point to Congress in 1970: "We will unlock new fundamental doors to knowledge, and will be able to use that knowledge for the benefit of man on earth."[4] Knowledge about space is important, said James Fletcher, because space represents "a new important resource that can be used for the benefit of people everywhere on earth."[5]

Pragmatism encourages people to rely on rational calculation rather than emotion in assessing the value of the space program. The image's unemotional, self-centered approach distinguishes it from both romanticism and nationalism. Pragmatism's accent on practical benefits clearly separates it from

romanticism, which focuses mainly on intangible rewards. While the nationalism approach argues that the space program helps America as a whole through
both tangible and intangible benefits, pragmatism highlights mainly the tangible dividends that space utilization brings to individuals at home and abroad.
In a 1973 pragmatic statement, Fletcher called space a resource to be used "for
the benefit of people everywhere on earth."[6]

As with its other images, NASA has used pragmatism at various times
throughout its history. The agency employed pragmatism most heavily from
around 1970 until the mid-1980s. NASA promoted its major program of that
era, the space shuttle, primarily through a pragmatic image.

MAJOR THEMES IN PRAGMATISM

The goal of pragmatism has been to convince citizens that they personally
benefit from the space program and should therefore support NASA. The image has thus entailed cataloguing and explaining those benefits and showing
how they improve life on earth. Although NASA has tended to concentrate on
benefits to the general public, some of the items NASA has listed affect most
citizens only indirectly. NASA's pragmatic claims have generally related to
the benefits provided in the following areas: technological stimulus, spinoffs,
satellites, economic returns, science, education, and space transportation. The
agency's explanations of each group of benefits constitute the major themes in
pragmatism.

Technological Stimulus

NASA has argued that the space program helps push technology forward, a
process that ultimately pays a variety of dividends. Pursuing a space program,
NASA explained, is a complicated task fraught with many technological obstacles. To make progress in the program, those obstacles must be overcome.
This compels people to confront the problems and, eventually, to solve them.
Thus, the space program provides a "forcing function" that drives technology
forward and leads to new technological benefits.[7]

NASA pointed to the Apollo program as an example of how the space program stimulates technology. The agency argued that Apollo would force technological development that otherwise might not be achieved. James Webb
went so far as to say that "learning how to get to the moon, developing the
technology which will be required to get there, . . . is more important than the
lunar landing itself."[8] In general, James Fletcher wrote in 1972, "Our space
work will be a major factor in . . . United States technological leadership."[9]

Advances in technology contribute to some of the other benefits NASA has
described. Technological strides provide economic returns because the private

sector is heavily involved in achieving the advances and then applying them. Technological advances stimulate "the development of improved products and processes that increase our ability to compete in world markets," and hence make the nation more economically competitive.[10] Furthermore, NASA has argued, technological progress is essential to solving "the many complex problems which face the world," such as energy and food shortages, pollution, and transportation difficulties.[11] It also leads to spinoffs.

Spinoffs

When a product or technique originally developed for the space program is subsequently used in another field, that use is known as a "spinoff." Spinoffs have surfaced throughout society, NASA has stressed. As one agency publication said, "It is difficult to find a facet of everyday life into which spinoffs have not penetrated, even though sometimes their origins in aeronautics and space research are not easily recognizable."[12] NASA has done its best to point out those spinoffs.

In fact, referring to spinoffs has been one of the most common types of pragmatic appeal employed by NASA. According to James Fletcher, NASA has always named spinoffs as one *raison d'etre* of the space program.[13] Many of the agency's publications have been devoted partly or entirely to extolling the multitude of space program spinoffs, and there is an office within NASA with the sole purpose of identifying spinoffs and making the public aware of them. Although some of the 10,000 spinoffs NASA has identified are highly specialized, others more visibly influence the everyday lives of citizens.[14]

Some of the space program's more esoteric spinoffs include improved electrical switching systems, pollution control devices, agricultural grain dryers, electronics miniaturization, computer software, fire safety techniques, and spray-on foam insulation. The long list of more familiar spinoffs encompasses freeze-dried dinners, quartz watches, cordless power tools, improved batteries, microwaves, better dental drills, powdered fruit drinks, and Teflon.[15] NASA has placed particular emphasis on the numerous advances in medical technology that have been spurred by spinoffs.[16]

As early as 1960, NASA was stressing that "it is virtually certain that practical application of space vehicles can be made for the benefit of the taxpayer who will pay the bill."[17] Two years later the agency asserted:

The exploration of space affects your life today; it will continue to affect your life more and more. . . . Whatever age you may be it is probable that you come into almost daily contact with some product or by-product which is the result of space research.[18]

In 1981, NASA heralded the successful completion of the first shuttle flight as the beginning of "a new era in space promising countless benefits for people everywhere."[19] Highlighting spinoffs has been a pillar of NASA's pragmatic image.

Satellites

Launching satellites is a big part of NASA's business, and the agency has emphasized how useful it is to have satellites in orbit. Satellites play such an important role, James Fletcher contended in 1972, that their worth "can be measured almost immediately in terms of dollars, or convenience, or even in terms of human lives saved."[20] NASA has often named meteorology, communications, and the study of the earth as fields of endeavor greatly benefiting from satellites.

NASA has described how satellites enable meteorologists to study weather patterns with great ease and efficiency. For example, the agency said, much has been learned about how storms form and move since satellite observation began. That knowledge, coupled with the ability to track by satellite the progress of storms, helps meteorologists predict where potentially damaging storms will occur. As described by NASA, "These 'sentinels in the sky' are constantly on guard for those inevitable moments when friendly weather turns to foe."[21]

NASA has also praised the use of satellites as a way to improve the accuracy of weather forecasts. According to the agency, more accurate and longer-term forecasts would almost certainly result in fewer deaths due to unexpected storms, in large savings in crop and property damage, greater efficiency in utilities, construction, transportation, and other industries, and even in better vacation planning.[22] NASA asserted in the early 1970s that satellite technology would eventually allow meteorologists to develop weather forecasts accurate up to two weeks.[23]

The advent of satellites has brought about "a new era in communications," claimed NASA.[24] The use of satellites enhances communication in numerous ways. Intercontinental telephone calls are much cheaper and more reliable than previously, while instant intercontinental television is possible only through the use of satellites. The agency said its "programs in satellite communications and information systems are committed to the advancement of the state of the art."[25]

Finally, satellites provide unparalleled ability to examine the earth and its environment. A variety of satellite photographic techniques can reveal a tremendous amount of information about the planet and its condition. Endeavors such as urban planning, the search for and utilization of natural resources, oceanography, geology, and agriculture apply this technology, NASA has noted.

Because of their unique ability to provide information about the earth, satellites play an increasingly important role in the growing environmental movement, NASA has stated. The agency's proposed "Mission to Planet

Earth," an in-depth study of the environment and its problems, would rely heavily on satellite technology. As a NASA official put it: "Space is the place to gather most of the data we need to understand the Earth for the first time in all its beauty, glory and increasingly recognized vulnerability."[26] Such information about the earth is vital because "understanding the dynamics and limitations of our environment is essential to our long term survival."[27]

Economic Returns

NASA has asserted that the space program results in several kinds of economic benefits. The technological stimulus and spinoffs produce important economic returns. Fletcher declared in 1972 that "the space effort will be serving a prime economic role" in the coming decades because of the way it drives technological advances.[28] NASA has argued that spinoffs from the space program have a salutary effect on the overall economy by creating new industries, jobs, and markets. This in turn increases America's economic productivity.[29] In addition, NASA spending directly influences the economy by employing tens of thousands of people in government and industry.

NASA has eagerly described the positive influence that spending on the space program has on the overall economy. The agency commissioned a study in the mid-1970s to assess the economic effect of its spending. The results, which the agency submitted to Congress in support of its fiscal 1977 budget request, indicated that the return on NASA spending has historically been about 43 percent.[30] Along those same lines, astronaut Rhea Seddon said in a 1989 speech that for every dollar budgeted for NASA in that year, society could expect a return in knowledge and technology worth about nine dollars.[31] NASA has frequently quoted the figure of a seven-to-one return on space investment.[32]

Since 1984, when the Reagan administration announced a National Commercial Space Policy, NASA has contended that space and the private sector make a good match (although the 1986 *Challenger* disaster dampened the enthusiasm of both NASA and the private sector). In a pragmatic statement couched in romantic terms, NASA asserted that "space represents an economic frontier, a new territory of commercial opportunity."[33] Corporations, serving as contractors for many of the products and services required by NASA, have been deeply involved in the space program since its beginning. The agency has encouraged the private sector to make commercial use of space in addition to serving the space program.

NASA has particularly urged business to investigate using the "unique conditions of space" to manufacture products "that are difficult or impossible to make on Earth."[34] The agency also exhorted industry to make full use of the new technology developed by the space program, and the agency has an office charged with the responsibility of facilitating that process. In general, NASA declared in 1989, increased commercialization of space will mean "an opportunity for new industries, new jobs, new products and services to benefit people on Earth; continuing leadership in civil space activities, and, a strengthened competitive position in the world economy."[35]

One example of the business potential of space that NASA has often used involves protein crystals, which are used in the manufacture of pharmaceuticals. These crystals can be grown most effectively under conditions of zero gravity. NASA has claimed that the ability to produce these superior crystals could have major implications for the pharmaceutical industry, with one possible result being "advances in the development of new life-saving drugs."[36] This is the kind of advantage, NASA has said, that can help make America more economically competitive.

Science

NASA has also emphasized the tremendous amount of scientific knowledge generated by its activities. In the last few decades, NASA noted, "Spacecraft have already vastly expanded scientific frontiers."[37] This knowledge, which may eventually lead to practical applications, is cherished by academics and other researchers in its own right. Fields of study in both the earth and life sciences have been greatly enriched by the information discovered by NASA. As James Fletcher said in 1989, NASA's "goals emphasize concerted attacks on those critical questions of physics, astronomy, global climate and environment, and biology to which space activities can make great and unique contributions."[38]

Examples of scientific knowledge acquired by NASA are many and varied. Mercury and Gemini, for instance, provided insights into how humans function in space. NASA devoted much of a 1976 publication to describing the tremendous amount of new information about the moon provided by the Apollo program.[39] Unmanned missions, including Viking, Voyager, Magellan, and Galileo, have sent back new photographs and data about the other planets in our solar system or will do so in the future. The shuttle has allowed fruitful new study of the both the earth and the heavens. The Hubble Space Telescope, specially designed to be launched and serviced by the shuttle, "will dispel much of the mystery and uncertainty that limit our knowledge" about the universe, said NASA before the telescope's launch.[40]

While acknowledging the intrinsic value of scientific knowledge, NASA has also discussed practical applications of that information. One important fact is that science makes technological advancement and all its concomitant benefits possible.[41] More generally, NASA has argued, science helps us comprehend our surroundings and ways to influence them. "As we understand more about the forces affecting the solar system and the Earth," a NASA publication noted, "we are learning more about man's immediate environment and how to predict and control many of the forces which affect human life."[42]

Education

NASA has contended that its various academic projects help educate Americans. The agency runs instructional programs, administers grants, awards fellowships, and provides materials to help educate students from grade school to graduate school about space and science. NASA also assists teachers in a variety of ways. It runs courses and workshops attended by thousands of teachers annually and provides a range of up-to-date curriculum supplements.[43]

Another way NASA aids education, it has stated, is by appealing to the curiosity of youngsters and perhaps interesting them in science careers. According to a 1986 agency publication, "NASA programs have traditionally served to stimulate the imaginations of our young people, to stimulate them to become interested in scientific endeavors and in the world of constantly emerging new technologies."[44] This is vital because America is, or at least is perceived to be, falling behind in science and needs more people entering careers in that area. As a NASA education specialist remarked, today's students "are our future astronauts, engineers and scientists."[45]

NASA has listed an ambitious set of goals in education:

To encourage interdisciplinary training, research, and public-service programs related to aerospace; to recruit and train professionals, especially women and minorities, for careers in aerospace science . . . and to promote a strong science, math, and technology educational base from elementary through university levels.[46]

The net effect of NASA's educational activities is significant, the agency has asserted. James Webb made a bold statement in 1963: "We're strengthening the American educational process far more than any government program has ever done."[47]

Space Transportation

NASA has pointed out the obvious but fundamental fact that it is crucial to the nation's space transportation capability. The military plays a role, but NASA dominates America's space efforts. Therefore, unless the nation wants to eliminate its ventures in space or start its space program virtually from scratch, NASA must be supported. NASA has promised to continue to improve its space transportation expertise.

New means of transportation have historically had significant economic effects, NASA said, and the space program will be no different. According to a

1988 agency publication: "New methods of transportation have played a key role in expanding our economy. America's wilderness frontiers were opened by the railroad. International commerce was revolutionized by the airplane."[48] The next century will see a booming space economy because of its efforts at building America's space transportation capability, NASA claimed.

STYLES OF PRAGMATIC APPEALS

In addition to the preceding major themes, other patterns have appeared in pragmatism. Certain phrases and ideas, clearly designed to convey the image's message, recur throughout agency statements and publications. NASA has frequently contended that: the benefits of the space program cannot be entirely foreseen; NASA runs a "balanced" space program; space influences the daily lives of people; and a "new era" in space exploration dawned with the emphasis on practical benefits.

Unforeseen Benefits

NASA has often claimed that many of the practical benefits of the space program cannot be foreseen, which makes it impossible to know the full value of the current or future programs. "No one can yet comprehend the full dimensions of the possibilities to which space systems can be placed in the service of man," stated a NASA brochure.[49] A 1962 agency publication phrased it this way: "As it was impossible in 1492 to forecast the benefits of the voyages of Columbus, so it is impossible now to foretell what man will gain from the exploration of space."[50]

Why cannot many of the space program's benefits be foreseen? The main reason is that no one knows what sort of results the space program's technological and scientific research will bring. A 1960 NASA statement explained:

Science reflects in a very real fashion the injunction: "Seek and ye shall find." Whenever man has probed into strange and unknown fields of science, the discoveries have always exceeded the expectations of our ignorant state of mind when we began the search.[51]

The type of practical applications cannot be foreseen because those applications depend on the nature of the scientific and technological discoveries.

In addition, the potentially long lag between scientific breakthroughs and practical applications of those discoveries makes prediction of benefits difficult. As James Fletcher told Congress in 1971: "Historically, new discoveries and new basic science have resulted in practical benefits from 30 to 50 or more years later. We know this will happen even though we cannot now predict in detail what the benefits will be."[52] As a result, NASA said in 1960, "We cannot even begin to visualize" all of the applications flowing from the space program.[53]

What is certain, NASA has contended, is that those applications will be valuable. Investment in scientific research generally pays dividends worth many times the cost of research, the agency has argued: "The many returns from space research and exploration will indeed repay over and over again the value of our investment."[54]

Stressing that many benefits of the space program cannot be foreseen is an effective argument for two reasons. First, consistent with the central theme of pragmatism, it emphasizes the practical benefits of space activity. Second, it cannot be easily refuted. Since NASA is not specifying the benefits in question, critics cannot easily dispute the value of the benefits or whether they could have been achieved some other way.

Balance

NASA has frequently stressed that it runs a "balanced" program. In fact, "balanced" seems to be one of NASA's favorite adjectives for itself and its activities. For example, the word appeared five times in one 1988 NASA publication with only about thirteen pages of text.[55]

NASA has applied the word in various contexts. The agency has spoken of balances between manned and unmanned missions, between cost and achievement, between programs that look to the future and programs that tackle contemporary problems, and among exploration, applications, and aeronautics.[56] Often, however, the word has simply been bestowed on the space program in general.[57]

It is easy to see why the word "balance" would attract NASA as a pragmatic description. It evokes notions of practicality, moderation, and rationality—all watchwords of pragmatism. The notion of balance presumably appeals to people living in the relatively hard financial times when pragmatism has been emphasized.

Everyday Life

NASA has indicated that the benefits of its programs affect people in their everyday lives. A 1966 agency publication averred that "the space program contributes to improvements and benefits in day-to-day living" in thousands of ways.[58] Another NASA booklet emphasized that "both the daily lives of people and the long-term future of mankind" are enhanced through space dividends.[59] This emphasis on everyday benefits is almost certainly used to convince people that the space program helps them personally and directly, thus giving them additional incentives to support the agency.

A New Era

Finally, NASA frequently proclaimed, especially in the 1970s and 1980s, that a "new era" in space activities was on the horizon.[60] Most of NASA's references to a "new era" in space operations referred to the shuttle program, which was to be the vehicle of the new era. These references symbolized what NASA presented as an entirely new approach to space operations—one emphasizing practical results. NASA naturally wanted to underline its switch in images after it became clear that romanticism was counterproductive. Announcing the dawning of a "new era" in space operations was one way to do that.

CONCLUSION

Pragmatism has stressed that the space program provides an array of practical benefits to all citizens. The many such benefits NASA has enumerated fall into several categories: technological stimulus, spinoffs, satellites, economic returns, science, education, and space transportation. NASA has noted that people may not realize all the dividends from the space program because some of them reach the citizens indirectly.

The agency's effort to promote the space shuttle, and to win political support generally in the 1970s and much of the 1980s, centered on an image of pragmatism. Accenting the practical benefits provided by NASA's programs seemed appropriate given the agency's relatively hostile political environment in those years.

NOTES

1. James C. Fletcher, "Space Program to Aim at Practical Needs," *New York Times*, 4 December 1972, 50.

2. NASA, *Putting Satellites to Work*, by William R. Corliss, EP-53 (Washington, D.C.: GPO, 1969), 1.

3. Congress, House, Committee on Science and Astronautics, Subcommittee No. 4, *1961 NASA Authorization*, 86th Cong., 2d sess., 19 February 1960, 159.

4. Congress, Senate, Committee on Aeronautical and Space Sciences, *Space Program Benefits*, 91st Cong., 2d sess., 6 April 1970, 39.

5. John Noble Wilford, "NASA, on 15th Birthday Today, Finds Itself in an Identity Crisis," *New York Times*, 1 October 1973, 70.

6. Ibid.

7. NASA, *America's Next Decades in Space*, (Washington, D.C.: GPO, 1969), 75.

8. Vernon Van Dyke, *Pride and Power: The Rationale of the Space Program* (Urbana: University of Illinois Press, 1964), 100.

9. Fletcher, "Space Program to Aim at Practical Needs," 50.

10. NASA, *Questions About Aeronautics and Space*, (Washington, D.C.: GPO, 1976), 3.

11. Congress, House, Committee on Appropriations, Subcommittee on HUD—Independent Agencies, *Department of Housing and Urban Development—Independent Agencies Appropriations for 1976*, Part 2, 94th Cong., 1st sess., 4 March 1975, 11.

12. NASA, *Space Program Spinoffs*, PMS-023 (Washington, D.C.: GPO, 1987), 1.

13. Dr. James C. Fletcher, interview by author, Washington, D.C., 5 October 1990.

14. Congress, Senate, Committee on Appropriations, Subcommittee on HUD—Independent Agencies, *Department of Housing and Urban Development—Independent Agencies Appropriations for Fiscal Year 1988*, 100th Cong., 1st sess., 10 April 1987, 1124.

15. NASA, *Space Benefits*, by Denver Research Institute (Washington, D.C.: GPO, 1981).

16. For example, Senate Committee on Appropriations, 10 April 1987 hearing, 1125; and NASA, *Space Benefits and Older Citizens* (Washington, D.C.: GPO, 1972).

17. Richard E. Horner, speech to the annual convention of the Society of Technical Writers and Editors, Chicago, Illinois, 21-22 April 1960, NASA History Office, Washington, D.C., 5.

18. NASA, *Space: The New Frontier* (Washington, D.C.: GPO, 1962), 5.

19. NASA, *Mission Report*, MR-001 (Washington, D.C.: GPO, 1981), 1.

20. Congress, Senate, Committee on Aeronautical and Space Sciences, *NASA Authorization for Fiscal Year 1973*, 92d Cong., 2d sess., 14 March 1972, 23.

21. NASA, *Sentinels in the Sky: Weather Satellites*, by Robert Haynes, NF-152(s) (Washington, D.C.: GPO, n.d.), 2.

22. NASA, *This Is NASA*, EP-22 (Washington, D.C.: GPO, 1971), 4; NASA, *NASA: National Aeronautics and Space Administration* (Washington, D.C.: GPO, 1971), 6; Congress, Senate, Committee on Aeronautical and Space Sciences, *NASA Authorization for Fiscal Year 1974*, Part 1, 93d Cong., 1st sess., 6 March 1973, 270.

23. NASA, *Space Shuttle*, EP-96 (Washington, D.C.: GPO, 1972), 1; Senate Committee on Aeronautical and Space Sciences, 6 March 1973 hearing, 270.

24. NASA, *NASA: National Aeronautics and Space Administration*, 3; NASA, *The Space Shuttle at Work*, by Howard Allaway, EP-156 (Washington, D.C.: GPO, 1979), 25.

25. NASA, *Aeronautics and Space Report of the President: 1987 Activities* (Washington, D.C.: GPO, 1989), 34.

26. Douglas Isbell, "Space 'Mission' to Study Global Environment," *Washington Flyer*, January/February 1990, 6.

27. Congress, Senate, Committee on Commerce, Science, and Technology, *NASA Authorization for Fiscal Year 1980*, Part 1, 96th Cong., 1st sess., 1979, 148.

28. Fletcher, "Space Program to Aim at Practical Needs," 50.

29. Congress, House, Committee on Appropriations, Subcommittee on HUD—Independent Agencies, *Department of Housing and Urban Development—Independent Agencies Appropriations for 1977*, Part 2, 94th Cong., 2d sess., 18 February 1976, 17-19.

30. Mary A. Holman and Theodore Suranyi-Unger, Jr., "The Political Economy of American Astronautics," in *Between Sputnik and the Shuttle*, ed. Frederick C. Durant III (San Diego: American Astronautical Society, 1981), 175.

31. "Seddon Targets Education Needs," *Murfreesboro (Tenn.) Daily News Journal*, 15 November 1989, 3.

32. Congress, Senate, Subcommittee of Committee on Appropriations, *Department of Housing and Urban Development and Certain Other Independent Agencies Appropriations for Fiscal Year 1976*, Part 1, 94th Cong., 1st sess., 10 March 1975, 223; Senate Committee on Appropriations, 10 April 1987 hearing, 1125.

33. NASA, *Commercial Use of Space: A New Economic Strength for America*, NP-113 (Washington, D.C.: GPO, 1989), 2.

34. NASA, *The Space Shuttle at Work*, EP-156, 26.

35. NASA, *Commercial Use of Space*, NP-113, 7.

36. NASA, *1987 Activities*, 9; and NASA, *Commercial Use of Space*, NP-113, 16.

37. NASA, *Space Station: The Next Logical Step*, by Walter Froehlich, EP-213 (Washington, D.C.: GPO, 1984), 23.

38. NASA, *NASA Highlights 1986-1988* (Washington, D.C.: GPO, 1988), 1.

39. NASA, *What's New on the Moon?* EP-131 (Washington, D.C.: GPO, 1976).

40. NASA, *Exploring the Universe with the Hubble Space Telescope*, NP-126 (Washington, D.C.: GPO, 1990), 7.

41. Congress, House, Committee on Science and Technology, Subcommittee on Space Science and Applications, *1978 NASA Authorization*, Part 2, 95th Cong., 1st sess., 9 February 1977, 778.

42. NASA, *Space Physics and Astronomy*, by William R. Corliss, EP-51 (Washington, D.C.: GPO, 1969), 22.

43. NASA, *This Is NASA*, EP-22, 14.

44. NASA, *The Partnership: Space Shuttle, Space Science, and Space Station*, by Philip E. Culbertson and Robert F. Frietag (Washington, D.C.: GPO, 1986), 12.

45. Leigh Ann Eagleston, "Kids Ask and NASA Answers," *Nashville Tennessean*, 20 September 1990, 3B.

46. NASA, *National Space Grant College and Fellowship Program* (Washington, D.C.: GPO, n.d.), 1.

47. "Spending on Space Defended by Webb," *New York Times*, 24 October 1963, 14.

48. NASA, *Discovering Space for America's Economic Growth* (Washington, D.C.: GPO, 1988), 4.

49. NASA, *Space Station: Key to the Future*, EP-75 (Washington, D.C.: GPO, 1970), 1.

50. NASA, *Space: The New Frontier*, 1962, 1.

51. House Committee on Science and Astronautics, 19 February 1960 hearing, 160.

52. Congress, Senate, Committee on Appropriations, *Department of Housing and Urban Development, Space, and Science Appropriations for Fiscal Year 1972*, 92d Cong., 1st sess., 23 June 1971, 471.

53. House Committee on Science and Astronautics, 19 February 1960 hearing, 160.

54. Ibid.

55. NASA, *Space Shuttle: The Journey Continues*, by Richard Truly, NP-117 (Washington, D.C.: GPO, 1988).

56. Ibid., 7; Congress, Senate, Committee on Aeronautical and Space Sciences, *NASA Authorization for Fiscal Year 1973*, Part 1, 92d Cong., 2d sess., 15 March 1972, 334; Congress, House, Committee on Appropriations, Subcommittee on HUD— Independent Agencies, *Department of Housing and Urban Development—Independent*

Agencies Appropriations for 1978, Part 5, 95th Cong., 1st sess., 29 March 1977, 45; Congress, Senate, Committee on Aeronautical and Space Sciences, *NASA Authorization for Fiscal Year 1974*, Part 1, 93d Cong., 1st sess., 28 February 1973, 61.

57. For example: Senate Committee on Aeronautical and Space Sciences, 14 March 1972 hearing, 14; Congress, House, Committee on Science and Technology, *1980 NASA Authorization*, Part 2, 96th Cong., 1st sess., 6 February 1979, 541; Congress, Senate, Committee on Appropriations, Subcommittee on HUD—Independent Agencies, *Department of Housing and Urban Development—Independent Agencies Appropriations for Fiscal Year 1988*, 100th Cong., 1st sess., 9 April 1987, 1026.

58. NASA, *Space: The New Frontier* (Washington, D.C.: GPO, 1966), 4.

59. NASA, *This Is NASA*, EP-155 (Washington, D.C.: GPO, 1979), 26.

60. For example, NASA, *Man in Space: Space in the Seventies*, by Walter Froehlich, EP-81 (Washington, D.C.: GPO, 1971), 12; Congress, House, Committee on Appropriations, Subcommittee on HUD—Independent Agencies, *Department of Housing and Urban Development—Independent Agencies Appropriations for 1979*, Part 1, 95th Cong., 2d sess., 25 January 1978, 71; NASA, *Space Shuttle* (Washington, D.C.: GPO, 1981), 4.

6

The Shuttle Era

The space shuttle dominated NASA's attention in the years after Apollo ended. NASA conducted other programs during the period, but the shuttle was the centerpiece of the agency's manned space flight efforts. This chapter defines the shuttle era as stretching from 1973, just after the last Apollo flight, to 1990.[1]

NASA sought backing for the space shuttle in a political environment much less favorable than in previous years. By 1970, the bottom had dropped out of NASA's political support. America's decisive victory in the race to the moon greatly eased Americans' fear of Soviet space domination and, in the process, made NASA's image of nationalism much less compelling. The other image NASA used extensively in the 1960s, romanticism, had also failed to stop the ebb of support.

NASA therefore executed a drastic shift in its image making. In the early 1970s, the agency began to concentrate overwhelmingly on pragmatism, while sharply curtailing its use of nationalism and romanticism. Administrator James Fletcher signaled NASA's image shift with remarks like this one: "We have entered a period of increasing earthly benefits from the space program. We can now turn our hard-won new abilities to increasingly practical use."[2]

THE 1970s

The shuttle did not fly in space during the 1970s, but it occupied much of NASA's time and attention nevertheless. The reusable shuttle was fundamentally different from NASA's previous projects, and hence the agency faced difficult technical problems as well as political ones.

NASA Activities

Development of the shuttle was NASA's primary focus during most of the 1970s, but the agency did pursue some other projects. Using Apollo hardware, NASA launched a small orbital "workshop" called Skylab in May 1973, which was visited by three crews over the following year. The primary goal of Skylab was to study humans' ability to live and work in space for extended periods.[3] Public and congressional reaction to Skylab was "tepid at best,"[4] probably in part because the project seemed mundane compared with Apollo. After astronauts repaired damage done to the laboratory during lift-off, Skylab's crews successfully performed a wide variety of experiments.[5] NASA was highly embarrassed in 1979, however, by the furor preceding Skylab's unplanned re-entry into the atmosphere.[6] When NASA admitted that pieces of the station large enough to injure people would probably fall somewhere on earth, a barrage of unflattering news stories and jokes erupted.[7] Fortunately, the debris fell to earth harmlessly, mostly in uninhabited areas of Australia.

The decade also featured the 1975 Apollo-Soyuz Test Project (ASTP), a joint American-Soviet project that sprang from the detente of the period.[8] ASTP entailed an American Apollo spacecraft docking in space with a Soviet Soyuz spacecraft, exchanging crews, and performing experiments. The 1970s also saw NASA exploring the planets through a series of unmanned projects, including the Viking probes that sent back spectacular photos of the surface of Mars.[9]

NASA's Political Environment

The early 1970s brought NASA a drastically less favorable political environment, as support from all sources was much lower than it had been throughout most of the 1960s. The precipitous political decline shocked NASA. Coming from a spectacular success that many thought was merely the beginning of NASA's glory days, the agency was surprised to find itself attacked rather than rewarded. In addition, NASA's enviable political environment in the 1960s meant the agency was not accustomed to the relentless struggle for political support that government agencies typically have to wage. As two historians of NASA phrased it, "Until 1970 NASA had been tampered with from time to time but was, politically speaking, a virgin."[10] That changed in the 1970s.

The news was not all bad for NASA, however. Table 1 shows that while public support for space spending was quite low in the early 1970s, it gradually increased throughout the decade. A 1973 Roper poll found that 66 percent of those surveyed believed that too much was being spent on space, while only 3 percent thought expenditures were too low. By 1980, however, only 36 percent considered space spending too high, while the group believing spending

Table 1
Public Opinion in the Early Shuttle Era

Question: Are we spending too much, too little, or about the right amount on [the] space exploration program?

Poll Date	Too Little	About Right	Too Much	Don't Know	Number Polled	Poller
Mar 1973	7	29	58	5	1503	GSS
Dec 1973	3	24	66	6	1768	Roper
Mar 1974	8	28	61	4	1480	GSS
Dec 1974	7	28	56	9	2005	Roper
Mar 1975	7	30	58	4	1490	GSS
Dec 1975	9	28	55	9	2002	Roper
Mar 1976	9	28	60	2	1496	GSS
Dec 1976	11	33	46	9	2000	Roper
Mar 1977	10	34	50	6	1530	GSS
Dec 1977	12	34	43	10	2001	Roper
Mar 1978	12	35	47	6	1532	GSS
Dec 1978	13	32	44	10	1742	Roper
Dec 1979	15	33	42	10	2003	Roper
Mar 1980	18	35	39	8	1466	GSS
Dec 1980	19	33	36	12	2000	Roper
Average	11	31	51	7		

Source: Richard G. Niemi, John Mueller, and Tom W. Smith, *Trends in Public Opinion: A Compendium of Survey Data* (New York: Greenwood Press, 1989), 77.

Note: GSS refers to the General Social Survey.

was too low jumped to 19 percent. In addition to the incremental gains in popular opinion, NASA was bolstered in the 1970s by the establishment of a variety of pro-space exploration interest groups.[11]

Presidential support was not very strong during the 1970s. Richard Nixon grudgingly endorsed the shuttle program, but did not follow through with much political support. Gerald Ford backed NASA more enthusiastically, but his brief tenure in office minimized his influence on the agency.[12] Jimmy Carter was, at best, a lukewarm supporter of space exploration.[13] Although keenly interested in space science, Carter doubted the value of manned space flight, as did his science adviser Frank Press and Vice President Walter Mondale. Carter trimmed the number of shuttle orbiters from the planned seven to four.[14] James Fletcher characterized Carter as "not very strongly supportive of the shuttle."[15]

Congress was fairly cool toward NASA in the 1970s. Although Congress eventually approved it, the shuttle program was subjected to some withering criticism on Capitol Hill. In the Senate, Walter Mondale (before he became vice president), William Proxmire, Edward Kennedy, and Jacob Javits led the charge.[16] Proxmire called the shuttle plan "an outrageous distortion of budgetary priorities," while Mondale dismissed the shuttle as "a manned extravaganza to get public support."[17] The House also held some critics. In sharp contrast to the days when congressmen took NASA statements "on faith," Rep. Joseph Karth said about the agency's extremely optimistic budget estimates for the shuttle: "NASA must consider the Members of the Congress a bunch of stupid idiots. Worse yet, they may believe their own estimates—and then we really are in bad shape."[18]

SELLING THE SHUTTLE WITH PRAGMATISM

NASA statements in the early 1970s signaled a fundamental shift in the way the agency presented itself to the public. NASA Associate Administrator Dale Myers told Congress in 1971 that while the Apollo era had been thrilling,

We must now leave the excitement behind and proceed along new paths in space. Until now, we have been intrepid explorers traveling into the unknowns of space and we have made great strides. . . . However, if we are to reap the benefits of space, we must do things differently than we are doing today.[19]

James Fletcher explained in 1973 that it was time for NASA "to move back from the spectacular" and "become more like one of the service agencies of government."[20] He said the new space program would be "relevant to the needs of modern America."[21]

The way to make this shift toward a practical space program, NASA contended, was the space shuttle. Fletcher said that the shuttle would be "a historic step in the nation's space program" and would "change the nature of what man can do in space." He continued, "We can and must look upon the space shuttle as a major investment in America's future."[22] As a 1972 NASA publication proclaimed, the shuttle would "provide dividends that will continue for decades to come."[23]

The benefits provided by the shuttle, NASA asserted, would "contribute substantially in improving the way of life for all the peoples of our world."[24] Continued space exploration spearheaded by the shuttle would result in "a new and better destiny" for everyone.[25] NASA sold the shuttle by describing the virtues of the vehicle and explaining how those virtues would translate into practical payoffs.

Improved Space Transportation

Many of NASA's statements about the shuttle spoke of its attributes as a space transportation system. NASA highlighted several expected shuttle characteristics: routine operation, high reliability, versatility, and rapid availability.

Routine Access to Space. The primary justification NASA gave for the shuttle was that it would provide routine, reliable, and economical access to space. Virtually every NASA description of the shuttle during the 1970s and early 1980s stressed that point. NASA publications and official statements of the time explaining the shuttle were peppered with phrases such as "economical, routine and simplified access to Earth orbit," "reliable, frequent, flexible, economical two-way freight and passenger service," and "reliable, economic, and routine round-trip transportation between Earth and orbit."[26] NASA identified the vehicle's ability to provide routine and economical access to space as "the fundamental reason for developing the space shuttle."[27] Most of the other rationales NASA used to try to win support for the shuttle emanated from this central thesis.

James Fletcher said, for example, that the shuttle would give the nation "the means of getting men and equipment to and from space routinely, on a moment's notice if necessary, and at a small fraction of today's cost."[28] Similarly, a NASA publication said, "The Shuttle will turn formidable and costly space missions into routine, economical operations generating maximum benefits for people everywhere."[29]

To emphasize the expected routine operation of the shuttle, NASA often compared the system with commercial aviation. The agency predicted in the early 1970s that shuttle flights would become nearly as commonplace as airline flights. The shuttle was to operate much like airliners; the ground equipment needed to service the shuttle would "eventually become as standard as the conventional equipment at major airports" and the "orbiter would land on Earth like airplanes."[30]

People would probably ride the shuttle with the nonchalance of the airline frequent flier, NASA asserted. "For passengers," a agency publication said, "a shuttle trip to or from space stations may be similar to a business trip by air to a distant city. . . . While the astronauts pilot the craft, the passengers will relax in comfort comparable to flight in today's airliners." The publication went on to say that shuttle flights would become so routine that they eventually might "fly into space on timetables like those of buses, trains, ships and airliners."[31]

NASA referred to the shuttle itself as an "aircraft type space vehicle," a "vehicle that will combine the advantages of airplanes and spacecraft," and the "spaceliner of tomorrow."[32] The shuttle was also heralded as the "DC 3 of the Space Age,"[33] a reference to the first truly reliable and successful commercial airplane. NASA Administrator Thomas Paine summarized this notion: "We stand at the start of a new era which will see space flight become as safe, as reliable and as economical as aircraft flight through the atmosphere is today."[34] The decidedly pragmatic view of space travel conveyed through these comparisons with aviation was epitomized in a NASA publication that said, "The Shuttle will function as a 'freight' carrier."[35] Thus, in stark contrast to America's earlier space activities, the defining image of the space shuttle centered on routine efficiency.

The name of the program also contributed to its practical image. The term "space shuttle" did not inspire great excitement or awe about the program, but it did convey the pragmatic message that NASA was trying to send: The system would be a routine method of shipping, or "shuttling," people and cargo from one destination to another. The name was more likely to remind people of short airplane trips, such as the Washington, D.C., to New York to Boston shuttle route, or of crosstown buses, than of cutting-edge space technology. The official name of the entire program (including the shuttle itself and its ground support network)—the Space Transportation System—was also suitably pragmatic.

Reliability. An important part of NASA's promise that the shuttle would make travel to and from space routine was the assurance that the shuttle would be an extremely reliable vehicle. The shuttle could hardly be considered routine or economical, much less the "DC 3 of the Space Age," if there were a significant chance that it might suffer a catastrophic failure. Implied in the efforts to sell the shuttle was the notion that the chances of such a failure would be quite remote.

NASA also made a good many explicit promises on the reliability of the shuttle. The term "reliable" appears frequently in NASA descriptions of the shuttle.[36] NASA often asserted that the shuttle's reliability would compare favorably with that of earlier space systems. James Fletcher maintained that the shuttle would eliminate the "high risk, long lead times, and complex systems" that characterized previous space systems.[37]

While NASA exuded an overall air of confidence during this period regarding the shuttle's reliability, there was some acknowledgment that the shuttle was not entirely simple and risk-free. Early in the system's development phase, James Fletcher remarked that budget cuts forced the agency to make changes in the program that would "increase the technical risk somewhat but within prudent bounds."[38] Despite these occasional asides, however, the general tone of NASA's statements concerning shuttle reliability was quite optimistic.[39]

Versatility. NASA also accented the shuttle's flexibility and versatility in terms of operations performed, payloads delivered, users served, and passengers carried. The shuttle, NASA said, would be capable of a wide range of functions not possible or more difficult in earlier space systems. Fletcher told Congress that "there are a number of things that only the shuttle can do."[40] NASA highlighted these space shuttle capabilities:

The space shuttle can . . . serve as a launching vehicle for all manned and unmanned payloads and satellites to earth orbit, but at far lower cost; checkout satellite subsystems in orbit before releasing satellite; recover payloads in orbit and return them to earth; service and repair satellites; perform defense security missions; serve as a laboratory where specialists can conduct scientific and technological observations and experiments in earth orbit; [and] . . . rescue crews from crippled spacecraft.[41]

In addition, NASA noted that pilot maneuverability of the shuttle offered many potential benefits.[42] The shuttle's enhanced capability would create many possibilities for space exploration and exploitation, NASA asserted, and would do so economically. The shuttle promised to be "the one space tool which can accomplish the necessary balance between cost and achievement."[43]

NASA argued that the shuttle's roomy cargo space would allow flexibility in the size and weight of payloads carried, as would the shuttle's ability to adjust the orbits of satellites and otherwise service them in space or return them to earth. Flexibility in operations and payloads would also mean that many different users could be served by the shuttle. NASA predicted:

Users of the versatile Shuttle system will include communications networks, research foundations, universities, observatories, federal departments and agencies, state agencies, county and city planners, public utilities, farm cooperatives, the medical profession, the fishing industry, the transportation industry, and power generation and water conservation planners.[44]

The agency noted that the shuttle was "designed to meet the needs of all groups who will be using space in the 1980s and beyond."[45] Because of its versatility, NASA argued, "The Space Shuttle is overall the most capable vehicle built since the space program began."[46]

Part of the shuttle's flexibility would be its ability to carry non-astronauts into space. NASA pointed out that the cabin would be pressurized to maintain a "shirtsleeve environment," eliminating the need for bulky spacesuits throughout the flight.[47] That environment, and the relatively low gravitational forces experienced during a shuttle's launch and re-entry, would enable people lacking the extensive training and peak physical condition of astronauts to fly aboard the shuttle.

These non-astronauts would be people who could do important work in space. They could be scientists and engineers supervising on-board experiments; photographers, journalists, or others who could effectively communicate the experience and worth of space activities; or persons "with imagination enough to recognize new ways of substantially benefitting mankind by work in orbit."[48] People from many different organizations and nations would have the opportunity to fly aboard the shuttle.

The shuttle's versatility would make it especially valuable for scientific research, said NASA. The shuttle could be used as an in-orbit laboratory or as an observation post of the earth or the heavens, and its congenial environment would allow non-astronaut scientists to go along for the ride. The craft's satellite capabilities would also enable the launching and maintenance of specialized scientific satellites, such as the space telescope the agency was planning.[49]

Rapid Availability. Another benefit of the shuttle, NASA proclaimed, would be the speed with which the vehicle could be prepared for launch. NASA estimated that a shuttle returning from a mission could be readied to fly again in two weeks.[50] Thus, even with only four or five shuttles, the quick turnaround time would mean that NASA could sustain a high launch rate. As a result, the United States would be far more productive in its space efforts. For instance, James Fletcher mentioned the likelihood that "experiments will take 6 months instead of 6 years to get out into space."[51]

Further, since the "shuttle would require no elaborate launch preparations and no recovery forces" as did earlier spacecraft, once the basic maintenance was done, the shuttle could "be launched on short notice—perhaps within hours—if the need should arise." This meant that the shuttle could be used for rescue operations "to fetch marooned or injured astronauts from space or bring relief supplies to a stricken craft."[52] The shuttle could be "sent off quickly on a special mission to gather information needed in an emergency on Earth, such as a flood or crop blight."[53] It could also be used to gather vital information during environmental crises.

Economic Benefits of the Shuttle

NASA outlined a variety of economic benefits the space shuttle would produce, including lower space program operating costs, a return on space spending, satellite benefits, spinoffs, and an economical American presence in space.

Lower Operating Costs. NASA claimed that the shuttle's reusability would lower the costs of running the space program. Unlike earlier space projects, which relied on expendable launch vehicles, most components of the shuttle system would be recovered after each flight, refurbished, and used again. This reusability was central to the notion of the shuttle as a routine, airplane-like way of traveling to and from space. "After all," one agency publication said, "a

transcontinental airliner is not discarded after a single trip."[54] NASA estimated that each shuttle would be used one hundred times or more.[55]

Savings in the space program's operating costs would accrue from the
shuttle's reusability and its capability to land like an airplane, rather than
splashing down in the ocean. Costs would also be lower because most of
America's space needs could be accommodated through a small number of
fundamentally similar vehicles, keeping the program relatively simple and
easily manageable. NASA said that five shuttles would be enough "to take care
of the entire civilian and military space program" and would be the "most cost
effective" arrangement.[56] NASA emphasized that, overall, "the Shuttle system
is being developed by the United States to make space operations less complex
and less costly."[57]

The shuttle's reliability would also produce financial benefits. A NASA
statement to Congress stressed the agency's confidence that it was "pursuing
an optimum program from the standpoints of technical risk and program dollar utilization."[58] James Fletcher said, "The low risk access to space possible
with the shuttle will increase commercial interest in exploiting space in a wide
variety of beneficial applications."[59] A NASA brochure predicted that the
shuttle would result in "greatly reduced risk of costly total failures in spacecraft operations."[60]

Return on Investment in Space. Another economic justification of the shuttle was the contention that the money spent on the program would be an investment that would eventually pay dividends. NASA carefully noted that this
was not the sole or even the primary reason to build the shuttle, but frequently
put forth the argument nonetheless. A NASA official stated that the shuttle
would play a central part in "providing the taxpayer as large a return for his
space investment as possible."[61]

This argument is based on the economic theory that spending in research
and development spurs technological advances, which in turn lead to higher
productivity and economic growth. NASA adduced evidence indicating that
spending on high technology efforts has a particularly beneficial effect on the
economy. NASA also stressed that spending on the space shuttle undoubtedly
fell into this category of highly salubrious investment. In addition, NASA
claimed that the shuttle would improve America's balance of trade by stimulating technology-driven industries at home and by selling its satellite services to
other nations.[62] In general, the agency claimed, the space shuttle would
greatly help "advance the nation's technological capabilities."[63]

NASA commissioned several economic studies to pinpoint the effects of
space spending on the economy and then used the results of those studies in
selling the shuttle program. The agency quoted a variety of figures. NASA
often said that as long as a certain number of shuttle missions were flown a
year, there would be a 10 percent return on investment in the shuttle. However, the minimum number of flights NASA said were required to achieve this

result continually declined. In 1971 the number quoted was thirty-nine, in 1972 it was thirty to thirty-three, in 1973 it was thirty, and in 1975 it was twenty-five.[64]

NASA brandished another kind of statistic to establish the economic benefits of the space program. James Fletcher gave an example when he said, "The economists who have looked at the program find that for every $1 that you invest in a high technology program like the Shuttle, or like Apollo, you receive $7 back."[65] The point, however, is the same: The shuttle provides a good return on the investment. While, according to this argument, economic forces are largely responsible for the benefit, NASA took care to remark that it works hard to reach the same result. Fletcher averred that NASA puts forth "a conscious, determined effort to wring the most benefit for all out of every dollar spent on NASA research."[66]

NASA also sold the shuttle based on the jobs it would provide. The agency told the White House that the shuttle would result in 8,800 jobs in 1972 and 24,000 by 1973.[67] In addition, the space shuttle was touted as a boon for commerce. When asked in 1974 about the long-term value of the shuttle, Administrator Fletcher replied, "We do have in mind really making use of what we have learned in the past about the possibilities for using space for all kinds of things, particularly for commercial use."[68] Part of the shuttle's mission would be to serve the business community directly by transporting loads to space. The shuttle, NASA said, "will operate as a common carrier, serving essentially anyone who can buy a ticket or pay the freight cost."[69]

Satellites. The shuttle was also sold as a way to reduce the cost of the satellites put into space.[70] NASA predicted that "the Shuttle will place satellites in orbit for one-third to two-thirds the cost of launches" by expendable rockets.[71] If, as NASA argued, the shuttle were significantly cheaper to operate, then the costs to launch payloads into orbit would also be lower. One early NASA estimate placed the payload launch cost per pound by a fully loaded shuttle at $120, compared with $900 to $5,600 per pound by conventional launch vehicles.[72]

In addition, the shuttle's cargo space and lifting ability, both of which are large relative to expendable launch vehicles, meant that payloads would no longer have to be as "highly miniaturized and extensively tested and checked out at great expense" as they were before.[73] Satellites could be of significantly simpler designs, which would also translate into lower costs. Use of the shuttle would thus reduce the risk and time involved in developing payloads, NASA noted.[74] Furthermore, the ample cargo space would enable multiple missions to be accomplished on a single shuttle flight, with flight participants sharing the costs.[75]

The shuttle's ability to repair satellites in orbit or to retrieve them and return them to earth for refurbishment also were mentioned as ways to save money. Previously, if a satellite failed, it was a total loss. With the shuttle's ability to service satellites in orbit, however, such would not be the case. In the words of a top NASA leader, "With the Shuttle, we will no longer have to 'throw away' payloads."[76] In 1972, NASA claimed that the shuttle could have corrected seventy-eight of 131 payload failures that occurred in the pre-shuttle era.[77]

For all of these reasons, the shuttle promised to "carry out various missions in Earth orbit at a fraction of the cost of earlier systems."[78] NASA's Christopher Kraft told Congress, "This vehicle will be the transportation system to open the frontier of space on a regular and cost-effective basis."[79] NASA Administrator James Fletcher was more specific in his 1972 statement that "the total savings to NASA, [the Department of Defense], and other users are estimated to average a billion a year in the 1980's."[80]

Spinoffs. James Fletcher recalled that, along with satellites, NASA emphasized spinoffs in the early 1970s.[81] The agency argued that the new technology required by the shuttle would serve as technological inspiration for industry and would result in a wide array of spinoffs. For instance, NASA Deputy Administrator George Low testified to Congress in 1973 that spinoffs would "flow inevitably" from the shuttle program and described in detail the structure NASA had in place to assist that flow.[82] A NASA report to Congress at about the same time said,

We can say with confidence that the research and development expenditures for the Shuttle will provide a considerable number of new procedures and products that will benefit all of our people in the coming decades—and all as bonuses of a transportation system that is planned to save us money directly in its application to space.[83]

Although NASA did not predict the exact spinoffs the shuttle program would produce, it did list specific areas in which it believed spinoffs would occur. Those areas were: aerodynamics, combustion/propulsion, electronics, fuel cells, man/machine interactions, materials, and structural design.[84]

American Presence in Space. Another justification for the shuttle was that it ensured that the United States would continue to have a manned space program, and would do so economically. NASA presented the shuttle as a real space bargain in a time of severe budgetary constraints. Thus, NASA answered the question 'Why the space shuttle?' partly by saying: "The United States must continue to do useful things in space. The cost of doing business in space must be reduced. The space shuttle offers the most effective way."[85] An agency brochure asserted that "the shuttle is the only meaningful new manned space program which can be accomplished on a modest budget."[86]

Furthermore, the shuttle was the only scheme that received serious consideration as Apollo's long-term successor (the relatively brief Skylab program was already in the works, and the Apollo-Soyuz Test Project was a one-time event). If the shuttle were not developed, the United States would be out of the manned space business, NASA argued. The shuttle represented, in the words of James Fletcher, "the keystone to the Nation's future in space."[87] As Fletcher told Congress, "The shuttle is necessary to assure that the United States will have a continuing effective presence in space."[88]

NASA's various promises about the shuttle were extremely optimistic. The fundamental justification NASA gave for the shuttle was that it would provide routine and reliable access to space.[89] Many of the other shuttle benefits NASA discussed—versatility, rapid availability, lower operating costs, and ability to provide economic returns—depended on the shuttle being reliable. Yet the shuttle never became the routine and reliable system NASA had envisioned, and many of the promises NASA made never came true.

1981 TO 1985: THE EARLY YEARS OF SHUTTLE OPERATIONS

The space shuttle began flying in 1981, two years behind schedule. NASA's tight budgets exacerbated the development problems that caused the program's delay. The major engineering hurdles were the shuttle's engines and the tiles designed to protect the craft from the tremendous heat experienced during re-entry into the earth's atmosphere.[90] By spring 1981, however, NASA was ready for the first shuttle flight. The shuttle *Columbia* lifted off from Kennedy Space Center on April 12, 1981, spent two days in orbit testing the spacecraft, and landed safely at Edwards Air Force Base in California.[91]

NASA conducted twenty-two more shuttle flights by the end of 1985. Despite a few glitches, the shuttle performed well during these years.[92] NASA accomplished a string of space "firsts" in this period: first American spacecraft landing on the ground, first reusable space vehicle, first American woman and first African-American in space, largest number of crew members (eight) in a single spacecraft, and first members of Congress launched in space.[93] NASA also aggressively pursued its plan to use the shuttle for deploying satellites and conducting scientific experiments. The agency was especially delighted by the 1984 *Challenger* mission that retrieved, repaired, and returned a satellite to orbit.

Meanwhile, NASA made plans for its future. The agency had long wanted to build a large manned space station and proposed that as its next big project. NASA began seeking political support for the station in the early 1980s.

NASA's Political Environment

NASA's political situation improved somewhat in the early 1980s. The start of shuttle operations likely helped reinvigorate interest in and support for the agency. An estimated half-million people went to Edwards Air Force Base to watch the landing of the first shuttle mission.[94] Prior to the initial shuttle flight in 1981, no American manned missions had flown since Apollo-Soyuz in 1975.

By the early 1980s, public support for space had recovered fairly well from the devastating dip of the immediate post-Apollo period. Although polls indicated that most Americans still did not consider space exploration a priority, the overall trends in public opinion were encouraging for NASA.[95] Several 1981 opinion polls reflected NASA's improved standing. In May 1981, a Harris survey showed that a strong majority of 63 percent to 33 percent favored spending several billion dollars over ten years to refine the shuttle, a finding Harris called "even more significant in view of the current overwhelming preference for cutting Federal spending."[96] That same poll revealed that 76 percent of respondents thought the shuttle was "a major breakthrough for U.S. technology and know-how." An Associated Press-NBC poll conducted in August 1981 found that 66 percent believed the shuttle was a good national investment, while 60 percent thought the United States was either spending too little or about the right amount on space generally. An October 1981 Associated Press-NBC poll confirmed the earlier results.[97]

Table 2 also reflects improvement in NASA's political environment. By an average margin of 40 percent to 51 percent, fewer people in the early 1980s than in the 1970s believed too much was being spent on space exploration. More people in the early 1980s than in the 1970s, by an average of 41 percent to 31 percent, thought about the right amount was being spent on space exploration. The proportion of respondents who believed NASA was receiving too little funding, 11 percent in the 1970s and 12 percent in the early 1980s, remained fairly constant.

The newly elected president, Ronald Reagan, exhibited more enthusiasm about space than did his immediate predecessors. Reagan apparently was convinced that the shuttle program meshed with his political theme of renewed American confidence and pride.[98] His administration was also extremely interested in the military potential of space, and in 1984 Reagan listed "strengthened security and capability to maintain the peace" among American goals in space.[99] The Department of Defense handled much of that work because NASA was designated as a civilian agency, although several shuttle flights performed military missions.

In regard to NASA, Reagan spoke more often of the commercial possibilities of space.[100] He said in his 1984 State of the Union address, "Just as the oceans opened up a new world for clipper ships and Yankee traders, space holds enormous potential for commerce today."[101] He remarked later that year, "The benefits our people can receive from the commercial use of space literally dazzle the imagination."[102] Reagan proposed to stimulate private involvement in space by giving tax breaks and easing government regulations. Reagan also supported development of the National Aero-Space Plane, which would fly in low earth orbit and would be able to take off and land under its own power.

Table 2
Public Opinion in the Early 1980s

Question: Are we spending too much, too little, or about the right amount on [the] space exploration program?

Poll Date	Too Little	About Right	Too Much	Don't Know	Number Polled	Poller
Dec 1981	14	38	41	7	2000	Roper
Mar 1982	12	41	40	6	1505	GSS
Dec 1982	12	37	44	6	2000	Roper
Mar 1983	14	40	40	6	1598	GSS
Dec 1983	10	45	38	7	2000	Roper
Mar 1984	12	43	39	6	487	GSS
Mar 1985	11	44	41	4	748	GSS
Average	12	41	40	6		

Source: Richard G. Niemi, John Mueller, and Tom W. Smith, *Trends in Public Opinion: A Compendium of Survey Data* (New York: Greenwood Press, 1989), 77.

Note: GSS refers to the General Social Survey.

The plane would be able to fly between America and Asia in about three hours.[103]

Most important for NASA, in 1984 President Reagan endorsed the agency's plans to build a space station, directing NASA "to develop a permanently manned space station." In a phrase reminiscent of John F. Kennedy, Reagan told NASA to construct the station "within a decade."[104] Unlike Kennedy, however, Reagan did not ensure that NASA received adequate funding to do the job. This was typical of Reagan's attitude toward NASA: He generally gave the agency strong rhetorical support, but did not follow through with funding.

One positive sign for NASA's congressional relations in the early 1980s was the creation of a space caucus comprising members with strong interests in space.[105] NASA courted congressional support by enabling two influential congressmen to take the ultimate junket—a ride to space on board the shuttle. Sen. Jake Garn, chairman of the appropriations subcommittee with jurisdiction over NASA, had been pestering the agency to let him fly since 1981. He got his wish in 1985, serving as an observer and as a subject for tests on weight-lessness and space sickness. Rep. Bill Nelson, chairman of the Science and Technology Space Subcommittee and representative for the Cape Canaveral area, flew the next year.[106]

Overall, NASA slowly started to pull out of its post-Apollo political dol-drums in the early 1980s. NASA's political environment was still not nearly as favorable as it had been in the 1960s, but it was on the upswing. The future looked even brighter. After years of development, the space shuttle was finally flying. In a major coup, NASA persuaded President Reagan to approve, at least in principal, the space station—the big project the agency had wanted for years.[107]

Yet NASA still faced some difficulties. While it helped NASA politically in some ways, the shuttle had also created some problems. The shuttle's in-credible complexity and NASA's limited budgets made it very difficult to keep the program on schedule. In the 1970s NASA had promised that the shuttle would make sixty flights per year, but the most it ever made in a single year was nine in 1985.[108] In promoting the shuttle, NASA had repeatedly promised that the vehicle would be routine and reliable, thereby setting high standards for assessing the shuttle's performance. The delays and low flight rate made the agency look bad.[109]

The frequent launch postponements sparked increasing criticism from the media and complaints from Congress and the White House.[110] These admon-ishments placed heavy political pressure on NASA to try to stay on sched-ule.[111] In addition, NASA faced increasingly stiff competition for commercial payloads from the European Space Agency and its reliable Ariane launch ve-hicle. Shuttle launch delays made potential customers think twice about using the shuttle to launch their payloads.

Image Adjustments

NASA continued to use pragmatism as its primary image in the early 1980s, maintaining its position that the space program brought practical payoffs. Administrator James Beggs made a representative statement to Con-gress in 1983: "There is no doubt in my mind, Mr. Chairman, that the invest-ment this Nation has made in the Space Shuttle will pay off handsomely."[112]

The agency did have to make some changes to its image, however. In addi-tion to the frequent launch delays, the shuttle had taken longer to develop and suffered more technical problems than NASA had anticipated. Therefore, the agency slightly toned down its statements on the routine, reliable nature of the vehicle.

One way NASA qualified its stance was to indicate that reliability was not completely ensured until the shuttle was fully "operational." The term "operational" appeared regularly in agency statements and documents, although it never seemed to be defined. Yet NASA made it clear that it was striving to achieve the operational plateau. For instance, James Beggs said to Congress, "The highest priority we have set for NASA is to complete development of the Shuttle and to turn it into an operational system."[113] Beggs struck a similar chord by telling Congress that "NASA's first priority" was to make the shuttle "fully operational" and that NASA planning for the following several years would be devoted to achieving "operational maturity" for the shuttle.[114]

The early 1980s were characterized by numerous assurances from NASA that the shuttle was on its way to reaching its operational goal. "The Shuttle is approaching full operational status," reported James Beggs to Congress in 1984.[115] Later that same year, he said that the shuttle was "becoming truly operational."[116] Other statements pointed to the increasing "maturity" of the shuttle.[117] Beggs pointed out that any state-of-the-art program is going to experience difficulties, and that the shuttle program was "pushing the state-of-the-art probably even harder" than the Apollo program had.[118] A NASA brochure touched on the same point by calling the shuttle "the largest and most complex technological project ever undertaken by our country during peacetime."[119]

Despite the changes, NASA maintained its basic portrayal of the shuttle as a reliable vehicle. A 1983 agency publication told potential commercial shuttle customers: "Twenty-five years of hands-on experience assures you of the most reliable, flexible, and cost-effective launch system in the world."[120] In 1985 the agency called the shuttle "a reliable and reusable workhorse that carries payloads and crews routinely to and from space" and even still referred to it as the "airline to space."[121]

At the direction of the Reagan administration in 1984, NASA stepped up its emphasis on the commercial use of space and the space shuttle. The agency created an Office of Commercial Programs to promote the commercial use of space. NASA cited satellite communications, earth and ocean observations, materials research and processing, industrial services, and space transportation as fruitful areas for private sector involvement.[122] NASA portrayed the shuttle as the "link to the new economic frontier of space, enabling NASA and U.S. industry to conduct joint research in this unique environment."[123]

In addition to adjusting its use of pragmatism in the early 1980s, NASA also slightly increased its use of nationalism. The agency again spoke of America's need to retain leadership in space.[124] NASA emphasized the economic competition in space, stressing that an active space program would play a vital part in keeping America competitive with the rest of the world.[125] A strong space program was required, said James Beggs, "so that this country can compete effectively in the international arena."[126]

THE *CHALLENGER* DISASTER AND ITS AFTERMATH

The second shuttle mission of 1986, to be flown by *Challenger*, generated unusually high prelaunch interest because its crew included a personable high school teacher. Christa McAuliffe, NASA's choice as the first "Teacher in Space," planned to transmit lessons from space to thousands of schoolchildren on earth. After several embarrassing launch delays, *Challenger* finally took off on the cold morning of January 28, 1986.

The Explosion and Its Investigation

Seventy-three seconds after lift-off, the *Challenger* exploded. The seven crew members aboard—Francis Scobee, Michael Smith, Judith Resnik, Ronald McNair, Ellison Onizuka, Gregory Jarvis, and Christa McAuliffe—were killed.[127] The tragedy was captured on film, which was shown repeatedly on television.

Americans were deeply shocked and sorrowed by the accident,[128] and NASA itself was badly shaken. The *Challenger* explosion undoubtedly marked the nadir of the agency's history. The dismay of the public and NASA soon intensified, however, when reports surfaced contending that the accident could and should have been prevented. Ronald Reagan appointed a panel, the Presidential Commission on the Space Shuttle *Challenger* Accident (chaired by former Secretary of State William P. Rogers, and better known as the Rogers Commission), to investigate the matter.[129]

The Rogers Commission identified the cause of the accident: A gasket, called an O-ring, between two sections of a solid rocket booster lost its resiliency because of the cold weather and failed to maintain its seal, allowing burning propellant to spew out of the booster and cause the explosion. The Rogers report sharply criticized NASA management and safety procedures, and it made numerous suggestions for changes both in the shuttle system and in NASA itself. The commission's report received wide praise, although numerous observers doubted its conclusion that NASA was under no demonstrable outside pressure to maintain its launch rate.[130] NASA Administrator James Fletcher, recalled to service by Reagan after the tragedy, welcomed the report and vowed to implement its recommendations.[131]

NASA's Political Environment

Ironically, NASA's political environment generally improved after the biggest disaster in its history. Political support for NASA generally increased after the *Challenger* accident and seemed to continue improving. *Challenger* did bring NASA some problems, however, as Congress became increasingly skeptical of the agency and stepped up oversight of it.

Public support for NASA and the shuttle program jumped considerably after the *Challenger* explosion and stayed high in the following years.[132] This wave of support was reminiscent of the "rally round the flag" phenomenon, in which the public rushes to back the president in times of crisis. Indeed, the accident seemed to rekindle the strong feelings of patriotism and national pride that Americans have tended to associate with the space program.[133]

Polls showed that despite the accident, most of the public still had confidence in NASA.[134] An overwhelming majority wanted to continue the shuttle program despite the risks involved.[135] For example, a *New York Times*/CBS News poll found that 85 percent of those surveyed believed the program should continue, and a Market Opinion Research poll found an astounding 89 percent wanted shuttle flights to resume.[136] Opinion on the issue did not change much over the next two years.[137] Polls also reflected higher percentages of the public who believed that the shuttle was a good investment.[138]

Table 3 shows that Americans were also more supportive of overall spending on space in the late 1980s. On average, 15 percent of the people surveyed believed that too little was being spent on space in this period, as compared with 12 percent in the early 1980s and 11 percent in the 1970s. An average of 42 percent of respondents supported the current funding levels, also an increase from the earlier findings of 41 and 31 percent. The proportion of respondents who thought too much was being spent declined to 38 percent, down from 40 percent in the early 1980s and 51 percent in the 1970s. Other post-*Challenger* polls generally confirm this picture, with several showing even greater public support for spending on space.[139]

The Reagan administration's support for NASA wavered somewhat in the post-*Challenger* period. As ever, Reagan's rhetorical support was strong. He spoke soothingly to the nation just hours after the explosion and attended the memorial service for the astronauts a few days later. Yet he delayed seven months before calling for the construction of a replacement shuttle, and even then his plan would have diverted funds from other NASA projects to pay for it.[140]

Reagan's stated space goals remained essentially the same as they had been throughout his tenure in office; his 1988 space policy highlighted the military and commercial potential of space and reaffirmed his commitment to the space station.[141] However, his administration responded to rising cost projections for the station by scaling back and stretching out the program.[142] Congressional critics continued to charge that the Reagan administration lacked a coherent overall space policy.[143]

The election of George Bush elevated some enthusiastic proponents of the space program to high places. Both President Bush and Vice President Dan Quayle were strong advocates of space exploration, as was Budget Director Richard Darman.[144] Quayle played a major role in space policy during the

Table 3
Public Opinion after the *Challenger* Accident

Question: Are we spending too much, too little, or about the right amount on [the] space exploration program?

Poll Date	Too Little	About Right	Too Much	Don't Know	Number Polled	Poller
Mar 1986	11	43	41	4	727	GSS
Mar 1987	16	38	40	6	484	GSS
Mar 1988	18	42	34	6	714	GSS
Mar 1989	15	44	35	6	766	GSS
Average	15	42	38	6		

Sources: Richard G. Niemi, John Mueller, and Tom W. Smith, *Trends in Public Opinion: A Compendium of Survey Data* (New York: Greenwood Press, 1989), 77; *General Social Surveys, 1972-1989: Cumulative Codebook* (Chicago: National Opinion Research Center, 1989), 104.

Note: GSS refers to the General Social Survey.

Bush administration. Bush delegated considerable authority over space to the vice president, who reportedly saw space policy as an area in which he could make a substantive mark.[145]

Bush's plan, announced in July 1989, that NASA build a manned base on the moon and pursue manned exploration of Mars excited NASA but elicited skepticism elsewhere. Bush did not set a deadline or explain the financing of the plan, estimated to cost $500 billion or more.[146] Aside from the tremendous fiscal obstacles, several observers wondered whether NASA, beset by troubles from much less ambitious programs, had the technical competence to attain such a lofty goal.[147]

The *Challenger* disaster led to important changes in NASA's relations with Congress. The House Science and Technology Committee held its own hearings into the disaster and reached generally harsher conclusions about NASA's performance than did the Rogers Commission.[148] Numerous members, including some of the agency's strongest supporters, admitted that congressional oversight of NASA had been lax. As one legislator said, Congress "may have been too trusting of NASA."[149]

The *Challenger* episode spurred Congress to conduct more vigorous oversight of NASA. Rep. Robert A. Roe, who chaired the House hearings on the accident, explained the change:

Because of its great success story, Congress has been too shy in finding fault with NASA. As a result of the *Challenger* accident, Congress and NASA must begin a new era, one in which Congress must apply the same strong oversight to NASA that it does to any other government agency.[150]

The increase in congressional scrutiny prompted some NASA officials to complain that Congress was delving too deeply into the details of NASA operations. Such "micromanagement" by Congress makes it much harder to run NASA, agency leaders contended.[151] Fletcher said this "is something that the country ought to be worried about."[152]

Aside from the stricter oversight, Congress's attitude toward the post-*Challenger* NASA was mixed. On the positive side, Congress did appropriate funds to build a replacement orbiter and, in general, funded the agency more generously than in the recent past. Yet Congress demonstrated considerable skepticism about NASA and the space program in this period. While NASA had long faced some congressional opposition, the *Challenger* catastrophe seemed to unleash a continuing wave of fault-finding. For the most part, Congress met President Bush's proposal for a manned trip to Mars with incredulity rather than support, criticizing the lack of a funding plan.[153]

Congress may have been forced into the role as the villain, however. According to one observer, the "new reality" of American space policy is that the president makes exciting plans, leaving Congress to handle the financing and other dirty work. In addition, space funding decisions are made more difficult because NASA's budget is considered in the same appropriations bill as such politically appealing agencies as the Environmental Protection Agency, the Department of Veterans Affairs, and the Department of Housing and Urban Development.[154]

Another important result of the *Challenger* episode was the decline in NASA's autonomy. Congress and the executive branch, their faith in NASA shaken, placed institutional restraints on NASA and invited other agencies to participate more in space policy making.[155] NASA officials protested the encroachment on their bureaucratic turf but were unable to stop it.[156] As a member of the Reagan administration put it, "NASA is upset because they can see their empire being carved up."[157]

Because Congress approved a replacement orbiter for the *Challenger*, NASA enjoyed a brief upsurge in funding after the accident. Yet overall funding for the agency in the shuttle era was relatively stable. Its budget authority in current dollars rose from $3.4 billion in fiscal 1973 to $12.3 billion in fiscal 1990, but in constant 1987 dollars the climb in that period was only from $8.6 billion to $10.9 billion. In most of the intervening years, NASA's budget authority in constant dollars ranged between $6.8 billion and

$8.2 billion. After fiscal 1973, the agency's budget authority did not again top $10 billion until fiscal 1987. (See the Appendix for more extensive data on NASA funding.) Figure 3 illustrates NASA's budget authority in the shuttle era.

Post-*Challenger* Image Changes

The United States was deeply committed to the shuttle program long before 1986, and there was little chance the nation would abandon the program in the wake of the *Challenger* explosion. Yet NASA still had to be extremely concerned with the shuttle's image because of the shuttle's role in the agency's next big project—the space station. Plans called for the station to be assembled in orbit using people and material transported there by the shuttle. Thus, to some extent, selling the space station meant continuing to sell the space shuttle. NASA therefore faced a serious problem because much of the credibility of the arguments the agency had been using for over fifteen years to support the shuttle blew up with the *Challenger*.

Handling that problem fell to James Fletcher, who had been recalled to a second term as administrator. Fletcher described his strategy for doing so:

The initial strategy was to take the high ground, so to speak. Say that we had an accident, it was a combination of errors that led to the accident, we're going to fix all the problems that we know about that led to the accident, . . . and then, last but not least, we'll not fly till we're ready to fly, till we think it's safe to fly.[158]

Fletcher's remarks upon receiving the Rogers Commission report exemplified that approach: "Where management is weak, we will strengthen it. Where engineering or design or process need improving, we will improve them. Where our internal communications are poor, we will see that they get better."[159] This approach blunted overall criticism of NASA but did little to gain political support for specific programs.

When NASA did speak about its activities after *Challenger*, it referred to the shuttle only infrequently. The agency constantly extolled the virtues of the space station but said little about the benefits of the shuttle, which had been hailed throughout the 1970s and early 1980s. Fletcher explained that the shift in emphasis from the shuttle toward the station "wasn't because of the accident so much as we needed a new goal."[160]

In fact, when NASA did discuss the shuttle, the agency often used the space station as a justification for it. NASA argued that the country needed the shuttle because the space station, with its "enormous potential," was not possible without it.[161] The shuttle "underlies the very concept of a Space Station," which must depend on "an efficient, man-rated transportation system."[162] Therefore, "the shuttle is the fundamental link in a space transportation infrastructure which will carry this Nation into the 21st century."[163] This tactic is

Figure 3
NASA Funding in the Shuttle Era: Budget Authority in Constant 1987
Dollars

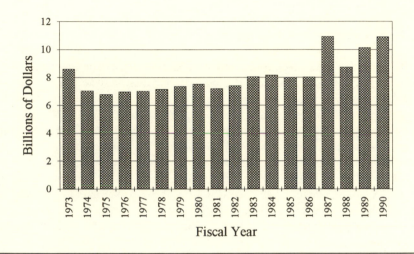

Sources: Adapted from Office of Management and Budget, *Budget of the United States Government: Fiscal Year 1995, Historical Tables* (Washington, D.C.: GPO, 1994); and Office of Management and Budget, *Budget of the United States Government* (Washington, D.C.: GPO, 1971-77).

quite ironic because many of the arguments used to justify the space station—its versatility, its economic and commercial importance, its influence on technology, and its scientific potential—were the same ones NASA deployed to sell the shuttle two decades earlier.

Otherwise, NASA's justifications of the shuttle were somewhat diluted versions of the arguments used before the accident. NASA described many of the same shuttle benefits it enumerated before 1986, but it did so in a much more tentative manner. Thus NASA still used pragmatism in selling the shuttle, but its pragmatic claims were noticeably less assertive than before the *Challenger* explosion.

The *Challenger* disaster forced NASA to alter radically its stance on some shuttle issues. The claim that the shuttle would make space flight routine and highly reliable, which was at the heart of NASA's portrayal of the shuttle during the 1970s and early 1980s, was obviously no longer credible, and NASA did not attempt to salvage it. In the aftermath of the disaster, the agency began freely admitting that it was involved in risky work and that the shuttle was a highly complex machine.

NASA re-emphasized the inherent risk of its activities in a 1989 brochure: "Veteran astronauts and engineers alike know that sending men and women into the space frontier will continue to involve risk, just as it has since America's first manned suborbital flight in 1961."[164] As astronaut John Young put it: "Riding a rocket is definitely not routine."[165]

In 1989 Fletcher described the shuttle to Congress in terms that would certainly not have been used before the accident. He called the shuttle "a highly technical, highly R&D, highly risky business, and we aim to make it as safe as we can, but it's still going to be a big risk. And some people are willing to take that risk, and I applaud them for it. But it is not routine."[166]

Fletcher thus spurned the label "routine" and recoiled at the idea of the shuttle as a trucking operation, an idea NASA had relished in the early 1970s. Astronaut Bryan O'Connor commented on the complexity of the craft in 1991 after technical problems twice delayed his shuttle mission: "We all realize that there are millions of parts involved in this vehicle and that it's a miracle when we do launch."[167]

NASA made repeated pledges to make the shuttle as safe as possible. It declared safety and reliability the top priorities at the agency.[168] In response to charges that with *Challenger* NASA had sacrificed safety to maintain its ambitious flight schedule, the agency also vowed not to fly a shuttle until it was as safe as possible, regardless of the schedule.[169]

Other of NASA's previous claims about the shuttle's performance—its low operating costs, high launch rates, and rapid availability—were also less tenable after the explosion, and the comparisons of the shuttle to commercial aviation disappeared. A top agency official refuted that description by asserting that the shuttle "will never be 'operational' and it will never be an airliner. . . . We can't make it as safe as an airliner."[170]

However, NASA clung to its fundamental argument that the shuttle— "currently the nation's only means of sending astronauts into orbit"[171] —was a valuable space transportation system. A 1988 NASA brochure read:

To realize the vast potential of space and to achieve the benefit from space in science, technology, and commerce, you must first get there. Transportation, as always, is critical. Payloads must be placed in orbit. The Space Shuttle is important because it carries these payloads into space.[172]

The image of the shuttle as a freight carrier also survived to some extent. According to the same publication, the shuttle "is a truck to transport things into space."

NASA contended that the shuttle did, in fact, succeed in easing access to space. The agency noted that there were twice as many shuttle flights in five years as there were manned Mercury, Gemini, and Apollo flights in ten years, and that the shuttle transported twice as many astronauts into space. "By that measure," NASA asserted, "the Space Shuttle fulfilled its goal of improving access to space."[173] Administrator James Fletcher told Congress in 1986 that improved access to space, which "was always the object of the shuttle program, . . . has been achieved."[174] Fletcher went even further in his defense of the shuttle in later testimony before Congress:

Really, the space shuttle is a viable vehicle. It is a super flying machine. It can do all the things it was advertised to do. The cost per flight is higher than we used to think of it. But in every other respect, it is a super machine.[175]

Fletcher said the shuttle would enable NASA to achieve its plan to "operate an effective and efficient space transportation system and develop advanced space transportation capabilities."[176]

Thus, the fundamental argument used to sell the shuttle both before and after *Challenger*, and the one that lies at the heart of pragmatism, is that the shuttle would yield practical benefits for the people on earth. As astronaut Rhea Seddon said: "People want to see the practical aspects. . . . We tried to sell the shuttle as a practical thing."[177]

Other Problems for NASA

The *Challenger* disaster grounded the U.S. manned space program for over two and a half years. In the meantime, NASA modified the shuttle's design and worked to fulfill the Rogers Commission's suggestions. To NASA's great relief, the shuttle program resumed successfully in September 1988 with the flight of *Discovery*.

Yet a new round of problems soon beleaguered the agency. NASA's design for the space station received harsh criticism on several points. First, critics charged that NASA had not made a clear case why the station was needed.[178] Second was the enormous cost of the project; estimates of the cost of the station as designed ballooned to $38 billion.[179] Finally, space experts were aghast when a NASA study revealed the station would require 2,200 hours of EVA (extra-vehicular activity, or spacewalks) for maintenance each year; NASA had only planned on 130 hours annually. The finding was especially shocking because, in the entire history of the American space program, there had been only about 400 hours of EVA.[180]

In addition to the travails of the space station, NASA suffered continued problems with the shuttle program. After discovering potentially deadly hydrogen leaks in the spacecrafts' fuel lines, NASA temporarily grounded the shuttle in 1990, prompting yet another round of criticism.[181] NASA seemed to be in a no-win situation. It was criticized after the *Challenger* accident for not being cautious enough; now it was being criticized for being too cautious. Administrator Richard Truly complained: "It is very frustrating to be castigated, to end up in political cartoons and to be made fun of when the agency . . . judiciously cancels flights to ensure the safety of astronauts."[182]

Probably the biggest political flap, however, concerned the Hubble Space Telescope. The $1.5 billion telescope, which NASA promised would be "the greatest advance in astronomy since Galileo," was devised to orbit above the earth's distorting atmosphere and peer deeply into the universe.[183] Yet soon after the Hubble was deployed in April 1990, NASA discovered that one of the telescope's mirrors had a manufacturing flaw that blurred its vision and admitted that the agency had not thoroughly tested the mirrors before launch.[184] James Fletcher called the episode "devastating to NASA" because the public had been excited about the telescope.[185]

Public outcry over the Hubble fiasco, combined with the criticism sparked by the other problems, left NASA staggering. Vice President Quayle formed a committee to study NASA's future. That committee, chaired by Norman Augustine, reported in December 1990 that although NASA was deeply troubled and major changes were needed, the agency should still run the nation's civilian space program.[186]

The events of 1986 to 1990 made this an highly unsettled time for NASA, both operationally and politically. NASA's reputation as a "can-do" agency took a serious beating. Just as the agency seemed to have recovered from the *Challenger* disaster, it suffered the highly embarrassing Hubble Space Telescope problem. In addition, the space shuttle delays and the flaws in the space station design harmed the agency. Questions about NASA's competence to fulfill its mission began to appear.[187] The problems also damaged NASA's credibility in Congress. For example, Sen. Al Gore wondered: "What are the implications of these repeated errors for the ambitious program NASA has mapped out for the 1990s?"[188]

Had NASA not suffered any more major problems after *Challenger*, the agency's political environment would probably have stabilized. Fletcher had seen improvement by 1988: "The bottom line is that NASA is in pretty good shape right now."[189] But the other problems did occur and NASA's credibility, badly tarnished by *Challenger*, continued to fade. NASA was clearly on the defensive.

NOTES

1. NASA statements made before 1973 specifically about the shuttle are included in this chapter, however. The shuttle remained NASA's only manned space program into the 1990s.

2. L. B. Taylor, Jr., *For All Mankind: America's Space Programs of the 1970s and Beyond* (New York: E. P. Dutton & Co., 1974), 5.

3. Roger E. Bilstein, *Orders of Magnitude: A History of the NACA and NASA, 1915-1990*, SP-4406 (Washington, D.C.: GPO, 1989), 100-101.

4. William H. Schauer, *The Politics of Space: A Comparison of the Soviet and American Space Programs* (New York: Holmes & Meier, 1976), 188.

5. Bilstein, *Orders of Magnitude*, SP-4406, 102-103; *Congressional Quarterly Almanac 1973* (Washington, D.C.: Congressional Quarterly, 1974), 878.

6. Through a series of events over which NASA had little or no control, Skylab could not be saved as planned.

7. Joseph J. Trento, *Prescription for Disaster* (New York: Crown Publishers, 1987), 165-66.

8. Walter A. McDougall, . . . *The Heavens and the Earth: A Political History of the Space Age* (New York: Basic Books, 1985), 431.

9. Bilstein, *Orders of Magnitude*, SP-4406, 93-98, 113-17.

10. Richard Hirsch and Joseph John Trento, *The National Aeronautics and Space Administration* (New York: Praeger, 1973), 183.

11. Congress, Office of Technology Assessment, *Civilian Space Policy and Applications* (Washington, D.C.: GPO, 1982), 139.

12. Trento, *Prescription for Disaster*, 144, 146; Eugene M. Emme, "Presidents and Space," in *Between Sputnik and the Shuttle*, ed. Frederick C. Durant III (San Diego: American Astronautical Society, 1981), 111-13.

13. Larry Light, "One Decade After the Moon Landing, Space Program Gets Little Attention or Interest," *Congressional Quarterly Weekly Report*, 28 April 1979, 780; Jonathan Spivak, "Apathy is NASA's Biggest Foe," *Wall Street Journal*, 25 February 1977, 12.

14. Trento, *Prescription for Disaster*, Chapter 7.

15. Dr. James C. Fletcher, interview by author, Washington, D.C., 5 October 1990.

16. Alex Roland, "The Shuttle: Triumph or Turkey?" *Discover*, November 1985, 35; "Space Shuttle: NASA Versus Domestic Priorities," *Congressional Quarterly Weekly Report*, 26 February 1972; Malcolm McConnell, *Challenger: A Major Malfunction* (Garden City, N.Y.: Doubleday & Co., 1987), 35; Thomas R. McDonough, *Space: The Next 25 Years* (New York: John Wiley & Sons, 1987), 29; *Congressional Quarterly Almanac* (Washington, D.C.: Congressional Quarterly), various years.

17. "Space Shuttle: NASA Versus Domestic Priorities," 435, 439.

18. Ken Hechler, *The Endless Space Frontier: A History of the House Committee on Science and Astronautics, 1959-1978* (San Diego: American Astronautical Society, 1982), 246.

19. Congress, House, Committee on Science and Astronautics, Subcommittee on Manned Space Flight, *1972 NASA Authorization*, Part 2, 92d Cong., 1st sess., 4 March 1971, 59.

20. John Noble Wilford, "NASA, on 15th Birthday Today, Finds Itself in an Identity Crisis," *New York Times*, 1 October 1973, 70.

21. Taylor, *For All Mankind*, 8.

22. Ibid., 12-13.

23. NASA, *Space Shuttle* (Washington, D.C.: GPO, 1972), 4.

24. NASA, *Space Shuttle: For Down to Earth Benefits* (Washington, D.C.: GPO, 1974), 3.

25. Congress, Senate, Committee on Aeronautical and Space Sciences, *NASA Authorization for Fiscal Year 1973*, Part 1, 92d Cong., 2d sess., 15 March 1972, 334.

26. NASA, *New Horizons*, EP-117 (Washington, D.C.: GPO, 1975), 26; NASA, *The Space Shuttle at Work*, by Howard Allaway, EP-156 (Washington, D.C.: GPO, 1979), 24; NASA, *Space Station: The Next Logical Step*, by Walter Froehlich, EP-213 (Washington, D.C.: GPO, 1984), 2.

27. Congress, House, Committee on Science and Astronautics, *1973 NASA Authorization*, Part 1, 92d Cong., 2d sess., 8 February 1972, 15.

28. Taylor, *For All Mankind*, 12.

29. NASA, *Space Shuttle* (Washington, D.C.: GPO, 1977), 1.

30. NASA, *Space Station: Key to the Future*, EP-75 (Washington, D.C.: GPO, 1970), 36; NASA, *This Is NASA*, EP-22 (Washington, D.C.: GPO, 1971), 2.

31. NASA, *Man in Space: Space in the Seventies*, by Walter Froehlich, EP-81 (Washington, D.C.: GPO, 1971), 11.

32. NASA, *Space Shuttle*, EP-77 (Washington, D.C.: GPO, 1971), 1; NASA, *Space Shuttle*, EP-96 (Washington, D.C.: GPO, 1972), 1; NASA, *Space in the Seventies*, EP-81, 11.

33. Congress, House, Committee on Appropriations, Subcommittee on HUD—Independent Agencies, *Department of Housing and Urban Development—Independent Agencies Appropriations for 1976*, Part 2, 94th Cong., 1st sess., 4 March 1975, 23.

34. NASA, *Space in the Seventies*, EP-81, 11.

35. NASA, *Aboard the Space Shuttle*, by Florence S. Steinberg, EP-169 (Washington, D.C.: GPO, 1980), 3.

36. For example: NASA, *The Next Logical Step*, EP-213, 2, 15; Congress, House, Committee on Appropriations, Subcommittee on HUD—Independent Agencies, *Department of Housing and Urban Development—Independent Agencies Appropriations for 1986*, Part 6, 99th Cong., 1st sess., 2 April 1985.

37. Congress, Senate, Committee on Aeronautical and Space Sciences, *NASA Authorization for Fiscal Year 1974*, Part 1, 93d Cong., 1st sess., 28 February 1973, 212.

38. House Committee on Appropriations, 4 March 1975 hearing, 5.

39. Fletcher recalled in 1990: "We knew there were risks on the shuttle too, and why we didn't emphasize them I'm not sure, because we all knew that the risks were there." Fletcher interview.

40. House Committee on Science and Astronautics, 8 February 1972 hearing, 39.

41. Senate Committee on Aeronautical and Space Sciences, 15 March 1972 hearing, 336.

42. Congress, House, Committee on Appropriations, Subcommittee on HUD—Independent Agencies, *Department of Housing and Urban Development—Independent Agencies Appropriations for 1978*, Part 5, 95th Cong., 1st sess., 29 March 1977, 5.

43. Senate Committee on Aeronautical and Space Sciences, 15 March 1972 hearing, 334.

44. NASA, *This Is NASA*, EP-155 (Washington, D.C.: GPO, 1979), 26.

45. John E. Naugle, "Research with the Space Shuttle," *Physics Today*, November 1973, 31.

46. NASA, *Space Shuttle*, PMS-013A (Washington, D.C.: GPO, 1989), 9.

47. NASA, *Space in the Seventies*, EP-81, 11; NASA, *Space Shuttle*, EP-77, 8.

48. NASA, *NASA: National Aeronautics and Space Administration*, 2; NASA, *Space Shuttle*, EP-77, 8; NASA, *Space Shuttle*, EP-96, 6.

49. NASA, *Science in Orbit: The Shuttle & Spacelab Experience: 1981-1986*, NP-119 (Washington, D.C.: GPO, 1988), 3.

50. NASA, *Space in the Seventies*, EP-81, 12; NASA, *Down to Earth*, 3.

51. House Committee on Science and Astronautics, 8 February 1972 hearing, 39.

52. NASA, *Space in the Seventies*, EP-81, 12.

53. NASA, *The Space Shuttle at Work*, EP-156, 23.

54. NASA, *Space Shuttle* (1972), 2.

55. NASA, *Space Shuttle*, EP-77, 3.

56. House Committee on Appropriations, 4 March 1975 hearing, 23; Congress, House, Committee on Appropriations, Subcommittee on HUD—Independent Agencies, *Space Shuttle Appropriations for Fiscal Year 1979*, 95th Cong., 2d sess., 9 March 1978, 29.

57. NASA, *New Horizons*, EP-117, 26.

58. Senate Committee on Aeronautical and Space Sciences, 15 March 1972 hearing, 337, 340.

59. Senate Committee on Aeronautical and Space Sciences, 28 February 1973 hearing, 212.

60. NASA, *The Space Shuttle at Work*, EP-156, 22.

61. Congress, House, Committee on Science and Astronautics, Subcommittee on Manned Space Flight, *1973 NASA Authorization*, Part 2, 92d Cong., 2d sess., 17 February 1972, 87.

62. NASA, *Space Shuttle*, SP-407 (Washington, D.C.: GPO, 1976), 82-83.

63. Congress, House, Committee on Science and Astronautics, Subcommittee on Manned Space Flight, *1973 NASA Authorization*, Part 2, 92d Cong., 2d sess., 16 March 1972, 830.

64. Congress, Senate, Committee on Aeronautical and Space Sciences, *NASA Authorization for Fiscal Year 1973*, 92d Cong., 2d sess., 14 March 1972, 228; Senate Committee on Aeronautical and Space Sciences, 28 February 1973 hearing, 73; House Committee on Appropriations, 4 March 1975 hearing, 64.

65. Senate Committee on Aeronautical and Space Sciences, 28 February 1973 hearing, 218.

66. NASA, *New Horizons*, EP-117, 3.

67. Leon Jaroff, "Spinning Out of Orbit," *Time*, 6 August 1990, 27.

68. Congress, House, Committee on Appropriations, Subcommittee on HUD—Space—Science—Veterans, *HUD—Space—Science—Veterans Appropriations for 1975*, Part 3, 93d Cong., 2d sess., 26 March 1974, 57.

69. NASA, *Space Shuttle*, EP-96, 6.

70. See, for example, James C. Fletcher, "Space Program to Aim at Practical Needs," *New York Times*, 4 December 1972, 50.

71. NASA, *The Space Shuttle at Work*, EP-156, 21.

72. House Committee on Science and Astronautics, 8 February 1972 hearing, 15.

73. NASA, *Space Shuttle*, EP-77, 3.

74. House Committee on Science and Astronautics, 16 March 1972 hearing, 830.

75. NASA, *Down to Earth*, 3.

76. House Committee on Appropriations, 4 March 1975 hearing, 23.

77. NASA, *Space for Mankind's Benefit*, SP-313 (Washington, D.C.: GPO, 1972), 15.

78. NASA, *Questions About Aeronautics and Space* (Washington, D.C.: GPO, 1976), 4.

79. Congress, House, Committee on Science and Astronautics, Subcommittee on Manned Space Flight, *1973 NASA Authorization*, Part 2, 92d Cong., 2d sess., 2 March 1972, 301.

80. House Committee on Science and Astronautics, 8 February 1972 hearing, 13.

81. Fletcher interview.

82. Congress, Senate, Committee on Science and Astronautics, *1974 NASA Authorization*, Part 1, 93d Cong., 1st sess., 20 March 1973, 63.

83. Senate Committee on Aeronautical and Space Sciences, 28 February 1973 hearing, 216.

84. Ibid., 215.

85. House Committee on Science and Astronautics, 8 February 1972 hearing, 15.

86. NASA, *Space Shuttle* (1972), 2.

87. House Committee on Science and Astronautics, 8 February 1972 hearing, 12.

88. Congress, Senate, Subcommittee of Committee on Appropriations, *Department of Housing and Urban Development, Space, Science, Veterans, and Certain Other Independent Agencies Appropriations for Fiscal Year 1973*, 92d Cong., 2d sess., 12 April 1972, 156.

89. In 1990, Fletcher gave this assessment of NASA's portrayal of the shuttle: "I think we used the word 'routine' because there were a lot more flights scheduled for the shuttle than were ever scheduled for Apollo, but I don't remember ever saying more reliable—but it may have given that impression." Fletcher interview.

90. Bilstein, *Orders of Magnitude*, SP-4406, 110-12.

91. NASA, *On the Wings of a Dream: The Space Shuttle*, EP-269 (Washington, D.C.: GPO, n.d.), 27.

92. Bilstein, *Orders of Magnitude*, SP-4406, 132.

93. Ibid.; NASA, *On the Wings of a Dream*, EP-269, 27.

94. Jon D. Miller, "Is There Public Support for Space Exploration?" *Environment*, June 1984, 29; Bilstein, *Orders of Magnitude*, SP-4406, 132.

95. Office of Technology Assessment, *Civilian Space Policy*, 142; Miller, "Is There Public Support for Space Exploration?," 26; National Commission on Space, *Pioneering the Space Frontier* (Toronto: Bantam Books, 1986), 178-79.

96. Office of Technology Assessment, *Civilian Space Policy*, 141.

97. Ibid.

98. Thomas J. Frieling, "The Reagan Report Card," *Space World*, March 1988, 10.

99. W. Henry Lambright and Dianne Rahm, "Ronald Reagan and Space Policy," *Policy Studies Journal* 17 (Spring 1989): 524; NASA, *The Next Logical Step*, EP-213, 1.

100. See, for example, his radio address of 28 January 1984 in *Weekly Compilation of Presidential Documents* (6 February 1984): 113; his radio address of 21 July 1984 in *Weekly Compilation* (30 July 1984): 1057; and his speech, "United States Space Plan," in *Weekly Compilation* (12 July 1982): 872-74.

101. 1984 State of the Union Address, *Congressional Quarterly Almanac 1984* (Washington, D.C.: Congressional Quarterly, 1985), 7-E.

102. Carol A. Shifrin, "Reagan Backs Space Commerce," *Aviation Week & Space Technology*, 30 July 1984, 16.

103. Ibid.; Bilstein, *Orders of Magnitude*, SP-4406, 142.

104. 1984 State of the Union address, *Congressional Quarterly Almanac 1984*, 7-E.

105. Office of Technology Assessment, *Civilian Space Policy*, 142.

106. *Congressional Quarterly Almanac 1985* (Washington, D.C.: Congressional Quarterly, 1986), 34. The flights of the congressmen forced NASA to juggle its schedule somewhat. Gregory Jarvis, an engineer for the Hughes Aircraft Company, was

bumped from both flights and eventually reassigned to the ill-fated *Challenger* mission (see Trento, *Prescription for Disaster*, 279).

107. John M. Logsdon, "A Response to Alex Roland," *Space Policy*, May 1987, 113.

108. Marcia Dunn, "From 'Gee Whiz' to 'So What' for NASA," *Nashville Tennessean*, 16 December 1990, 2D; Jaroff, "Spinning Out of Orbit," 27; "NBC Nightly News," NBC-TV, 6 April 1991.

109. John M. Logsdon, "The Space Shuttle Program: A Policy Failure?" *Science*, 30 May 1986, 1104; Sylvia D. Fries, "2001 to 1994: Political Environment and the Design of NASA's Space Station System," *Technology and Culture* 29 (July 1988): 585; Michael Potter, "Shuttle's Success Masks Space Program's Troubles," *Atlanta Constitution*, 2 October 1988, 2B.

110. Karen M. Hult and Charles Walcott, *Governing Public Organizations: Politics, Structures, and Institutional Design* (Pacific Grove, Calif.: Brooks/Cole Publishing Co., 1990), 3; William Boot, "NASA and the Spellbound Press," *Columbia Journalism Review* 25 (July/August 1986): 25; Fletcher interview.

111. Fletcher interview; Alex Roland, "Priorities in Space for USA," *Space Policy*, May 1987, 108; Hult and Walcott, *Governing Public Organizations*, 3.

112. Congress, House, Committee on Appropriations, Subcommittee on HUD— Independent Agencies, *Department of Housing and Urban Development—Independent Agencies Appropriations for 1984*, Part 6, 98th Cong., 1st sess., 22 March 1983, 8.

113. Congress, Senate, Committee on Appropriations, Subcommittee on HUD— Independent Agencies, *Department of Housing and Urban Development, and Certain Independent Agencies Appropriations for Fiscal Year 1983*, Part 2, 97th Cong., 2d sess., 5 May 1982, 1029.

114. Congress, House, Committee on Appropriations, Subcommittee on HUD— Independent Agencies, *Department of Housing and Urban Development—Independent Agencies Appropriations for 1986*, Part 6, 99th Cong., 1st sess., 2 April 1985, 8.

115. Congress, House, Committee on Appropriations, Subcommittee on HUD— Independent Agencies, *Department of Housing and Urban Development—Independent Agencies Appropriations for 1985*, Part 6, 98th Cong., 2d sess., 27 March 1984, 3.

116. NASA, *Space Station: The Next Logical Step*, by James M. Beggs (Washington, D.C.: GPO, 1984), 5.

117. For example, House Committee on Appropriations, 2 April 1985 hearing, 2.

118. House Committee on Appropriations, 22 March 1983 hearing, 39.

119. NASA, *Daring What Others Dream* (Washington, D.C.: GPO, 1984), 10.

120. NASA, *We Deliver* (Washington, D.C.: GPO, 1983), 1.

121. NASA, *Space Shuttle: NASA's Answer to Operations in Near-Earth Orbit*, NF-144 (Washington, D.C.: GPO, 1985), 2, 5.

122. NASA, *Commercial Use of Space: A New Economic Strength for America*, NP-113 (Washington, D.C.: GPO, 1989), passim.

123. Ibid., 5.

124. See, for example, NASA, *The Next Logical Step*, EP-213, 17, 34; House Committee on Appropriations, 2 April 1985 hearing, 8.

125. Beggs, *Space Station*, 1; Senate Committee on Appropriations, 5 May 1982 hearing, 1032; Congress, House, Committee on Science and Technology, Subcommittee on Space Science and Applications, *1986 NASA Authorization*, 99th Cong., 1st sess., 5 March 1985, 739.

126. House Committee on Appropriations, 2 April 1985 hearing, 8.

127. *Congressional Quarterly Almanac 1986* (Washington, D.C.: Congressional Quarterly, 1987), 327.

128. Jon D. Miller, "The Challenger Accident and Public Opinion," *Space Policy*, May 1987, 126-27; *The Harris Survey*, 6 February 1986, 1.

129. Steve Blakely and John R. Cranford, "Lawmakers Weigh In on Shuttle Safety Issue," *Congressional Quarterly Weekly Report*, 14 June 1986, 1324.

130. Ibid.; Congress, House, Committee on Science and Technology, *Investigation of the Challenger Accident*, 99th Cong., 2d sess., 1986; Fletcher interview; Hult and Walcott, *Governing Public Organizations*, 3; R. P. Feynman, *What Do You Care What Other People Think?* (New York: W. W. Norton, 1988), 217.

131. Blakely and Cranford, "Lawmakers Weigh In on Shuttle Safety Issue," 1324.

132. Miller, "The Challenger Accident and Public Opinion," 128-30, 139; James Fisher, "America Loves NASA, Budget Writers Don't," *Orlando Sentinel*, 24 November 1987, 12; Jon Van, "Americans Still Back Space Program, but NASA's Goals Remain Sketchy," *Chicago Tribune*, 1 February 1987, sec. 4, p. 4; Fletcher interview.

133. Miller, "The Challenger Accident and Public Opinion," 134; Fisher, "America Loves NASA, Budget Writers Don't," 13.

134. Kevin Klose and Barry Sussman, "NASA Gets 'Fair Amount' of Blame in Poll," *Washington Post*, 25 February 1986, A3; *The Harris Survey*, 15 September 1986, 1; *The Gallup Report*, No. 246, March 1986, 12.

135. *The Gallup Report*, No. 246, 10; Klose and Sussman, "NASA Gets 'Fair Amount' of Blame in Poll," A3.

136. "Opinion Roundup," *Public Opinion* 9 (February/March 1986): 27; "Public Opinion Survey Shows Increase in Support of Space Program," *Langley Researcher*, 21 November 1986, 5.

137. See Michael R. Kagay, "Poll Finds Increased Support for Nation's Space Program," *New York Times*, 5 October 1988, B4; "Poll Finds Backing for Space Spending," *New York Times*, 26 July 1988, C10.

138. "Most in U.S. Still Endorse Space Program, Poll Finds," *Wall Street Journal*, 11 February 1986, 29; "What the Public Thinks," *Space World*, April 1986, 6; Miller, "The Challenger Accident and Public Opinion," 128-29.

139. For similar results, see the *Wall Street Journal*/NBC News poll in "Most in U.S. Still Endorse Space Program," 29; the *New York Times*/CBS polls in Adam Clymer, "Public Blames NASA Officials," *New York Times*, 28 January 1987, D27, and in "Poll Finds Support for Space Shuttle, But Doubts Persist," 29 January 1988, A15; and *The Gallup Poll, 1989*, 209-10. For indications of somewhat higher support, see the *Newsweek* poll, in "The Public's View," *Newsweek*, 10 February 1986, 37; the *Time* survey in Michael D. Lemonick, "Goodbye to NASA's Glory Days," *Time*, 22 February 1988, 54; the Associated Press survey in "Poll Finds Backing for Space Spending," C10; and the Washington Post/ABC poll in Richard Morin, "A Sea Change on Federal Spending," *Washington Post Weekly Edition*, 28 August 1989, 37.

140. Frieling, "The Reagan Report Card," 10-11; *Congressional Quarterly Almanac 1986*, 330.

141. White House, Office of the Press Secretary, "The President's Space Policy and Commercial Space Initiative to Begin the Next Century," press release, 11 February 1988.

142. Frieling, "The Reagan Report Card," 11.

143. *Congressional Quarterly Almanac 1987* (Washington, D.C.: Congressional Quarterly, 1988), 368, 370.

144. William J. Broad, "Diverse Factors Propel Bush's Space Proposal," *New York Times*, 30 July 1989, 16.

145. Bruce Reed, "Rocket Man," *The New Republic*, 15 May 1989, 12; John Noble Wilford, "Steadier Orbit for NASA," *New York Times*, 11 December 1990, B9; David C. Morrison, "Vice-President for Space," *National Journal*, 29 July 1989, 1910-11; Paul A. Gigot, "NASA's Flyboys Have Grown Old and Fat," *Wall Street Journal*, 13 July 1990, A8.

146. George Johnson, "The Long Way to Outer Space," *New York Times*, 23 July 1989, sect. 4, p. 5; Bernard Weinraub, "President Calls for Mars Mission and a Moon Base," *New York Times*, 21 July 1989, A1; Phil Kuntz, "Pie in the Sky: Big Science is Ready for Blastoff," *Congressional Quarterly Weekly Report*, 28 April 1990, 1255.

147. See, for example, William J. Broad, "Pervasive Decline of Staff Stunts NASA, Critics Say," *New York Times*, 9 September 1990, 1; Jaroff, "Spinning Out of Orbit," 27.

148. *Congressional Quarterly Almanac 1986*, 329.

149. Ibid.

150. John R. Cranford, "A New Tone Heard in Congressional Dealings with NASA," *Congressional Quarterly Weekly Report*, 14 June 1986, 1325.

151. Theresa M. Foley, "Departing NASA Manager Criticizes Micromanagement of Space Agency," *Aviation Week & Space Technology*, 4 April 1988, 51; Leonard David, "NASA at T + 30 Years," *Space World*, October 1988, 8; Fletcher interview; Craig Covault, "NASA Managers Fear Loss of Space Program Leadership," *Aviation Week & Space Technology*, 2 February 1987, 22.

152. Fletcher interview.

153. Phil Kuntz, "Bush Goes on the Counterattack Against Mars Mission Critics," *Congressional Quarterly Weekly Report*, 23 June 1990, 1958.

154. David S. Cloud, "U.S. Space Flight Ambitions Face New Ground Rules," *Congressional Quarterly Weekly Report*, 22 July 1989, 1848-49.

155. Wayne Biddle, "NASA: What's Needed to Put It on Its Feet?" *Discover*, January 1987, 48; Philip M. Boffey, "Space Agency Image: A Sudden Shattering," *New York Times*, 5 February 1986, A25; Foley, "Departing NASA Manager," 53; Covault, "NASA Managers Fear Loss," 21-22; Barbara S. Romzek and Melvin J. Dubnick, "Accountability in the Public Sector: Lessons from the Challenger Tragedy," *Public Administration Review* 47 (May/June 1987): 236.

156. Covault, "NASA Managers Fear Loss," 21; Foley, "Departing NASA Manager," 51; Craig Covault, "NASA Plans to Fight Threats to Its Role in Space Program," *Aviation Week & Space Technology*, 26 October 1987, 61.

157. Covault, "NASA Managers Fear Loss," 21.

158. Fletcher interview.

159. *Congressional Quarterly Almanac 1986*, 328.

160. Fletcher interview.

161. NASA, *Space Station: The Next Logical Step*, by Andrew J. Stofan (Washington, D.C.: GPO, 1987), 5; Congress, House, Committee on Science, Space, and Technology, Subcommittee on Space Science and Applications, *1990 NASA Authorization*, 101st Cong., 1st sess., 2 February 1989, 14.

162. NASA, *The Partnership: Space Shuttle, Space Science, and Space Station*, by Philip E. Culbertson and Robert F. Frietag (Washington, D.C.: GPO, 1986), 2.

163. House Committee on Science, Space, and Technology, 2 February 1989 hearing, 14.

164. NASA, *Space Shuttle: The Renewed Promise*, by Neil McAleer, PAM-521 (Washington, D.C.: GPO, 1989), 5.

165. Henry S. F. Cooper, Jr., *Before Liftoff: The Making of a Space Shuttle Crew* (Baltimore: Johns Hopkins University Press, 1987), 12.

166. House Committee on Science, Space, and Technology, 2 February 1989 hearing, 23.

167. Warren E. Leary, "Space Shuttle Launching Delayed by Navigational Equipment Flaw," *New York Times*, 2 June 1991, sec. 1, p. 36.

168. "Safe Flight NASA's Top Concern," *NASA Activities*, March/April 1988, 6; NASA, 4-26-86, 9; NASA, *The Next Logical Step*, EP-213, 5; Don Phillips and Boyce Rensberger, "Astronaut Says NASA Cut Corners," *Washington Post*, 9 March 1986, A1.

169. See, for example, Peter N. Spotts, "NASA Needs Better Tools for Reducing Shuttle Risks, Study Says," *Christian Science Monitor*, 9 March 1988, 5.

170. Foley, "Departing NASA Manager," 51.

171. NASA, *NASA*, NP-111 (Washington, D.C.: GPO, 1989), 21.

172. NASA, *Space Shuttle: The Journey Continues*, by Richard Truly, NP-117 (Washington, D.C.: GPO, 1988), 4.

173. NASA, *The Renewed Promise*, PAM-521, 5.

174. Congress, House, Committee on Appropriations, Subcommittee on HUD—Independent Agencies, *Department of Housing and Urban Development—Independent Agencies Appropriations for 1987*, Part 7, 99th Cong., 2d sess., 13 May 1986, 58.

175. Congress, House, Committee on Appropriations, Subcommittee on HUD—Independent Agencies, *Department of Housing and Urban Development—Independent Agencies Appropriations for 1989*, Part 7, 100th Cong., 2d sess., 19 April 1988, 63.

176. NASA, *Agenda for Tomorrow* (Washington, D.C.: GPO, n.d.), 3.

177. Astronaut Rhea Seddon, interview by author, Murfreesboro, Tennessee, 23 November 1989.

178. Roland, "Priorities in Space for USA," 108; Bob Davis and Laurie McGinley, "Why a Space Station That Costs $25 Billion May Never Leave Earth," *Wall Street Journal*, 1 September 1988, 4; Michael D. Lemonick, "The Next Giant Leap for Mankind," *Time*, 24 July 1989, 50.

179. Warren E. Leary, "New Plan for Space Station Cuts Cost, Size and Flights," *New York Times*, 22 March 1991, A11.

180. William J. Broad, "NASA Defends Space Station Building Plans," *New York Times*, 20 March 1990, C8. An independent study of the station placed the number of EVA hours required annually at 3,800. See Jaroff, "Spinning Out of Orbit," 27.

181. Broad, "Decline of Staff," 1, 32.

182. Jaroff, "Spinning Out of Orbit," 27.

183. NASA, *Exploring the Universe with the Hubble Space Telescope*, NP-126 (Washington, D.C.: GPO, 1990), 31.

184. Sharon Begley, "Heaven Can Wait," *Newsweek*, 9 July 1990, 48-51; David Bjerklie, "Roots of the Hubble's Troubles," *Time*, 10 December 1990, 78.

185. Fletcher interview.

186. See Warren E. Leary, "U.S. Advisers Urge Sweeping Change in Shuttle Program," *New York Times*, December 1990, A1; Wilford, "Steadier Orbit for NASA."

187. See, for example, Broad, "Decline of Staff," 1.

188. Phil Kuntz, "Hubble, Shuttle, and Moon-Mars Add Up to Bad Week for NASA," *Congressional Quarterly Weekly Report*, 30 June 1990, 2054.

189. Mdu Lembede, "Fletcher Says NASA Gains Support," *Washington Post*, 19 October 1988, A21.

7

Transmitting the Images

NASA's heavy reliance on image-building to generate political support means that the transmission of its images—conveying the desired information to the public—is crucial. If no one receives the information, the agency's efforts are wasted and its political standing is not improved. A fundamental problem facing almost any agency seeking to communicate with outsiders is that most people are only marginally affected by the agency's actions and therefore are not particularly interested in communications from it.[1] Citizens generally have other things on their minds besides government bureaus and their activities.

Agencies can do two things to increase the chance of citizens paying attention to their messages: They can make the information free and easily obtainable, and they can make it interesting enough that people want to receive it.[2] NASA has attempted to do these things by working with the media, controlling the flow of information, using astronauts as spokesmen, and emphasizing the spectacular aspects of its mission. These techniques are designed to disseminate whatever message NASA wants to send, and therefore NASA's use of them has been fairly constant and not usually tied to any particular type of image.

WORKING WITH THE MEDIA

The media have served as vital conduits of NASA's images. While the agency also has spread its messages through publications, reports, congressional testimony, and other means,[3] using the media has enabled NASA to reach a large audience at little cost to either NASA or the recipients. Whatever information most Americans receive from and about NASA has generally come through the media. This has made the media extremely useful messengers for the agency. As two observers noted, "NASA has been unusually dependent on the media since its birth in 1958."[4]

From its earliest days, NASA has encouraged media coverage of its activities.[5] Such attention keeps the agency's public visibility high, which is a prerequisite for the effective spreading of its message. NASA has always worked hard to keep the press happy by providing what it most needs—good stories. Especially early in its history, NASA's activities supplied a great deal of exciting and fresh material, which fed reporters' hunger for stimulating and glamorous space stories.[6]

In addition to generating media attention by running interesting programs, NASA has sought to transmit its images by providing reporters and their news agencies with copious amounts of briefing material. Such material is, naturally, geared toward NASA's point of view. Reporters are briefed before, during, and after each space flight. NASA also furnishes general background information on space.

NASA has enjoyed considerable success in getting its message to the public. In 1969, for example, 734 of the 840 American television stations on the air showed film provided by NASA, while about half of all U.S. radio stations broadcast NASA-produced features.[7] In the shuttle era, NASA has made available to the media live audio and video "feeds" of shuttle flights.[8] In addition, some cable television systems provide continuous coverage of shuttle flights and other NASA activities.

Another way NASA has courted reporters has been to make them feel like a part of the agency. These efforts to co-opt the press have been quite effective; some scholars have charged that reporters have often behaved more as participants in the space program than observers of it.[9] NASA officials and the reporters covering the agency have tended to share the same technical and scientific jargon, which draws them closer and fosters a "team" spirit.[10] NASA's ultimate plan to co-opt the press was the "Journalist in Space" program, in which a journalist would ride aboard the space shuttle and send dispatches back to earth. The program, which was canceled in the wake of the *Challenger* disaster, attracted 1,705 applicants from the press.[11] In general, NASA enjoyed very good relations with the media from its creation until the 1980s.

Several observers commented on NASA's favorable treatment from the press. Some accused the media of succumbing to the glamour of space program and cheerleading for NASA instead of scrutinizing it.[12] One writer, for instance, said that the press generally boosted NASA "with chamber of commerce fervor."[13] That sort of criticism of the media intensified after the *Challenger* tragedy, which graphically revealed problems within the agency.[14] A *New York Times* reporter argued in 1986 that most space reporters had been "popularizers . . . rather than investigators."[15]

Yet the honeymoon between NASA and the media had already ended by the time of the 1986 *Challenger* explosion. The agency got a spate of unfavorable coverage when Skylab made an uncontrolled re-entry into the atmosphere in 1979.[16] NASA's real difficulties with the media began with the shuttle pro-

gram, however. Prior to the *Challenger* disaster, the press treated the numerous shuttle launch delays as "costly bumbling" by NASA.[17] For example, a
New York Times article spoke of the "comedy of errors" as NASA tried to
launch a flight, while Dan Rather of CBS News described a postponement as
"yet another costly, red-faces-all-around space shuttle launch delay."[18]

Former NASA Administrator James Fletcher attributed the increased media criticism of NASA and the shuttle partly to the fact that, unlike most of
NASA's earlier vehicles, the shuttle often did not launch on schedule.[19] Reporters assemble at Kennedy Space Center for a launch, Fletcher argued, and
if the launch is postponed, the delay is all they have to report. Both Fletcher
and Kennedy Space Center Director Richard Smith contended that badgering
from the press created much of the pressure on NASA to maintain the shuttle
launch schedule, which contributed to the *Challenger* disaster.[20]

Since *Challenger*, press coverage of NASA has definitely been harsher,
according to NASA officials. Former Deputy Director Hans Mark asserted that
the "attitude of the press has changed" to a much more critical one.[21] Fletcher
concurred with that assessment.[22] In 1988, he explained that NASA was
harder to run because of the press:

The media . . . is almost impossible to deal with. They go after the news, whatever it
is, and it's usually bad news that seems to sell. . . . So when NASA is having a problem, they bore in and highlight those problems, regardless of what the public thinks.[23]

As the 1990s opened, Fletcher characterized NASA as "really under fire" from
the press.[24]

NASA clearly has had a rockier relationship with the media after *Challenger* than in its early years. Until the end of the Apollo program, reporters
covering NASA acted like part of the family and lavished favorable attention
on the agency. NASA encouraged this friendly relationship and relied on it to
transmit the agency's image. NASA still received plenty of media attention in
later years, but much of it was negative. That prompted NASA to try to control
the damage to its public image—a task that, ironically, involved using the
media.

NASA may never regain the favor from the press it had early in its history.
Much news coverage of the agency's latest major project, the space station, has
had a critical tone. Yet working with the media will likely remain a valuable
communications technique for NASA simply because most Americans form
their opinions based on information provided by the media.

CONTROLLING THE FLOW OF INFORMATION

NASA has long boasted that its operation is open to the world.[25] Central to
this openness is the release of information to the public, which also contributes

to building public interest.[26] Yet formulating a specific public image requires some control of the flow of information. NASA officials, ever mindful of their agency's image and its effect on political support, have traditionally carefully controlled the information released to the public.[27]

Creative use of language is one way NASA has controlled its flow of information. Scholars of the bureaucracy note that agencies often use jargon or euphemisms to bolster their images or to obscure their meanings when politically expedient.[28] NASA has provided numerous examples of both jargon and euphemisms. Anyone who has ever listened to broadcasts of launches, flights, or NASA press conferences can attest to agency employees' propensity to use jargon.

NASA is renowned for its abbreviations and acronyms, which number an estimated 16,000.[29] After the *Challenger* disaster, NASA relied heavily on euphemisms. A spokesman referred to the explosion as an "anomaly," while the astronauts' bodies were called "recovered components" and their coffins described as "crew transfer containers."[30]

Scholars also note that agencies try not to disclose information that makes them look bad.[31] NASA has sometimes avoided or delayed releasing facts it would prefer to keep quiet. A General Accounting Office official who audited NASA said of the space agency: "It's just their management philosophy over there. They want to provide a minimum of information, and it takes a great deal of effort to get the records we need."[32] A joke circulating in Washington, D.C., in the 1960s said that NASA's initials stood for "never a straight answer."[33]

In the wake of its two biggest tragedies, NASA withheld the release of unpleasant information that presumably would have tainted the agency's image.[34] After the 1967 fire that killed three astronauts training in an Apollo capsule, NASA stood by its initial erroneous report that the astronauts had perished instantly.[35] In fact, as dozens of people had heard over an open voice circuit, the crew members lived for several minutes after the fire started, screaming and scrambling to get out before eventually dying of asphyxiation.[36]

In 1984 NASA issued a contingency plan for the release of information to the public in case of a shuttle accident. Although the plan called for providing "accurate, timely and factual information to the news media," NASA's behavior after the *Challenger* accident mirrored its actions after the Apollo fire.[37] It released very little information at all, and it obfuscated the issue of how the astronauts died.[38] NASA officials were extremely slow to admit that evidence suggested the *Challenger* crew members were aware of their fate and may well have been conscious in the nearly three minutes between the explosion and the crew cabin's impact on the ocean surface.

Another way NASA has sometimes controlled its information, according to several observers, is through exaggeration or misstatement. In the 1960s, reported one critic, NASA "had a reputation for looseness with the truth."[39]

President Kennedy's science adviser, Jerome Wiesner, charged NASA with manipulating data to support the method the agency wanted to use to go to the moon.[40] Similarly, Alex Roland, former NASA historian, contended that in the 1970s the agency simply "cooked the data" to show how economical the space shuttle would be.[41]

Physicist Richard Feynman, a member of the presidential board (known as the Rogers Commission) that investigated the *Challenger* disaster, accused NASA of making numerous exaggerations to sell the shuttle. He alleged that the agency overstated the shuttle's economy, scientific usefulness, and flight rate, calling NASA's promise of sixty shuttle flights per year "complete P.R."[42] Feynman speculated that one reason NASA made these unrealistic claims may have been to "assure the government of NASA perfection and success in order to ensure the supply of funds."[43]

NASA has also tended to exaggerate how cheaply it can execute its programs. Max Faget, a high-level NASA engineer during the Apollo era, has said that to sell a program, "You always try to put the best picture on it. If you don't quote a low cost, you ain't going to get it to begin with."[44] Low initial cost estimates help programs survive long enough to win allies in Congress and industry who will help keep the programs alive even after their costs escalate.

When President Reagan endorsed the space station in 1984, for example, NASA projected the station's cost at $8 billion, but by 1990 the estimate had ballooned to $38 billion. In 1993, a NASA official admitted that the agency had not been candid about the station's price: "We never told the American people really how much the space station would cost."[45] The space shuttle, the Viking Mars probe, and the Hubble Space Telescope are among the NASA programs that ended up costing much more than NASA originally estimated.[46]

NASA's managers may have actually come to believe their exaggerations, thus hampering their judgment and their willingness to hear and speak the truth.[47] In 1986, a *New York Times* editorial on NASA said, "The agency has so long depended on currying of its public image that it has forgotten how to tell the exact truth."[48]

Handling the Issue of Risk

NASA has carefully controlled the information it releases about the riskiness of its programs, which are inherently risky. NASA has operated under at least four elements of risk: a high degree of personal danger to the people who participate most directly in the agency's missions—the astronauts; a tremendous financial investment riding on a relatively small number of projects; the probability that any major failure will be highly public; and the likelihood that major failures will cause lengthy delays in the agency's overall operations.

While NASA activities have been generally risky, some of its projects have been riskier than others. Yet assessing and comparing the riskiness of the various programs NASA has pursued over its history is not easy. Comparable quantitative information on the risk of NASA's various programs, if it exists at all, is not readily available. According to one report, NASA does not compare the riskiness of its programs.[49] The agency has frequently argued that statistical estimates of risk are meaningless on programs as complex as space projects, and it has not always conducted quantitative risk assessments of its programs.[50] Outside pressure, including Environmental Protection Agency requirements, forced NASA to use quantitative methods more often in the shuttle program, however, particularly after the *Challenger* disaster.[51]

Because adequate objective data on the relative riskiness of NASA's programs were unavailable, the author sent a questionnaire to a variety of space experts, asking for their personal subjective judgments. The respondents were: James M. Beggs (NASA administrator, 1981-86), James C. Fletcher (NASA administrator, 1971-77 and 1986-89), John M. Logsdon (director, Space Policy Institute, George Washington University), Frank Pizzano (chief, Reliability and Maintainability, Engineering Division, Marshall Space Flight Center, NASA), and Alex Roland (former NASA historian; professor of history, Duke University).

The questionnaire listed seven major NASA programs: Mercury, Gemini, Apollo, Skylab, Apollo-Soyuz Test Project, space shuttle, and space station. The questionnaire's instructions were:

I would like you to assess the riskiness of the listed programs. Risk is here defined as the probability of a mission suffering a catastrophic failure, resulting in loss of life or vehicle. Please categorize each program, compared to the other programs, as relatively high or relatively low risk.

In general, the experts said that the Mercury, Apollo, and shuttle programs involved relatively more risk than did the Gemini, Skylab, and Apollo-Soyuz programs. Complete results from the questionnaires are presented in Table 4.

The image NASA is cultivating at the time seems to shape its public portrayal of its programs' riskiness. Nationalism and romanticism have been better suited to accommodate admissions of risk than pragmatism. Nationalism has promoted programs serving the national interest in which risks are generally acceptable; the military is a prime example. Risks are also expected and acceptable in the kind of activities advocated by romanticism. The notion of risk is closely tied to the romantic themes of challenge, adventure, excitement, and so on. Conversely, pragmatism, with its emphasis on practicality and assured benefits, is not easily reconciled with admissions of program risk.

NASA seems to have wanted to emphasize the hazards of its particularly risky programs to prepare the public in the event of an accident. The agency may also have wanted to stress the danger because risky programs tend to attract greater public interest than routine ones. Astronaut Rhea Seddon spec-

Table 4
Results from Questionnaire on Relative Program Riskiness

Respondent	Program						
	Mercury	Gemini	Apollo	Skylab	Apollo-Soyuz Test Project	Space Shuttle	Space Station
Beggs	high	high	high	low to moderate	moderate	high	moderate
Fletcher	high	low[a]	high	low	low	high[b]	low[c]
Logsdon	high	low	high	low	low	high	low[d]
Pizzano	high	high	high	low	low	high	high
Roland	high	low	high	low	low	high	high

Source: Compiled by the author.

[a]Except for spacewalks.
[b]Later flights were low risk, although the large number of flights increased overall possibility of an accident.
[c]Low risk on any given flight; high risk overall.
[d]Low risk on any given launch.

ulated that part of the reason people find it exciting to watch launches is the risk involved.[52] The experience of Apollo 13 supports this notion; that mission, in which the lives of the astronauts were gravely endangered, attracted public interest rivaling that of the first lunar landing.

NASA could discuss the risks of the Mercury program, which was promoted through nationalism, and the Apollo program, which was sold through a combination of nationalism and romanticism, without damaging the credibility of its prevailing images. Before the *Challenger* explosion, however, NASA used pragmatism to sell the shuttle and therefore had to play down the risks of the shuttle. After the disaster, NASA scaled back its use of pragmatism and began freely admitting the risks of the shuttle program.

Mercury. In the Mercury era, NASA worried about the public's reaction if an accident occurred. NASA's Wernher von Braun was concerned that the public had been "conditioned" to believe that every manned flight would be entirely safe. Convinced that "there isn't such a thing" as a 100 percent safe space flight, von Braun directed in February 1961 that NASA's future publicity efforts emphasize that the Mercury program was indeed risky.[53]

Agency officials therefore stressed that, although safety was painstakingly built into the Mercury system, failure was definitely possible.[54] The agency noted that the extreme complexity of Mercury made problems likely.[55] It cautioned in 1960 that "there is a chance that the astronaut will be lost" despite "taking every precaution possible to protect" him.[56] In 1962 NASA's Robert Seamans said simply, "There is risk in our manned space program."[57] James Webb warned in 1962 that failures in the television age would be especially visible.[58] Overall, NASA expressed confidence in Mercury's reliability but clearly tempered that outlook with caution.

Apollo. Throughout the Apollo program, NASA officials stressed that it was a very difficult and risky enterprise.[59] As in the Mercury era, NASA conveyed its belief that its goals would be accomplished but also warned that disasters were quite possible. NASA emphasized, of course, that it would work hard to minimize Apollo's risk.[60]

NASA's stance on Apollo risk was typified by a statement from the agency's associate administrator to Congress in March 1969: "The road leading to success is narrow indeed, and it is bounded on both sides by potential problems, frustrations, and occasionally the possibility of catastrophe."[61] Two events confirmed the validity of NASA's warnings: the 1967 Apollo fire, and the aborted Apollo 13 mission in 1970.

Even though NASA frequently spoke of Apollo's risks, the agency was apparently skittish about releasing quantitative data suggesting that the risk was tremendous. A former NASA employee recalled that after some agency engineers in the 1960s calculated the odds of an Apollo astronaut returning safely to earth as approximately one in twenty, an agency manager ordered:

"Bury that number, disband that group, I don't ever want to hear about any-thing like this again!"[62] Similarly, George McKay, who worked at NASA's Marshall Space Flight Center, recounted that safety engineers there in the 1960s predicted that one in every twenty to twenty-five manned flights would fail. McKay said, "We didn't tell anybody about it at that time because it would have scared the hell out of everybody."[63] Despite NASA's reluctance to release negative quantitative data, the agency generally stressed to the public that Apollo was a difficult and risky endeavor.

The Shuttle. In the 1970s and early 1980s, NASA sold the space shuttle as a routine and reliable means of transportation to and from space.[64] For exam-ple, James Fletcher said in 1973, "The shuttle will provide quick and routine access to space and eliminate the constraints imposed by the present mode of space operations which is characterized by high risk, long lead times, and complex systems."[65]

After the *Challenger* disaster, however, the claim that the shuttle would make space flight routine was no longer credible. In the aftermath of the disas-ter, the agency began readily admitting that it was involved in risky work. For example, a 1989 agency publication said, "Veteran astronauts and engineers alike know that sending men and women into the space frontier will continue to involve risk, just as it has since America's first manned suborbital flight in 1961."[66] That statement clearly contradicted NASA's previous and long-held position that the shuttle would eventually mean routine space flight.

In addition, NASA revised its descriptions of the basic nature of the shut-tle. Before *Challenger*, NASA frequently compared the shuttle to a commer-cial airliner in space. Yet after the accident, the agency frequently stressed—almost to the point of boasting—that the shuttle was an extremely advanced and complicated craft. A 1989 NASA pamphlet said, "The Space Shuttle sys-tem remains the most technologically advanced and complex machine on planet Earth. NASA has never estimated even a ballpark figure for the mil-lions of parts that comprise its launch configuration."[67] Administrator James Fletcher told Congress that the shuttle was "highly technical, highly R&D, highly risky, . . . not routine."[68]

NASA also modified its statistical estimates of the shuttle's reliability. Richard Feynman of the Rogers Commission charged that prior to the acci-dent, NASA management exaggerated the reliability of the shuttle "to the point of fantasy."[69] NASA had claimed that the chance of a catastrophic shut-tle failure was about one in 100,000, Feynman said, when in reality the odds were closer to one in 100. NASA's post-*Challenger* estimate was more in line with Feynman's figure. In 1989 the agency estimated that the shuttle carried about a one in seventy-eight chance of catastrophic failure.[70]

Why did NASA downplay the shuttle's risks in the years before *Chal-lenger*? Admitting great riskiness would not have gone well with the overall image of pragmatism that the agency was pursuing, which emphasized economy, routine, and reliability. In addition, agency managers may have convinced themselves that the shuttle was as safe as they said it was.[71] The accident forced NASA to revise its portrayal of the shuttle's risk, and NASA's increased use of romanticism and nationalism after the explosion made that revision strategically possible.

USING ASTRONAUTS AS SPOKESMEN

NASA has used its astronauts to generate attention and to communicate its messages since the agency's early days. NASA carefully molded the Mercury astronauts' image so that they would represent NASA and the nation well.[72] The astronauts received tremendous publicity and achieved great prestige, which made them valuable public relations tools for NASA.[73] For instance, NASA Administrator James Webb believed the most important thing by far that John Glenn could do for the agency after his triumphant orbital flight was to help win political support for NASA by making public appearances.[74] President Kennedy also recognized Glenn's public appeal. He considered Glenn such a valuable political asset that he ordered him grounded when the Mercury program ended.[75]

After Mercury, individual astronauts generally attained less fame because their number grew and flights began to have more than one crew member. The public focus shifted more toward what the astronauts did and how they did it and away from who the astronauts were.[76] Yet the astronauts have remained an important part of NASA's efforts to communicate with the public.[77]

Dr. Rhea Seddon, who became an astronaut in 1978 and has flown on the shuttle three times, described the public relations duties of today's astronauts.[78] NASA makes it clear when interviewing prospective astronauts that doing public relations work is part of the job. Once selected, astronauts take one or two day-long courses on communicating with the public and learning to "show your program in the best light." Astronauts engage in more public relations as their flights approach. Seddon said she has "a lot" of contact with the media, including interviews, press conferences, educational programs, coverage of her personal appearances, and so on.

Astronauts generally make public speeches once or twice a month. NASA has an office to handle the requests for astronauts to speak, many of which have to be turned down due to the large number received. Astronauts speak to groups of many types and sizes, although NASA naturally prefers larger groups. Seddon usually talks about her own activities and therefore writes most of her own speeches, as do the other astronauts, although NASA provides support for speech research and writing.

Astronauts determine the content of their speeches and decide how to respond to questions. "No one tells us what we have to say," explained Seddon. NASA does give them guidance, however, and the astronauts try to work into their comments issues that the agency wants to stress. An astronaut who serves as chief of public appearances lets his or her colleagues know what those issues are. In addition, NASA thoroughly briefs any astronaut scheduled to testify before Congress.

Although most of today's astronauts are not major celebrities as were their Mercury predecessors, they still generate significant public interest and admiration. Seddon receives about five requests for autographs every day, for instance. Public interest and goodwill continue to make the astronauts effective as both spokesmen and symbols of the agency.

EMPHASIZING THE SPECTACULAR

Another way NASA has grabbed public attention is by emphasizing spectacular programs. While most space activity is interesting, some NASA projects create more excitement than others. These glamorous and spectacular programs tend to generate more public interest and therefore are more politically useful to NASA.[79] These programs, such as Apollo, the shuttle, and the proposed space station, are usually large manned projects that perform some new feat in space. NASA has devoted most of its energy and resources to spectacular programs.[80] According to one observer, "NASA wants big and politically glamorous [programs], even if small and boring will more than suffice."[81]

Alex Roland has argued that the agency sees the Apollo program as the paradigm of getting political and financial support. "Ever since," Roland contended, "NASA has built its agenda around a large, manned space spectacular, a project of high visibility and continuing congressional focus." NASA apparently reasons that because it prospered politically under such a program once, it can do so again. That logic is flawed, Roland said: NASA "never seemed to realize that Apollo was not the norm for civilian space activity but a fluke, a one-time crash programme designed primarily to achieve political goals."[82]

Some observers have contended that NASA also prefers large and glamorous projects because they are hard to cancel once begun.[83] A large project requires major expenditures of money and political capital to get going, and canceling it means both wasting those commodities and admitting that the project should not have been started in the first place—things politicians would rather not do. Large programs therefore provide the agency with an extra measure of political protection and help ensure institutional survival.[84]

NASA's hunger for big, new projects—and the attention and security they bring—seems insatiable. Even with all NASA's programmatic problems in the last few years, the agency still wants to pursue a permanently manned space station, a base on the moon, and a manned trip to Mars. Robert Hotz, a member of the Rogers Commission, commented: "NASA is like a guy with a bellyache. He can't digest what he's got in his stomach but he wants more. The space station is a big morsel. The Moon base is half a side of beef. And the mission to Mars is a whole steer."[85] Hotz's diagnosis agreed with that of then Sen. Al Gore, who remarked that "NASA's eyes are bigger than its stomach."[86] These statements highlight one of the results of NASA's emphasis on acquiring large new programs: The approach detracts from doing the more mundane work needed to keep the agency's old programs running smoothly.[87]

The tactic also leads to other problems. One is that it encourages NASA to attempt leaps in developing technology. Instead of building gradually, the agency wants to make spectacular strides forward. According to Roland, NASA seeks "quantum leaps to new operational technology instead of building up to it incrementally. They want revolution instead of evolution."[88] Roland said that NASA wants to make such steps to match or surpass the dramatic success of Apollo. The problem is that attempting such leaps can lead to disaster if they prove to be beyond NASA's capability. Bruce Murray and Robert Jastrow, other high-former level NASA officials, have also recognized and decried this tendency.[89]

Another result of pursuing spectaculars is that smaller NASA programs, however worthwhile, may suffer. Big space projects are expensive and often squeeze smaller programs out of NASA's budget.[90] Cost overruns on large programs exacerbate this problem. Such overruns have become common because NASA has tended to make overly optimistic initial cost projections to build support for its programs, and then must scramble to pay for the cost increases that occur when problems arise.[91] Smaller programs have usually been sacrificed because they have lower public visibility and because it is often more feasible to cancel an entire small program than to make cuts in a larger one.

Finally, NASA's experience with the shuttle demonstrates the danger of trying to run a spectacular program on a limited budget. Not only did the agency have to accept design modifications before the shuttle was approved, tight budgets forced NASA to make additional changes and take shortcuts during shuttle development and operations. Although the agency got its wish for a big new program, it did not get the political commitment needed to make the program succeed.[92] As a result, NASA has encountered numerous highly publicized problems with the shuttle, and the agency's image has been tarnished rather than enhanced by the program.

Manned Versus Unmanned Spaceflight

One of the fundamental controversies of space exploration is whether emphasis should be placed on manned or unmanned missions. Author James Michener summarized the issue nicely:

No intellectual speculation relating to space is more challenging than the contest between manned and unmanned flight, because civilian support of a space program seems to depend on the former and any meaningful exploration of the universe upon the latter.[93]

Manned missions usually generate much more public attention and excitement than unmanned ones.[94]

Many critics have asserted that NASA emphasizes manned flight because of its greater public appeal, which translates into greater political support.[95] According to this argument, NASA has played on the fact that the idea of humans in space excites the public. "NASA has always understood the P.R. value of human derring-do" in space, wrote one observer.[96] Another critic said, "Without humans, space would be like a circus without high-wire acts—bad for the box office."[97]

NASA has outlined many reasons that humans must go to space personally: to enhance national pride and prestige, to fulfill the urge to explore, to reap emotional rewards, to satisfy curiosity, to gather scientific information, to advance technology, and so on. The agency also has argued that manned flights offer unique advantages over unmanned missions. According to a 1962 NASA publication: "Man brings to space exploration certain attributes which no one has ever succeeded in building into a machine. He brings intelligence, judgment, determination, courage and creativity."[98] People can respond to unforeseen problems and do things in space that machines cannot, according to this argument.

Shuttle astronaut Rhea Seddon provides an example. During a 1985 flight she made an unscheduled attempt to start a malfunctioning satellite using a tool she improvised for the purpose. Even though the attempt failed, Seddon said of the incident: "It proves the point that people have a place in space. You can't program robots to do all the tasks that humans can do."[99] NASA made a similar point regarding the April 1991 *Atlantis* flight, when astronauts were able to extend a balky satellite antenna during an unscheduled spacewalk. NASA's Chuck Shaw told reporters: "You saw today the value of manned space flight. . . . We needed folks on the scene to finish up the job."[100]

Yet NASA officials have also admitted the political importance of having people in space. James Fletcher called manned flight "extremely important" in generating public support for NASA. "Really," he said, "you talk to people, that's the only part of NASA that they're aware of."[101] NASA Assistant Administrator Franklin D. Martin made a similar point in 1989:

Humans in space—that's an important thing. Don't believe for a minute that the American public is as excited about unmanned programs as they are about manned ones. There is something almost religious about it in a lot of people's minds.[102]

Fletcher agreed that unmanned missions rarely generate as much public interest or support as manned flights: "Middle America is more interested in the astronauts, the human element."[103] Nevertheless, unmanned missions do sometimes stimulate public interest, especially when—like the Mariner and Voyager missions—they send back spectacular photographs.

Despite its popularity, manned space flight has long come under some harsh criticism for its high cost and risks. The most prominent opponents have been politicians who want to divert funds from NASA to other government programs and scientists who believe that manned flight drains too many resources from other scientific endeavors. Walter Mondale, who as a senator opposed developing the space shuttle, is an example of the former. In 1972 he called the shuttle "a manned extravaganza to get public support."[104] Mondale also said that NASA needed "show business" to build support in Congress, "and manned flight was the drama."[105]

Scientific opposition to manned spaceflight goes back to NASA's early days. Prominent scientist Jerome Wiesner, who became John F. Kennedy's science adviser, blasted manned space flight as "an expensive and risky public-relations gimmick."[106] That attitude persists among many of today's scientists, including eminent astronomer James Van Allen. He has contended that America has wrongly emphasized "the misty-eyed concept that the manifest destiny of mankind is to live and work in space."[107] Van Allen argued that "almost all the truly important utilitarian and scientific achievements of our space program" have come from unmanned missions.[108]

Despite the criticisms of manned flight, NASA remains committed to pursuing it.[109] Manned projects consume the majority of NASA's budget, about 65 percent to 70 percent.[110] Most members of the public who pay attention to space seem to want a continued manned space presence despite the costs and risks involved.[111] Manned flight also appeals to journalists, who find that people in space make better stories than machines in space.[112] Because it attracts public interest, manned space activity pays NASA vital political dividends in addition to scientific and technical ones.

CONCLUSION

No matter how well conceived an agency's image is, it will not have much positive effect if it does not reach the intended audience. Thus, the process of transmitting the image is crucial in building political support for the agency. NASA has used four kinds of techniques to disseminate its images and to make them as interesting and flattering as possible.

First, NASA has always worked closely with the media, which provide the best access to the general public. Second, the agency has sought to protect the content of its images by controlling—and sometimes exaggerating—the information it releases to the public. Third, NASA has used astronauts as spokesmen to stimulate public interest and impart the agency's message. Fourth, by emphasizing spectacular programs, NASA has attracted tremendous public attention—a crucial step toward transmitting its images.

Skillfully packaged and delivered messages can pack a powerful punch. For example, Rogers Commission member Richard Feynman recalled seeing a dramatic NASA-produced movie at the National Air & Space Museum while he was in Washington, D.C., investigating the *Challenger* accident. He said the movie was so powerful that it almost moved him to tears. Moreover, his disposition toward NASA shifted. Feynman said: "After seeing this movie I was very changed, from my semi anti-NASA attitude to a very strong pro-NASA attitude."[113]

NASA would undoubtedly be thrilled if everyone who encountered its images were affected as Feynman was. Unfortunately for the agency, however, that has not always been the case. Indeed, NASA's difficulties have caused the agency tremendous public image problems in recent years. Because NASA places great weight on a good public perception, constructing and transmitting favorable images to the public has therefore become even more important for the space agency.

NOTES

1. Anthony Downs, *Inside Bureaucracy* (Boston: Little, Brown & Co., 1967), 239-40.

2. Ibid., 240.

3. The displays in the visitors' centers at various NASA installations also communicate the agency's message. In addition, the Smithsonian Institution's National Air & Space Museum, although not operated by NASA, glamorizes the agency's activities. The museum has become the most popular permanent exhibit in the nation. See Tom Logsdon, *Space, Inc.: Your Guide to Investing in Space Exploration* (New York: Crown Publishers, 1988), x.

4. Matt Moffett and Laurie McGinley, "NASA, Once a Master of Publicity, Fumbles in Handling Shuttle Crisis," *Wall Street Journal*, 14 February 1896, 23.

5. Loyd S. Swenson, Jr., James M. Grimwood, and Charles C. Alexander, *This New Ocean: A History of Project Mercury*, SP-4201 (Washington, D.C.: GPO, 1966), 350, 419-20.

6. William Boot, "NASA and the Spellbound Press," *Columbia Journalism Review* 25 (July/August 1986): 28.

7. Robert C. Seamans, Jr. and Frederick I. Ordway III, "Lessons of Apollo for Large-Scale Technology," in *Between Sputnik and the Shuttle*, ed. Frederick C. Durant III (San Diego: American Astronautical Society, 1981), 252.

8. Rick Norman Tumlinson, "Space in Your Living Room," *Space World*, February 1986, 21.

9. Boot, "NASA and the Spellbound Press," 29; Leon V. Sigal, *Reporters and Officials: The Organization and Politics of Newsmaking* (Lexington, Mass.: D.C. Heath & Co., 1973), 48-49.

10. James A. Skardon, "The Apollo Story: The Concealed Patterns," *Columbia Journalism Review* 6 (Winter 1967/68): 37; Sigal, *Reporters and Officials*, 49.

11. Boot, "NASA and the Spellbound Press," 29.

12. See Sigal, *Reporters and Officials*, 48-49; Erlend A. Kennan and Edmund H. Harvey, Jr., *Mission to the Moon: A Critical Examination of NASA and the Space Program* (New York: Morrow, 1969), 41-45; Michael L. Smith, "Selling the Moon: The U.S. Manned Space Program and the Triumph of Commodity Scientism," in *The Culture of Consumption*, ed. Richard Wightman Fox and T. J. Jackson Lears (New York: Pantheon Books, 1983), 198-99.

13. James A. Skardon, "The Apollo Story: What the Watchdogs Missed," *Columbia Journalism Review* 6 (Fall 1967): 12.

14. See Boot, "NASA and the Spellbound Press," 24-29; "Shuttle Lessons," *Science Digest*, September 1986, 18.

15. Boot, "NASA and the Spellbound Press," 26.

16. Jerry Grey, *Beachheads in Space: A Blueprint for the Future* (New York: Macmillan, 1983), 32-33.

17. Boot, "NASA and the Spellbound Press," 25.

18. Ibid.

19. Dr. James C. Fletcher, interview by author, Washington, D.C., 5 October 1990.

20. Ibid.; Boot, "NASA and the Spellbound Press," 25.

21. William J. Broad, "Troubles Raising Questions About Space Agency," *New York Times*, 1 July 1990, 14.

22. Fletcher interview.

23. Leonard David, "NASA at T + 30 Years," *Space World*, October 1988, 8.

24. Fletcher interview.

25. See Chapter 2 for a discussion of NASA's comparison of itself in this respect with the Soviet space program.

26. Mark Bloom, "NASA's Pie in the Sky," *The Nation*, 22 May 1972, 648; Ken Hechler, *The Endless Space Frontier: A History of the House Committee on Science and Astronautics, 1959-1978* (San Diego: American Astronautical Society, 1982), 168-70.

27. Moffett and McGinley, "Master of Publicity," 23.

28. Harold F. Gortner, Julianne Mahler, and Jeanne Bell Nicholson, *Organization Theory: A Public Perspective* (Chicago: Dorsey Press, 1987), 186.

29. Joseph Baneth Allen, "Mr. Acronym," *Final Frontier*, November/December 1990, 16.

30. "Doublespeak at NASA," *Space World*, February 1987, 7.

31. Harold W. Stoke, "Executive Leadership and the Growth of Propaganda," *American Political Science Review* 35 (June 1941): 499; Herbert A. Simon, Donald W. Smithburg, and Victor A. Thompson, *Public Administration* (New York: Alfred A. Knopf, 1950), 417.

32. Stuart Diamond, "NASA Wasted Billions on Space Projects," *New York Times*, 23 April 1986, A14.

33. Kennan and Harvey, *Mission to the Moon*, 43.

34. Skardon, "What the Watchdogs Missed," 13; Richard S. Lewis, *Challenger: The Final Voyage* (New York: Columbia University Press, 1988), 28; John Noble Wilford, "Challenger and NASA's 8th Casualty," *New York Times*, 14 February 1986, Y11; Moffett and McGinley, "Master of Publicity," 23.

35. Kennan and Harvey, *Mission to the Moon*, 47-49; Joseph J. Trento, *Prescription for Disaster* (New York: Crown Publishers, 1987), 66-67.

36. Trento, *Prescription for Disaster*, 66-67.

37. Wilford, "Challenger and NASA's 8th Casualty," Y11.

38. Ibid.; Lewis, *Challenger: The Final Voyage*, 35.

39. William Hines, "NASA: The Image Misfires," *The Nation*, 2 April 1967, 517.

40. Charles Murray and Catherine Bly Cox, *Apollo: The Race to the Moon* (New York: Simon & Schuster, 1989), 142.

41. Stephen Budiansky, "What's Wrong with America's Space Program," *U.S. News & World Report*, 28 December 1987, 34. See also Trento, *Prescription for Disaster*, 108-21; and Richard P. Feynman, *What Do You Care What Other People Think?* (New York: W. W. Norton, 1988), 214.

42. Sandra Blakeslee, "Feynman's Findings: They 'Fooled Themselves,' " *New York Times*, 11 June 1986, B6; Feynman, *What Do You Care What Other People Think?*, 214.

43. R. P. Feynman, "Personal Observations on Reliability of Shuttle" in United States, Presidential Commission on the Space Shuttle Challenger Accident, *Report to the President*, Vol. 2, (Washington, D.C.: GPO, 1986), F4.

44. Phil Kuntz, "Pie in the Sky: Big Science is Ready for Blastoff," *Congressional Quarterly Weekly Report*, 28 April 1990, 1254.

45. "NASA's Novel Idea to Get Funds: Honesty," *Nashville Tennessean*, 6 June 1993, 13A.

46. Kuntz, "Pie in the Sky," 1254-60.

47. "The Heart of the Matter," *Scientific American*, August 1986, 63-64; Blakeslee, "Feynman's Findings," B6; R. Jeffrey Smith, "Shuttle Problems Compromise Space Program," *Science*, 23 November 1979, 912. See also Charles Peters, "From Ouagadougou to Cape Canaveral: Why the Bad News Doesn't Travel Up," *Washington Monthly*, April 1986, 28.

48. "Nobility, and Knowledge, in Space," *New York Times*, 30 July 1986, A22.

49. William J. Broad, "High Risk of New Shuttle Disaster Leads NASA to Consider Options," *New York Times*, 9 April 1989, 24.

50. Trudy E. Bell and Karl Esch, "The Space Shuttle: A Case of Subjective Engineering," *IEEE Spectrum* 26 (June 1989): 42-46; Peter N. Spotts, "NASA Needs Better Tools for Reducing Shuttle Risks, Study Says," *Christian Science Monitor*, 9 March 1988, 5; Swenson et al., *This New Ocean*, SP-4201, 179; Murray and Cox, *Apollo: The Race to the Moon*, 101, 141-42; Congress, Office of Technology Assessment, *Round Trip to Orbit: Human Spaceflight Alternatives* (Washington, D.C.: GPO, 1989), 27; Kevin McKean, "They Fly in the Face of Danger," *Discover*, April 1986, 48-58.

51. Bell and Esch, "A Case of Subjective Engineering," 42-46; Spotts, "NASA Needs Better Tools," 5; Eliot Marshall, "Academy Panel Faults NASA's Safety Analysis," *Science*, 11 March 1988, 1233; Broad, "High Risk of New Shuttle Disaster," 24.

52. Astronaut Rhea Seddon, interview by author, Murfreesboro, Tennessee, 23 November 1989.

53. Swenson et al., *This New Ocean*, SP-4201, 328.

54. For statements on safety efforts, see NASA, *Exploring Space: Projects Mercury and Apollo of the United States Space Program* (Washington, D.C.: GPO, 1961), 5; NASA, *Space: The New Frontier* (Washington, D.C.: GPO, 1962), 29; Hugh L. Dryden, "Safety in the Space Age," speech to the National Safety Congress, Chicago, Illinois, 31 October 1962, NASA History Office, Washington, D.C., 2; NASA, *1-2-3 and*

the Moon (Washington, D.C.: GPO, 1963), 3; and NASA, *Mercury Project Summary* (Washington, D.C.: GPO, 1963), 105.

55. George M. Low, "Project Mercury Progress," speech to UPI Editors Conference, Washington, D.C., 9 September 1960, NASA History Office, Washington, D.C., 8; Dryden, "Safety in the Space Age," 4; T. Keith Glennan, speech at Wright Day dinner, Washington, D.C., 17 December 1958, NASA History Office, Washington, D.C., 10.

56. Congress, House, Committee on Science and Astronautics, *Review of the Space Program*, 86th Cong., 2d sess., 29 January 1960, 276.

57. Robert C. Seamans, "Reliability in Space Systems—A National Objective," speech to the I.A.S. National Propulsion Meeting, Cleveland, Ohio, 8 March 1962, NASA History Office, Washington, D.C., 7.

58. "Space Chief Talks," *New York Times*, 5 April 1962, 67.

59. See Chapter 4 for examples.

60. See, for example, Congress, House, Committee on Appropriations, Subcommittee on Independent Offices and the Department of Housing and Urban Development, *Independent Offices and Department of Housing and Urban Development Appropriations for 1969*, Part 3, 90th Cong., 1st sess., April 1967, 696; Congress, House, Committee on Science and Astronautics, *1968 NASA Authorization*, Part 1, 90th Cong., 1st sess., 28 February 1967, 14.

61. Congress, House, Committee on Science and Astronautics, *1970 NASA Authorization*, Part 1, 91st Cong., 1st sess., 4 March 1969, 14.

62. McKean, "They Fly in the Face of Danger," 48.

63. Congress, House, Committee on Science and Technology, *Investigation of the Challenger Accident*, Vol. 1, 99th Cong., 2d sess., 11 June 1986, 157.

64. See Chapter 6 for analysis and examples of NASA's strategic approach on the shuttle. Also see NASA, *Space Station: The Next Logical Step*, by Walter Froehlich, EP-213 (Washington, D.C.: GPO, 1984), 2, 15; and Congress, House, Committee on Appropriations, Subcommittee on HUD—Independent Agencies, *Department of Housing and Urban Development—Independent Agencies Appropriations for 1986*, Part 6, 99th Cong., 1st sess., 2 April 1985.

65. Congress, Senate, Committee on Aeronautical and Space Sciences, *NASA Authorization for Fiscal Year 1974*, Part 1, 93d Cong., 1st sess., 28 February 1973, 212.

66. NASA, *Space Shuttle: The Renewed Promise*, by Neil McAleer, PAM-521 (Washington, D.C.: GPO, 1989), 5. For similar statements, see Congress, House, Committee on Appropriations, Subcommittee on VA, HUD, and Independent Agencies, *Departments of Veterans Affairs and Housing and Urban Development, and Independent Agencies Appropriations for 1990*, Part 6, 101st Cong., 1st sess., 25 April 1989, 69; NASA, *Space Station: A Research Laboratory in Space*, PAM-512 (Washington, D.C.: GPO, 1988),7.

67. NASA, *The Renewed Promise*, 12.

68. Congress, House, Committee on Science, Space, and Technology, Subcommittee on Space Science and Applications, *1990 NASA Authorization*, 101st Cong., 1st sess., 2 February 1989, 23.

69. Feynman, "Personal Observations," F1.

70. Broad, "High Risk of New Shuttle Disaster," 24; "Shuttle Risk High NASA Admits," *Spaceflight*, June 1981, 187. Some private experts place the odds of cata-

strophic failure at about one in sixty. See William J. Broad, "NASA Budget Cuts Raise Concerns Over Safety of the Shuttle," *New York Times*, 8 March 1994, B5.

71. For a discussion of this issue, see Feynman, "Personal Observations," F1-F5. For an analysis of how organizational factors at NASA may have contributed to the *Challenger* explosion, see C.F. Larry Heimann, "Understanding the *Challenger* Disaster: Organizational Structure and the Design of Reliable Systems," *American Political Science Review* 87 (June 1993): 421-35.

72. See Chapter 2.

73. Frank Gibney and George J. Feldman, *The Reluctant Space-Farers: A Study in the Politics of Discovery* (New York: New American Library, 1965), 75-78; Hechler, *The Endless Space Frontier*, 163; Tom Wolfe, *The Right Stuff* (Toronto: Bantam Books, 1979), 160.

74. Wolfe, *The Right Stuff*, 331.

75. Dale Carter, *The Final Frontier: The Rise and Fall of the American Rocket State* (London: Verso, 1988), 190.

76. Smith, "Selling the Moon," 202-203.

77. Kennan and Harvey, *Mission to the Moon*, 54; Courtney G. Brooks, James M. Grimwood, and Loyd S. Swenson, Jr., *Chariots for Apollo*, SP-4205 (Washington, D.C.: GPO, 1979), 326-27.

78. Seddon interview. The rest of the material in this section is based on this interview.

79. Congress, Office of Technology Assessment, *Civilian Space Stations and the U.S. Future in Space* (Washington, D.C.: GPO, 1984), 25.

80. Ibid.

81. Paul A. Gigot, "NASA's Flyboys Have Grown Old and Fat," *Wall Street Journal*, 13 July 1990, A8.

82. Alex Roland, "Priorities in Space for USA," *Space Policy*, May 1987, 104-14.

83. See John S. Lewis and Ruth A. Lewis, *Space Resources: Breaking the Bonds of Earth* (New York: Columbia University Press, 1987), 341, 352; Leon Jaroff, "Spinning Out of Orbit" *Time*, 6 August 1990, 27; and Office of Technology Assessment, *Civilian Space Stations*, 26.

84. For a discussion of how large projects tend to take on lives of their own, see Aaron Wildavsky, *The New Politics of the Budgetary Process* (Glenview, Ill.: Scott, Foresman & Co., 1988), 115-16.

85. William J. Broad, "Pervasive Decline of Staff Stunts NASA, Critics Say," *New York Times*, 9 September 1990, 32.

86. Broad, "Troubles Raising Questions," 14.

87. Ibid.

88. Ibid.

89. Ibid.; Broad, "Decline of Staff," 32.

90. William J. Broad, "Shuttle's Stargazing Disappoints Astronomers," *New York Times*, 11 December 1990, B9; Office of Technology Assessment, *Civilian Space Stations*, 25.

91. Broad, "Decline of Staff," 1; Bob Davis and Laurie McGinley, "Why a Space Station That Costs $25 Billion May Never Leave Earth," *Wall Street Journal*, 1 September 1988, 4.

92. John M. Logsdon, "The Space Shuttle Program: A Policy Failure?" *Science*, 30 May 1986, 1105.

93. James A. Michener, foreword to Grey, *Beachheads in Space*, x.

94. William H. Schauer, *The Politics of Space: A Comparison of the Soviet and American Space Programs* (New York: Holmes & Meier, 1976), 128.

95. See, for example, Tina Rosenberg, "Mission Out of Control," *The New Republic*, 14 May 1984, 18; Frederick I. Ordway III, Carsbie C. Adams, and Mitchell R. Sharpe, *Dividends from Space* (New York: Thomas Y. Crowell Co., 1971), 4.

96. Rosenberg, "Mission Out of Control," 18.

97. Daniel S. Greenberg, "Space Politics and Useless Cargo," *Chicago Tribune*, 5 December 1985, 27.

98. NASA, *Space: The New Frontier* (Washington, D.C.: GPO, 1962), 28.

99. "Seddon So Busy with New Baby She Forgot 'Surgery' Anniversary," *Nashville Tennessean*, 13 April 1989, 7B.

100. Marcia Dunn, "Space Walk Repairs Antenna," *Murfreesboro (Tenn.) Daily News Journal*, 8 April 1991, 10.

101. Fletcher interview.

102. Stuart F. Brown, "20 Years After Apollo: Is the U.S. Lost in Space?" *Popular Science*, July 1989, 69.

103. "NASA: No Flight Plan," *Scientific American*, February 1987, 58.

104. "Space Shuttle: NASA Versus Domestic Priorities," *Congressional Quarterly Weekly Report*, 26 February 1972, 435.

105. Stuart Diamond, "NASA Cut or Delayed Safety Spending," *New York Times*, 24 April 1986, B4.

106. Murray and Cox, *Apollo: The Race to the Moon*, 67.

107. James A. Van Allen, "Myths and Realities of Space Flight," *Science*, 30 May 1986, 1076.

108. Ibid., 1075. See also Rosenberg, "Mission Out of Control," 20-21.

109. Craig Covault, "NASA Plans to Fight Threats to Its Role in Space Program," *Aviation Week & Space Technology*, 26 October 1987, 62; NASA, *Agenda for Tomorrow* (Washington, D.C.: GPO, 1988).

110. Office of Technology Assessment, *Round Trip to Orbit*, 3. See also Congress, Office of Technology Assessment, *Civilian Space Policy and Applications* (Washington, D.C.: GPO, 1982), 100.

111. John M. Logsdon, "A Response to Alex Roland," *Space Policy*, May 1987, 113.

112. Boot, "NASA and the Spellbound Press," 27.

113. Feynman, *What Do You Care What Other People Think?*, 138-39.

8

Conclusion

When the crew members of Apollo 11 returned to earth, they were quarantined for three weeks in case they had brought diseases back with them from the moon. One of the people sealed in with the astronauts was John Macleish, a NASA public relations official.[1] That act symbolizes the importance NASA has placed on communicating with the public throughout its history.

Astronaut Rhea Seddon said that there is "quite a bit" of awareness in NASA about the need for a good public image, and that the agency works hard to create and maintain one.[2] NASA leaders have often demonstrated their realization of the importance of the agency's public image. When James Fletcher returned to head NASA after the *Challenger* disaster, for instance, he brought in some outside experts to strengthen the agency's public relations program.[3] Another example came in 1987, when NASA's deputy administrator met with top agency managers to reiterate the need for a positive public image.[4]

NASA's public communications efforts have been geared toward generating political support for the space program and for the agency itself. As Rhea Seddon noted, "The way you sell [the space program] is however it's going to sell."[5] Choosing which images to use means deciding how to sell NASA and the space program. The agency's changing political environment has greatly influenced those image choices.

CHANGING NASA IMAGES

NASA's history clearly reveals that the agency has adjusted its images in response to changes in its political environment. This book has examined the agency's history in three segments: 1958 through 1963, the Mercury era; 1964 through 1972, the Apollo era; and 1973 through 1990, the shuttle era.

The Mercury Era

The launch of the Soviet Union's Sputnik satellite in 1957 shocked the United States and led to the creation of NASA in 1958. Americans' fear of Soviet domination of space persisted into the 1960s, which helped maintain strong political support for the agency designed to lead America's space effort—NASA. The Mercury program was NASA's first major project, lasting from 1958 until 1963.

Nationalism, with an emphasis on competition with the Soviets, was clearly NASA's dominant image during this period. NASA spoke repeatedly of the Soviet threat and the urgent need for an American reaction. In addition, the agency made frequent references to national pride and national prestige, two other strains of nationalism. Some romanticism, highlighting the adventure and opportunity for exploration offered by space exploration, appeared. NASA used little pragmatism in the early years.

NASA Administrator T. Keith Glennan's 1959 statement to Congress about American-Soviet competition is a striking example of the sort of nationalism NASA often employed during the period:

We are engaged in a struggle for the minds and hearts of men everywhere. The issue is simply whether our system of free government and responsible civic freedom is superior to the system of totalitarian communism and forcible direction of the lives of its captive peoples.

I believe it is becoming increasingly obvious to the world that Russia's space activities are devoted, as are most of their activities as a nation, in large part to the furthering of communism's unswerving designs upon mankind.[6]

Glennan urged that NASA be supported to counter the Soviet threat.

Nationalism was an appropriate image for NASA in this period given the Cold War context and the undeniable Soviet lead in space exploration. Americans feared the consequences if space were abandoned to the Soviets. That fear was a tremendous source of support for NASA, and the agency exploited the public's anxiety through repeated statements about the Soviet threat. Americans' demand for action in space made NASA's search for political backing much easier.

NASA's extraordinary success in obtaining program authorization and funding in the Mercury era meant that the agency had no reason to alter the images it was projecting. NASA could not expect to do much better than it already was doing.

The Apollo Era

During the middle and late 1960s, NASA focused on its goal of a manned lunar landing, which it achieved in 1969 through the Apollo program. The agency went on to conduct five more successful missions to the moon before Apollo ended in 1972. NASA's political support in this period was mixed. It enjoyed an all-time funding high early in the Apollo era, but then suffered a sharp budgetary decline. The strong support NASA enjoyed early in the period seemed to come mainly from the political momentum the agency had built during the Mercury years.

Nationalism remained NASA's primary image in the Apollo era, although the agency significantly increased its use of romanticism during the period. The romantic statements of the time accented the challenge, inspiration, and adventure of going to the moon. Another common romantic NASA theme described the Apollo program as heir to a great tradition of exploration. Pragmatism was not used extensively in the 1960s, although it began to appear more frequently as the 1970s opened.

NASA Administrator Thomas Paine gave a clear example of romanticism in 1968. Speaking of one Apollo flight, he said: "Apollo 8's pioneering flight into lunar orbit demonstrated to men everywhere the existence of a challenging new frontier for mankind in the vastness of extraterrestrial space."[7] The pioneering and frontier images raised in that statement are hallmarks of romanticism.

Nationalism was emphasized during this period because the Apollo program was America's entry in the race to the moon. The Cold War was still going on and many Americans considered the Soviet space program a threat to the free world. Yet the public also saw that the United States, despite its slow start, was overtaking the Soviets in the space race. The less dominant the Soviets seemed in space, the less compelling was NASA's nationalistic argument outlining the dire consequences of losing the race. Therefore NASA buttressed its communications efforts with the image of romanticism.

Romanticism fit the era for several reasons. First, it was more palatable than nationalism to those Americans who were disillusioned about government programs and nationalism by the Vietnam War. Romanticism emphasized idealism and intangible rewards, and it therefore corresponded to the political spirit of the time. Second, romanticism could deal effectively with the issue of risk, which had been dramatically raised by the 1967 Apollo fire. Finally, romanticism was a natural match for the Apollo program. The romantic themes of exploration, challenge, satisfying curiosity, and so on were undeniably appropriate for promoting Apollo.

Yet romanticism was not very effective in stopping the decline in NASA's political support. By the time NASA injected a significant amount of romanticism into its statements, the public mood may have changed enough that it was no longer receptive to romantic appeals. For instance, a 1980 analysis of poll data revealed that the public did not usually respond positively to justifications of the space program "based on emotional-idealistic statements."[8]

Alex Roland, former NASA historian, said: "What has passed is the romantic era of space flight, like the age of barn-storming for airplane flight.

People want to know: 'Where's the payoff?' They want more than just circus."[9] Another observer argued that by selling Apollo through romance,
NASA left itself vulnerable to social critics charging the program was frivo-
lous and to an overall drop in political support when the romance of space
flight diminished.[10]

NASA's budget authority (in constant 1987 dollars) peaked at $19.8 billion
in fiscal 1965, but then began to fall, plunging to $8.8 billion in fiscal 1972.
While the agency did obtain grudging approval for the shuttle program, that
was only a small part of the grand space exploration plan it had proposed for
the 1970s, and it had to struggle to get even that much. NASA had to go to the
military for help in getting the shuttle authorized, and in return was forced to
modify the shuttle design to meet the military's specifications. In addition, the
shuttle program received some stiff opposition in Congress. Overall, it was an
unpleasantly different experience for NASA, which had seen its earlier major
programs receive enthusiastic and uncritical approval.

Some drop in political support for NASA after the lunar landing was
probably inevitable. In a sense, NASA was a victim of its own success. Popular
excitement over the first moon landing was followed by a steep decline in
public interest in space.[11] America had won the race to the moon, the attitude
seemed to be, so it was time to move on to other things. According to Michael
Collins, "Apollo 11 was perceived by most Americans as being an end, rather
than a beginning."[12] In 1968, NASA's Rocco Petrone predicted, "When we
get to the moon I'm afraid there will be a big letdown. There'll be a parade up
Broadway, sure, but what will we do next?"[13]

The Shuttle Era

By the early 1970s, the bottom had dropped out of NASA's political support. NASA had achieved its heralded objective of landing on the moon, which
made the Soviet space program seem much less threatening. America's space
efforts in the 1970s therefore seemed less vital and less interesting than in the
past. Furthermore, the nation had other things to worry about, including the
war in Vietnam, domestic unrest, and the faltering economy.

The change in NASA's use of images was as stark as the change in its political environment. Pragmatism quickly became the dominant image, while
nationalism and romanticism nearly fell from view. The space shuttle, centerpiece of NASA's manned space activities, was sold overwhelmingly on the
basis of the practical benefits it would bring.

James Fletcher presided over this dramatic shift in NASA's image. A
statement he made in 1972 exemplifies the pragmatism NASA employed in
the 1970s:

We now look ahead to several decades of a highly rational use of space. The focus will be on domestic needs, and the turning of our rapidly developing space capabilities to useful work. We have made our new program relevant to the needs of modern America.[14]

That passage sharply contrasted with the kind of statements NASA usually made in earlier years.

By the early 1970s, the images most used in the 1960s were no longer appropriate for NASA's political environment. The variety of nationalism emphasizing competition with the Soviets was outdated because America had unquestionably won the race to the moon and had thereby proven its superiority in space. The few times NASA did use nationalism in the 1970s, a time of detente between the United States and the Soviet Union, it tended to stress international cooperation in space instead of competition. Cooperation in space was most clearly exemplified by the joint 1975 American-Soviet Apollo-Soyuz Test Project.

Americans did not appear to be in the mood for romanticism during the 1970s. People faced a variety of down-to-earth problems and were probably tired of high-sounding rhetoric. In addition, space exploration had been in the news frequently since 1957, and some of its excitement had worn off.

Pragmatism, however, seemed to fit the 1970s well. It stressed that spending for the space program was an investment that would pay concrete dividends. Pragmatism encouraged people to support the space program in return for the benefits they would receive personally—an appeal to self-centeredness that seemed to characterize the decade.

The space shuttle finally began flying in 1981, and NASA conducted a total of twenty-three flights by the end of 1985. The shuttle system performed well despite some glitches, and the agency began lobbying for authorization to build an orbiting space station. NASA's political environment improved somewhat, although it was not nearly as favorable as it had been in the Mercury era.

Pragmatism remained NASA's primary image, and the shuttle continued to be promoted on pragmatic grounds. Nationalism played a slightly larger role in the period, with greater emphasis on economic rivalry; the buzzword was "competitiveness." Romanticism appeared occasionally, but was still overshadowed by pragmatism.

An example of a typical statement of the time comes from Administrator James Beggs. He said in 1984, "NASA alone cannot assure our competitiveness, but the agency's programs can be—and I believe must be—an element in our nation's investment strategy."[15] This remark contained both pragmatism's theme of economic returns from space spending and nationalism's theme of economic competition. NASA's image did not change much in the early 1980s because its political environment had not changed much. NASA did increase its use of nationalism somewhat, especially regarding economic competition, to match the concerns of the Reagan years.

The January 1986 explosion of the shuttle *Challenger*, which killed all seven crew members aboard, badly tarnished NASA's image as a "can-do" agency. The accident also transformed NASA's political environment. The public, president, and Congress rallied around the agency in the wake of the explosion, and provided it with greater rhetorical and financial support.[16] Yet NASA and its activities also came under much more intense public, press, and political scrutiny in the wake of the accident.

No single image dominated in this period. NASA used all three images in roughly equal proportions. For example, a 1988 NASA booklet on the proposed space station read:

The Space Station is essential to regaining a position of leadership in space for the United States. Its practical benefits will be many. . . . Perhaps most importantly, as we steadfastly recover from the loss of Challenger and her crew, the Space Station symbolizes our national determination . . . to continue to explore the frontiers of space.[17]

That statement contained elements of all three images.

The post-*Challenger* period was a confused one for NASA, with much attention necessarily devoted to damage control. Each type of image offered something useful to NASA in that political environment, but none alone was sufficient. NASA had long sold the shuttle largely on the basis that it would eventually deliver the same sort of routine, reliable, and economical service provided by commercial aviation. The *Challenger* disaster dramatically discredited that notion. Nevertheless, NASA continued to make the pragmatic argument that the shuttle was a valuable space transportation system. In addition, NASA used some pragmatism in promoting the space station, the agency's next big project.

Nationalism was more evident in the post-*Challenger* period than in previous years. The image offered NASA suitable themes to seek support for the space station. NASA stressed competition by noting that the Soviet Union had two space stations in orbit and by trumpeting the economic advantages offered by its proposed station. Nationalism was also evident in NASA's suggestions that other nations participate in building and operating the station, which would promote peaceful international relations.

Romanticism also played a significantly larger part in NASA's image from 1986 to 1990. This too can be attributed to the *Challenger* disaster, which graphically illustrated that space exploration was still a very risky business. Romanticism was the image that best encompassed the issue of risk and the need to pursue risky programs because acceptance of risk is inherent in the romantic themes of exploration, challenge, adventure, and so on.

The 1970s and early 1980s were lean budgetary years for NASA. The agency's budget authority (in constant 1987 dollars) continued the decline that had started in the late 1960s, bottoming out at $6.8 billion in fiscal 1975. It then began a gradual rise, but reached only $7.5 billion by fiscal 1980. The agency's budget authority stayed between $7.2 billion and $8.2 billion from fiscal 1981 to 1985. NASA's funding improved after the *Challenger* disaster. Appropriations for a replacement shuttle bumped NASA's budget from $8 billion in fiscal 1986 to $10.9 billion in fiscal 1987. The next year's figure was $8.7 billion, which marked the beginning of a upward trend in the agency's budget authority. By fiscal 1990, NASA's authorization had reached $10.9 billion. Figure 4 illustrates NASA's funding history from 1958 to 1990.

After the shuttle began flying, NASA began its push for approval of its next large program, the permanently manned space station it had wanted to build immediately after Apollo. The agency convinced President Reagan, who in 1984 endorsed the space station. That was clearly a success for NASA, but Congress was skeptical of the station and by 1990 was considering canceling the program even though NASA had already spent over $5 billion for preliminary work on it.[18] NASA was also pleased with President Bush's 1989 Space Exploration Initiative, which called on the agency to construct a manned base on the moon and to pursue a manned mission to Mars by the year 2019. Yet Bush said nothing about paying for the plan, with an estimated $500 billion price tag.[19] Congress reacted with skepticism about the nation's willingness to finance the plan and NASA's ability to execute it.

The serious political problems NASA encountered beginning around 1970 prompted it to adopt pragmatism as its dominant image. Its unfavorable political environment in the 1970s made emphasizing the pragmatic, especially economic, value of its programs seem to be an appealing strategy.[20] In addition, the success of Apollo had made the Soviet space program seem much less threatening and the image of nationalism less powerful. As James Fletcher said, "The competition had gone away, and cooperation was the way we were going. So we had to emphasize the practical aspects" of the space program.[21]

Yet pragmatism did not seem to ignite the public's interest, and NASA stagnated politically for most of the 1970s and into the 1980s. Part of the problem may have been that pragmatism, as its name implies, is a more mundane image than nationalism and romanticism. Several observers have contended that NASA's efforts to stress the practical applications of space were not very successful.[22] As Apollo 11 astronaut Buzz Aldrin remarked, "People aren't eagerly glued to their television sets to find out how the latest submicroscopic circuitry evolved as a direct benefit of going to the moon."[23]

Some long-term decline in political support for NASA may have been unavoidable, however. In the late 1950s and early 1960s, a peculiar set of historical and political factors converged to give America's space program tremendous support. NASA skillfully exploited the situation, but it is unlikely that it could have generated that level of support no matter how good an image it had. After the initial burst of political enthusiasm for NASA subsided, the agency's image played to a less receptive audience.

Figure 4
NASA Funding, 1958 to 1990: Budget Authority in Constant 1987 Dollars

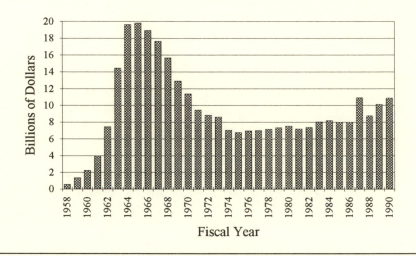

Sources: Adapted from Office of Management and Budget, *Budget of the United States Government: Fiscal Year 1995, Historical Tables* (Washington, D.C.: GPO, 1994); Bureau of the Budget, *Budget of the United States Government* (Washington, D.C.: GPO, 1959-70); and Office of Management and Budget, *Budget of the United States Government* (Washington, D.C.: GPO, 1971-77).

Generalizations

This study of NASA's history suggests some generalizations about the use of the agency's various images. The individual characteristics of the images have made them most suitable for use under particular political conditions.

The prevailing international situation seems to have been the most important influence on the use of nationalism, which has been quite compelling under the right international conditions. Americans have traditionally responded when called to assist their country, especially when they have perceived a threat to the nation. Thus nationalism was a powerful image in the years just after Sputnik, when Americans were deeply concerned about the nation's relative position in space, but it was not quite as effective in the 1980s, when NASA used the image to argue for the space station. By that time, the Cold War was fading and most Americans were much less scared of the Soviet Union than they were in the 1950s and 1960s. In general, the competitive themes of nationalism seem to have had greater effect than the peaceful theme.

NASA used romanticism most heavily during two periods: the Apollo era and the post-*Challenger* years. In both cases, events had clearly demonstrated to the actors in NASA's political environment that the agency was involved in risky work. NASA responded with romanticism, which admitted the risk and justified it on a variety of grounds.

Support for NASA decreased toward the end of the Apollo era but increased after *Challenger*. It may be that romanticism, because it plays to the audience's spirit and sense of adventure, has been more effective when the agency's political environment is more supportive and more flexible. The public had grown weary of the space race by the late 1960s, whereas the *Challenger* disaster rekindled the public's largely dormant interest in and support for the space program. In addition, while romanticism has sometimes been a powerful image, it probably has had a greater chance of falling flat than the other images. An agency enjoying strong public backing can better afford the uncertainty involved in employing a romantic approach.

Political difficulties seem to have encouraged NASA to use pragmatism, as it did after its political environment soured around 1970. Even under an unfavorable environment, an agency may win some measure of support if it can convince people that they have something material to gain through the agency's activities. Pragmatism did not bring NASA great political gains in the 1970s, but it did stabilize the agency's environment and thus may have prevented further erosion of support. Pragmatism has been a more conservative image than romanticism, but one that may offer more security in an hostile climate.

Additional Assessments. Observers have often regarded NASA as quite skillful at managing its public image.[24] For example, two reporters wrote in 1986 that NASA had a "longtime reputation as one of the slickest self-promoters in Washington."[25] Not everyone has agreed with that assessment, however.[26] One critic expressed amazement that NASA failed to maintain public interest in the Apollo program: "The inability of NASA to keep a few trips to the moon as interesting to a TV audience as years of soap operas and situation comedies represents a staggering triumph of ineptitude."[27] Similarly, the *New York Times* editorialized in 1990 that "space flight, once the most glamorous of enterprises, has become about as interesting as a crew of furniture deliverers at work."[28] After the *Challenger* disaster, several commissions studying NASA and the space program urged the agency to improve its public relations efforts.[29]

James Fletcher explained why he thought NASA has had communications problems. He said that NASA has not generally had much of a long-term strategy for communicating with the public, and that the agency has usually taken a year-by-year approach to getting political support.[30] In general, noted Fletcher, "We say 'the programs sell themselves'—that's the common theme in the NASA communications arena." He cited NASA's lack of a long-term communications strategy as a "major weakness." Fletcher explained that NASA is "composed primarily of a group of engineers and scientists that don't understand communications too well."[31]

OTHER POSSIBLE INFLUENCES ON NASA'S IMAGE CHOICES

This book argues that NASA has changed the images it projects in response to external political shifts, and that the agency's attempts to match its image to its prevailing political environment has been the fundamental determinant of the kind of image it pursues. However, other factors—including the skill and inclination of the agency's leadership, organizational aging, and the characteristics of the particular programs being sold—may also influence the agency's choice of image.

Agency Leadership

Even though they face an array of political restraints on their actions, the leaders of government agencies can greatly affect how their organizations function.[32] One way leaders exert this influence is by directing their agencies' external political relations; how well they perform that duty helps determine agency success.[33] According to one estimate, bureau chiefs spend 25 percent to 30 percent of their time on external matters.[34]

Managing an agency's external relations includes shaping its image.[35] James Fletcher recalled that during his tenure as NASA administrator, he directly oversaw the agency's public relations efforts. Fletcher said that those efforts in his second term as administrator were "mine alone and I didn't have much help."[36] An administrator also helps transmit the agency's image by testifying before Congress, making speeches, giving interviews, and issuing statements. The bureau chief's activities constitute an important part of the agency's total public relations effort.[37]

Agencies seek to maximize their political support by changing their images in response to external political shifts. Yet because agency leaders play such a major role in constructing their organizations' images, and because leaders generally decide how their bureaus react to changes in their external environments,[38] it is reasonable to assume that the characteristics of leaders influence their management of agency images. Individual leaders may respond somewhat differently because of their different attitudes, experiences, and skills.[39] Thus, the traits of the leader may influence how and how effectively the agency changes its public image.

NASA leaders have exhibited varying degrees of political and public relations skill. For example, James Webb, who ran NASA from 1961 to 1968 and led America's race to the moon, has been called "one of the giants of American public administration."[40] One reason Webb succeeded was that he clearly realized the importance of politics in his job. He later wrote about that issue: "Political relationships are not (nor can they be) something added on to the work of line managers or program officials as less important than other duties; these relationships are an integral part of their work."[41] Webb received wide praise for his skillful tenure as NASA administrator, particularly for his political sensitivity.[42]

Not all NASA administrators have demonstrated Webb's political acumen. James Fletcher, for instance, received mixed reviews on his political performance. According to one observer, Fletcher was "a competent but unexciting manager" who had "no flair for politics or publicity."[43] Fletcher admitted that he had little public relations experience before running NASA, but said he had to take the lead because there was no one else to do it. He added, "I don't think I was very good at it, either, but nevertheless, it got done."[44]

While the skills and choices of individual leaders do matter, the agency's political environment still sets its overall boundaries of action. Webb probably did exercise greater political skill than Fletcher, but he also ran NASA under much more favorable political conditions, which gave him greater freedom of action. Whatever the skill or inclination of NASA's administrator, he or she must still make image choices that work within the agency's political environment.

Organizational Aging

Changes that occur within an agency as it ages may also affect its choice of images. Anthony Downs describes changes in agencies throughout their "life cycle."[45] Agencies are created in a burst of enthusiasm and are usually dominated early on by "zealots," employees eager to fulfill agency missions. The new agencies begin ambitious programs, seek quick successes to prove their worth, and strive hard to win political support. These efforts usually lead to a period of rapid agency growth.

As agencies grow and require more resources and authority, however, they run into increasing opposition from organizational rivals and from the public, which is footing the bill. Growth slows or stops, the level of talent within the agency begins to decline, and the average age of employees increases. Agencies also become more bureaucratized as they age: More formal rules are instituted, organizational structure becomes more complex, agency emphasis shifts more toward institutional survival than fulfilling social functions, and employees tend to be less zealous and more conservative. Overall, Downs argues, "All organizations tend to become more conservative as they get older."[46]

NASA's organizational changes over its history have epitomized Downs' life cycle theory. The capable, dynamic, rapidly growing agency of the early 1960s has evolved into a less technically competent and much more ossified and conservative organization.[47] John L. McLucas, chair of a panel that advises NASA on policy, said of the agency: "There's been a hardening of the arteries. They've gotten more cautious. People have adopted a way of laying back. Bureaucratic lethargy has set in."[48]

In NASA's case, the increasing caution that normally accompanies organizational aging was understandably heightened by the fear of committing another mistake of the magnitude that caused the *Challenger* disaster.[49] As a result, said James Fletcher in 1990, "CYA [Cover your ass], if you know what that means, is quite a factor in NASA nowadays."[50]

NASA's journey through its life cycle may have influenced its use of images. Such an argument might go like this: In its early, ambitious phase, NASA stressed the need to tackle the crucial problem—the Soviet lead in space—that sparked the creation of the agency. NASA used an image of nationalism to hammer the point home. Yet as the 1960s progressed and NASA chipped away at the Soviet lead, the agency supplemented nationalism with a large dose of romanticism, which well represented the lofty ambitions of the zealots who then dominated the organization. As NASA aged, however, its increasingly cautious leadership turned to pragmatism, a less dramatic and more conservative image.

Conservative agency leaders would probably have disdained romanticism. With its emphasis on exploration, adventure, and great deeds, romanticism was flashy and emotional. Furthermore, romanticism may have been a riskier image because to accept it, the audience must be open-minded, imaginative, and willing to support projects that do not offer concrete payoffs. Americans have not always exhibited these characteristics, and there is no guarantee they will at any given time.

The public response to nationalism and pragmatism has probably been more predictable. Citizens have generally responded favorably to nationalistic appeals if convinced that the programs at issue will truly benefit their country. Pragmatism has probably always generated some support because people have usually been quite interested in personal benefits, even though the image has never aroused much public fervor.

Whatever influence organizational aging has had on NASA's choice of images, the agency's political environment still has carried more weight. NASA's recent image changes demonstrated this. The *Challenger* disaster drastically altered NASA's political environment, and the agency reacted by downplaying the conservative image of pragmatism and increasing its use of nationalism and romanticism. The quakes in the agency's political environment demanded a dramatic strategic shift from NASA's cautious managers.

Characteristics of Programs

The nature of the major program being sold at the time also may have influenced NASA's choice of image to sell it. Sometimes the inherent characteristics of a program seem tailor-made for promotion by a particular image. For instance, the Apollo project was a natural match for a romantic image. Apollo's bold objective of sending humans to the moon embodied many romantic elements: exploration, expanding the frontier, adventure, satisfying curiosity, and so on. Similarly, the predicted versatility and cost-effectiveness of the space shuttle may have made pragmatism seem like the logical image with which to sell that program.

In addition, NASA has occasionally adjusted its image to spark public support for hard-to-sell programs. Some kinds of programs have generally been easier to sell than others. Manned space exploration has tended to generate more public interest and excitement—and therefore has been easier to promote—than unmanned projects. Programs designed for pure research (that is, research not intended to pay immediate practical dividends) have been difficult to sell.[51] To overcome the obstacles involved in promoting hard-to-sell programs, NASA has sometimes made special efforts in its images. For instance, NASA highlighted the tantalizing search for extraterrestrial life in fostering support for the Viking program, which sent unmanned probes to explore Mars.

While the characteristics of individual programs likely have come into consideration when NASA leaders make image decisions, the political environment has exerted more influence. First, NASA has not always chosen the image that most obviously fits the primary program it is selling. For instance, had the nature of the program been the major consideration in selecting the image, romanticism may well have been the logical choice to sell Mercury, because it represented America's pioneering space exploration effort. The agency chose nationalism and concentrated on the competition with the Soviet Union, however, because its political environment made that the most politically powerful approach.

Second, the three images have been broad enough to be reasonably applied to virtually any space project. This has given NASA strategic leeway both at the outset of a project and later on. For example, in the early 1970s NASA could have chosen any image to sell the shuttle and highlighted the aspects of the program that best fit the image. The agency selected pragmatism because its political environment had changed, making romanticism and nationalism much less politically appealing, and emphasized the practical benefits of the shuttle. Yet after the *Challenger* explosion caused upheaval in NASA's political environment, the agency used all three images to sell the same shuttle program.

POLITICS AND AGENCY IMAGES

Former Vice President Dan Quayle was renowned for making misstatements. Yet Quayle, who took a definite interest in America's space program, made a perceptive comment about the subject in 1989. Speaking of the prerequisites for an ambitious American space effort, he remarked: "The bottom line is, what kind of political support can we garner in the country?"[52] That has been the eternal question for NASA, as it has for virtually all government agencies.

In its search for political support, NASA has always relied, and continues to rely, heavily on projecting favorable images of itself. Yet although its reliance on these images has been constant, the way it has used them has been far from constant. The agency has often adjusted its mix of images, sometimes emphasizing one, sometimes another. NASA has also changed which themes within the images it stresses at certain times.

NASA has made these changes in response to shifts in its political environment, with the goal of maximizing its political support. When the agency's environment has changed, NASA has altered its image in attempt to make it as effective as possible under the new conditions. Such strategic changes cannot ensure it—or any agency—of political success, but they do make it more likely.

Scholars have noted that different agencies use different images but have not said much about how and why agencies change their images over time. Based on the case study of NASA, this book argues that agencies change their images over time in response to changes in their political environments, and that they do so to maximize their political backing.

Government agencies adjust their images as part of their overall reactions to their environments. Agencies must respond to the political changes around them if they are to survive and prosper. No matter how great agencies' past successes or how promising their future endeavors, the political system in which they exist rewards those with present-day political backing. NASA has sent people to the moon and plans to send them to Mars, but its most enduring quest is the one for political support. Even though NASA's mission points it toward the heavens, the agency cannot lose sight of politics on the earth, for that is where its fate is determined.

NOTES

1. Michael Collins, *Carrying the Fire: An Astronaut's Journeys* (New York: Farrar, Straus and Giroux, 1974), 447-48.

2. Astronaut Rhea Seddon, interview by author, Murfreesboro, Tennessee, 23 November 1989.

3. Dr. James C. Fletcher, interview by author, Washington, D.C., 5 October 1990.

4. Craig Covault, "NASA Plans to Fight Threats to Its Role in Space Program," *Aviation Week & Space Technology*, 26 October 1987, 62.

5. Seddon interview.

6. Congress, House, Committee on Science and Astronautics, *1960 NASA Authorization*, 86th Cong., 1st sess., 20 April 1959, 3.

7. NASA, *Apollo: Man Around the Moon* (Washington, D.C.: GPO, 1968), 1.

8. "Public Support for Space," *Space Futures Newsletter*, March 1980, 3.

9. Kathy Sawyer, "Back in Space, But Where to Go?" *Washington Post National Weekly Edition*, 10 October 1988, 7.

10. Richard S. Lewis, "End of Apollo: The Ambiguous Epic," *Bulletin of the Atomic Scientists* 28 (December 1972), 39-44.

11. Thomas R. McDonough, *Space: The Next 25 Years* (New York: John Wiley & Sons, 1987), 27; Paul Hoversten, "World Saw 'Eagle' Land in 1969," *Sunday Tennessean*, 16 July 1989, 1G; Frederick I. Ordway III, Carsbie C. Adams, and Mitchell R. Sharpe, *Dividends from Space* (New York: Thomas Y. Crowell Co., 1971), 3.

12. Collins, *Carrying the Fire*, 464.

13. John Noble Wilford, "NASA, on 10th Birthday, Faces Uncertain Future," *New York Times*, 1 October 1968, 2.

14. L.B. Taylor, Jr., *For All Mankind: America's Space Programs of the 1970s and Beyond* (New York: E. P. Dutton & Co., 1974), 8.

15. NASA, *Space Station: The Next Logical Step*, by James M. Beggs (Washington, D.C.: GPO, 1984), 1.

16. Jon D. Miller, "The Challenger Accident and Public Opinion," *Space Policy*, May 1987, 128-30, 139; James Fisher, "America Loves NASA, Budget Writers Don't," *Orlando Sentinel*, 24 November 1987, 12; Jon Van, "Americans Still Back Space Program, but NASA's Goals Remain Sketchy," *Chicago Tribune*, 1 February 1987, sec. 4, p. 4.; Fletcher interview; John R. Cranford, "A New Tone Heard in Congressional Dealings with NASA," *Congressional Quarterly Weekly Report*, 14 June 1986, 1325.

17. NASA, *Space Station: A Research Laboratory in Space*, PAM-512 (Washington, D.C.: GPO, 1988), 1.

18. NBC Nightly News, 6 April 1991.

19. Leon Jaroff, "Spinning Out of Orbit," *Time*, 6 August 1990, 27; Phil Kuntz, "Pie in the Sky: Big Science is Ready for Blastoff," *Congressional Quarterly Weekly Report*, 28 April 1990, 1255; and "No Free Launch," *Time*, 31 July 1989, 21.

20. John S. Lewis and Ruth A. Lewis, *Space Resources: Breaking the Bonds of Earth* (New York: Columbia University Press, 1987), 98; Sylvia D. Fries, "2001 to 1994: Political Environment and the Design of NASA's Space Station System," *Technology and Culture* 29 (July 1988), 585-86; Barbara S. Romzek and Melvin J. Dubnick, "Accountability in the Public Sector: Lessons from the Challenger Tragedy," *Public Administration Review* 47 (May/June 1987), 232.

21. Fletcher interview.

22. D.S. Greenberg, "Space Program," *Science*, 8 March 1963, 890-91; Charles Murray and Catherine Bly Cox, *Apollo: The Race to the Moon* (New York: Simon & Schuster, 1989), 448.

23. Jeff Goldberg, "Lunar Reflections," *Omni*, July 1989, 40.

24. See, for example, David Howard Davis, *How the Bureaucracy Makes Foreign Policy: An Exchange Analysis* (Lexington, Mass.: Lexington Books, 1972), 39; Philip

M. Boffey, "Space Agency Image: A Sudden Shattering," *New York Times*, 5 February 1986, A1.

25. Matt Moffett and Laurie McGinley, "NASA, Once a Master of Publicity, Fumbles in Handling Shuttle Crisis," *Wall Street Journal*, 14 February 1896, 23.

26. See, for example, Frank Gibney and George J. Feldman, *The Reluctant Space-Farers: A Study in the Politics of Discovery* (New York: New American Library, 1965), 77-78; Ordway et al., *Dividends from Space*, 3; R. Jeffrey Smith, "Uncertainties Mark Space Program of the 1980s," *Science*, 14 December 1979, 1285-86; Covault, "NASA Plans to Fight Threats," 62.

27. David Bamberger, "NASA and Watergate: How the Publicists Lost the Public," *America*, 19 July 1975, 33.

28. "Reveille for Sophomores," *New York Times*, 17 January 1990, A24.

29. National Commission on Space, *Pioneering the Space Frontier* (Toronto: Bantam Books, 1986), 169-80; "NASA Changes Management Structure," *Aviation Week & Space Technology*, 26 January 1987, 75; National Academy of Public Administration, *Effectiveness of NASA Headquarters* (Washington, D.C.: NAPA, 1988), 47.

30. Fletcher interview. See also Vernon Van Dyke, *Pride and Power: The Rationale of the Space Program* (Urbana: University of Illinois Press, 1964), 255-56.

31. Fletcher interview.

32. See Jameson W. Doig and Erwin C. Hargrove, " 'Leadership' and Political Analysis," in *Leadership and Innovation: A Biographical Perspective on Entrepreneurs in Government*, ed. Jameson W. Doig and Erwin C. Hargrove (Baltimore: Johns Hopkins University Press, 1987), 1-7.

33. Erwin C. Hargrove, *The Missing Link: The Study of the Implementation of Social Policy* (Washington, D.C.: Urban Institute, 1975), 113; Philip B. Heymann, *The Politics of Public Management* (New Haven: Yale University Press, 1987), 47; James Q. Wilson, *Bureaucracy: What Government Agencies Do and Why They Do It* (New York: Basic Books, 1989), Chapter 11; Doig and Hargrove, " 'Leadership' and Political Analysis," 8; Steven Thomas Seitz, *Bureaucracy, Policy, and the Public* (St. Louis: C. V. Mosby Co., 1978), 140.

34. Herbert Kaufman, *The Administrative Behavior of Federal Bureau Chiefs* (Washington, D.C.: Brookings Institution, 1981), 78.

35. Heymann, *Politics of Public Management*, 46-47; Doig and Hargrove, " 'Leadership' and Political Analysis," 16.

36. Fletcher interview.

37. Kaufman, *Administrative Behavior*, 66.

38. Herbert A. Simon, Donald W. Smithburg, and Victor A. Thompson, *Public Administration* (New York: Alfred A. Knopf, 1950), 396.

39. Astronaut Rhea Seddon noted in her interview with the author that different NASA administrators have framed issues differently, making a "company line" less likely.

40. W. Henry Lambright, "James Webb and the Uses of Administrative Power," in *Leadership and Innovation*, ed. Doig and Hargrove, 174.

41. James E. Webb, foreword to *Managing NASA in the Apollo Era*, SP-4102, by Arnold S. Levine (Washington, D.C.: GPO, 1982), xii.

42. In addition to Lambright, "James Webb and the Uses of Administrative Power," see Joseph J. Trento, *Prescription for Disaster* (New York: Crown Publishers, 1987), Chapter 2; Murray and Cox, *Apollo: The Race to the Moon*, 71-72; Nancy Petrovic,

"Design for Decline: Executive Management and the Eclipse of NASA" (Ph.D. dissertation, University of Maryland, 1982), 238-39; Jonathan Spivak, "NASA's Jim Webb—A Rare Bureaucrat," *Wall Street Journal*, 11 October 1968, 16; James W. Fesler and Donald F. Kettl, *The Politics of the Administrative Process* (Chatham, N.J.: Chatham House Publishers, 1991), 247.

43. Jonathan Spivak, "Apathy is NASA's Biggest Foe," *Wall Street Journal*, 25 February 1977, 12.

44. Fletcher interview.

45. Anthony Downs, *Inside Bureaucracy* (Boston: Little, Brown & Co., 1967), 5-23. See also Gerald S. Gryski, *Bureaucratic Policy Making in a Technological Society* (Cambridge, Mass.: Schenkman Publishing Co., 1981), 99-105.

46. Downs, *Inside Bureaucracy*, 20.

47. See Howard E. McCurdy, *Inside NASA: High Technology and Organizational Change in the American Space Program* (Baltimore: Johns Hopkins University Press, 1993); William J. Broad, "Pervasive Decline of Staff Stunts NASA, Critics Say," *New York Times*, 9 September 1990, 1, 32; Paul A. Gigot, "NASA's Flyboys Have Grown Old and Fat," *Wall Street Journal*, 13 July 1990, A8; McDonough, *Space: The Next 25 Years*, 38; Romzek and Dubnick, "Accountability in the Public Sector;" Marcia Dunn, "From 'Gee Whiz' to 'So What' for NASA," *Nashville Tennessean*, 16 December 1990, 2D; Jaroff, "Spinning Out of Orbit," 26; Fletcher interview.

48. Broad, "Decline of Staff," 1.

49. Fletcher interview.

50. Ibid.

51. Smith, "Uncertainties Mark Space Program," 1285.

52. David C. Morrison, "Vice-President for Space," *National Journal*, 29 July 1989, 1911.

Appendix

NASA Budget Authority, 1958 to 1990		
Fiscal Year	Current Dollars (Millions)	Constant 1987 Dollars (Millions)
1958	117	551
1959	305	1,356
1960	524	2,229
1961	964	4,005
1962	1,825	7,449
1963	3,673	14,438
1964	5,100	19,646
1965	5,250	19,811
1966	5,175	18,942
1967	4,966	17,660
1968	4,587	15,671
1969	3,997	12,927
1970	3,746	11,414
1971	3,311	9,438
1972	3,306	8,849
1973	3,406	8,599
1974	3,036	7,049
1975	3,229	6,786
1976	3,552	6,967
1977	3,876	7,018
1978	4,244	7,159
1979	4,743	7,364
1980	5,350	7,533
1981	5,634	7,207
1982	6,200	7,408
1983	7,065	8,050
1984	7,458	8,173
1985	7,573	8,012
1986	7,807	8,020
1987	10,923	10,923
1988	9,062	8,746
1989	10,969	10,144
1990	12,324	10,922

Sources: Office of Management and Budget, *Budget of the United States Government: Fiscal Year 1995, Historical Tables* (Washington, D.C.: GPO, 1994); Bureau of the Budget, *Budget of the United States Government* (Washington, D.C.: GPO, 1959-70); Office of Management and Budget, *Budget of the United States Government* (Washington, D.C.: GPO, 1970-71).

Note: The author calculated constant dollar amounts by applying the composite deflators found in Table 1.3 of the *Historical Tables* to the current dollar amounts found in the sources listed above.

Bibliography

BOOKS

Altheide, David L., and John M. Johnson. *Bureaucratic Propaganda*. Boston: Allyn & Bacon, 1980.

Ambrose, Stephen E. *Eisenhower*. Vol. 2. *The President*. New York: Simon & Schuster, 1984.

Arnold, R. Douglas. *Congress and the Bureaucracy: A Theory of Influence*. New Haven: Yale University Press, 1979.

Barnard, Chester I. *The Functions of the Executive*. Cambridge: Harvard University Press, 1940.

Benson, Charles D., and William Barnaby Faherty. *Moonport: A History of Apollo Launch Facilities and Operations*. SP-4204. Washington, D.C.: GPO, 1978.

Bergerson, Frederic A. *The Army Gets an Air Force: Tactics of Insurgent Bureaucratic Politics*. Baltimore: Johns Hopkins University Press, 1980.

Bilstein, Roger E. *Orders of Magnitude: A History of the NACA and NASA, 1915-1990*. SP-4406. Washington, D.C.: GPO, 1989.

Blau, Peter M., and Marshall W. Meyer. *Bureaucracy in Modern Society*. 3d edn. New York: Random House, 1987.

Brooks, Courtney G., James M. Grimwood, and Loyd S. Swenson, Jr. *Chariots for Apollo*. SP-4205. Washington, D.C.: GPO, 1979.

Buchanan, James M., and Gordon Tullock. *The Calculus of Consent*. Ann Arbor: University of Michigan Press, 1962.

Carter, Dale. *The Final Frontier: The Rise and Fall of the American Rocket State*. London: Verso, 1988.

Cater, Douglass. *The Fourth Branch of Government*. Boston: Houghton Mifflin, 1959.

Collins, Michael. *Carrying the Fire: An Astronaut's Journeys*. New York: Farrar, Straus and Giroux, 1974.

Converse, Philip E., Jean D. Dotson, Wendy J. Hoag, and William H. McGee III. *American Social Attitudes Data Sourcebook, 1947-1978*. Cambridge: Harvard University Press, 1980.

Cooper, Henry S.F., Jr. *Before Liftoff: The Making of a Space Shuttle Crew*. Baltimore: Johns Hopkins University Press, 1987.

Davis, David Howard. *How the Bureaucracy Makes Foreign Policy: An Exchange Analysis*. Lexington, Mass.: Lexington Books, 1972.

Divine, Robert A., ed. *The Johnson Years*. Vol. 2. Lawrence: University of Kansas Press, 1987.

———. *The Sputnik Challenge*. New York: Oxford University Press, 1993.

Downs, Anthony. *An Economic Theory of Democracy*. New York: Harper & Row, 1957.

———. *Inside Bureaucracy*. Boston: Little, Brown & Co., 1967.

Dunn, Delmer D. *Public Officials and the Press*. Reading, Mass.: Addison-Wesley Publishing, 1969.

Edelman, Murray J. *The Symbolic Uses of Politics*. Urbana: University of Illinois Press, 1964.

———. *Politics as Symbolic Action: Mass Arousal and Quiescence*. New York: Academic Press, 1971.

Eisenhower, Dwight D. *Waging Peace, 1956-1961; The White House Years*. Garden City, N.Y.: Doubleday & Co., 1965.

Etzioni, Amatai. *The Moon-Doggle*. New York: Doubleday & Co., 1964.

Fenno, Richard, Jr. *The Power of the Purse: Appropriations Politics in Congress*. Boston: Little, Brown & Co., 1966.

Fesler, James W., and Donald F. Kettl. *The Politics of the Administrative Process*. Chatham, N.J.: Chatham House Publishers, 1991.

Feynman, R. P. *What Do You Care What Other People Think?* New York: W.W. Norton, 1988.

Freeman, J. Leiper. *The Political Process: Executive Bureau-Legislative Committee Relations*. Rev. edn. New York: Random House, 1965.

Gallup, George Horace. *The Gallup Poll: Public Opinion, 1935-1971*. New York: Random House, 1972.

Gawthorp, Louis C. *Bureaucratic Behavior in the Executive Branch: An Analysis of Organizational Change*. New York: Free Press, 1969.

Gibney, Frank, and George J. Feldman. *The Reluctant Space-Farers: A Study in the Politics of Discovery*. New York: New American Library, 1965.

Ginzberg, Eli, James W. Kuhn, Jerome Schnee, and Boris Yavitz. *Economic Impact of Large Public Programs: NASA Experience*. Salt Lake City: Olympus Publishing, 1976.

Goodsell, Charles T. *The Case for Bureaucracy: A Public Administration Polemic*. Chatham, N.J.: Chatham House Publishers, 1983.

Gordon, George J. *Public Administration in America*. 3d edn. New York: St. Martin's Press, 1986.

Gortner, Harold F., Julianne Mahler, and Jeanne Bell Nicholson. *Organization Theory: A Public Perspective*. Chicago: Dorsey Press, 1987.

Grey, Jerry. *Beachheads in Space: A Blueprint for the Future*. New York: Macmillan, 1983.

Grissom, Virgil I. *Gemini: A Personal Account of Man's Venture into Space*. New York: Macmillan, 1968.

Gryski, Gerald S. *Bureaucratic Policy Making in a Technological Society*. Cambridge, Mass.: Schenkman Publishing, 1981.

Hargrove, Erwin C. *The Missing Link: The Study of the Implementation of Social Policy*. Washington, D.C.: Urban Institute, 1975.

Harris Survey Yearbook of Public Opinion, 1970. New York: Louis Harris & Associates, 1971.

Hechler, Ken. *The Endless Space Frontier: A History of the House Committee on Science and Astronautics, 1959-1978.* San Diego: American Astronautical Society, 1982.

Heymann, Philip B. *The Politics of Public Management.* New Haven: Yale University Press, 1987.

Hirsch, Richard, and Joseph John Trento. *The National Aeronautics and Space Administration.* New York: Praeger, 1973.

Hult, Karen M., and Charles Walcott. *Governing Public Organizations: Politics, Structures, and Institutional Design.* Pacific Grove, Calif.: Brooks/Cole Publishing, 1990.

Katz, Daniel, and Robert L. Kahn. *The Social Psychology of Organizations.* 2d edn. New York: John Wiley & Sons, 1978.

Kaufman, Herbert. *Are Government Organizations Immortal?* Washington, D.C.: Brookings Institution, 1976.

———. *The Administrative Behavior of Federal Bureau Chiefs.* Washington, D.C.: Brookings Institution, 1981.

Kennan, Erlend A., and Edmund H. Harvey, Jr. *Mission to the Moon: A Critical Examination of NASA and the Space Program.* New York: Morrow, 1969.

Lambright, W. Henry. *Governing Science and Technology.* New York: Oxford University Press, 1976.

Levine, Arnold S. *Managing NASA in the Apollo Era.* SP-4102. Washington, D.C.: GPO, 1982.

Levine, Arthur L. *The Future of the U. S. Space Program.* New York: Praeger, 1975.

Lewis, John S., and Ruth A. Lewis. *Space Resources: Breaking the Bonds of Earth.* New York: Columbia University Press, 1987.

Lewis, Richard S. *The Voyages of Apollo: The Exploration of the Moon.* New York: Quadrangle, 1974.

———. *Challenger: The Final Voyage.* New York: Columbia University Press, 1988.

Light, Paul C. *The President's Agenda.* Baltimore: Johns Hopkins University Press, 1983.

Logsdon, John M. *The Decision to Go to the Moon: Project Apollo and the National Interest.* Cambridge: MIT Press, 1970.

Logsdon, Tom. *Space, Inc.: Your Guide to Investing in Space Exploration.* New York: Crown Publishers, 1988.

Long, Norton. *The Polity.* Chicago: Rand McNally, 1962.

Lutrin, Carl E., and Allen K. Settle. *American Public Administration: Concepts and Cases.* Palo Alto, Calif.: Mayfield Publishing, 1976.

Mark, Hans. *The Space Station: A Personal Journey.* Durham, N.C.: Duke University Press, 1987.

McConnell, Malcolm. *Challenger: A Major Malfunction.* Garden City, N.Y.: Doubleday & Co., 1987.

McCurdy, Howard E. *The Space Station Decision: Incremental Politics and Technological Choice.* Baltimore: Johns Hopkins University Press, 1990.

———. *Inside NASA: High Technology and Organizational Change in the American Space Program.* Baltimore: Johns Hopkins University Press, 1993.

McDonough, Thomas R. *Space: The Next 25 Years*. New York: John Wiley & Sons, 1987.

McDougall, Walter A. . . . *The Heavens and the Earth: A Political History of the Space Age*. New York: Basic Books, 1985.

Meier, Kenneth J. *Politics and the Bureaucracy: Policymaking in the Fourth Branch of Government*. 2d edn. Monterey, Calif.: Brooks/Cole Publishing, 1987.

Michaud, Michael A. G. *Reaching for the High Frontier: The American Pro-Space Movement, 1972-84*. New York: Praeger, 1986.

Murray, Charles, and Catherine Bly Cox. *Apollo: The Race to the Moon*. New York: Simon & Schuster, 1989.

National Academy of Public Administration. *Effectiveness of NASA Headquarters*. Washington, D.C.: NAPA, 1988.

National Commission on Space. *Pioneering the Space Frontier*. Toronto: Bantam Books, 1986.

Nelson, Bill, with Jamie Buckingham. *Mission: An American Congressman's Voyage to Space*. San Diego: Harcourt Brace Jovanovich, 1988.

Niemi, Richard G., John Mueller, and Tom W. Smith. *Trends in Public Opinion: A Compendium of Survey Data*. New York: Greenwood Press, 1989.

Niskanen, William A. *Bureaucracy and Representative Government*. Chicago: Aldine-Atherton, 1971.

Nixon, Richard M. *RN: The Memoirs of Richard Nixon*. New York: Grosset & Dunlap, 1978.

Ordway, Frederick I., III, Carsbie C. Adams, and Mitchell R. Sharpe. *Dividends from Space*. New York: Thomas Y. Crowell, 1971.

Perrow, Charles. *Complex Organizations: A Critical Essay*. 3d edn. New York: Random House, 1986.

Peter, Laurence J. *The Peter Pyramid: Or Will We Ever Get the Point?* New York: William Morrow, 1986.

Price, James L. *Organizational Effectiveness: An Inventory of Propositions*. Homewood, Ill.: Richard D. Irwin, 1968.

Rosholt, Robert L. *An Administrative History of NASA, 1958-1963*. SP-4101. Washington, D.C.: GPO, 1966.

Rourke, Francis E. *Secrecy and Publicity: Dilemmas of Democracy*. Baltimore: Johns Hopkins University Press, 1961.

———. *Bureaucracy, Politics, and Public Policy*. 3d edn. Boston: Little, Brown & Co., 1984.

———, ed. *Bureaucratic Power in National Policy Making*. 4th edn. Boston: Little, Brown & Co., 1986.

Schauer, William H. *The Politics of Space: A Comparison of the Soviet and American Space Programs*. New York: Holmes & Meier, 1976.

Schulman, Paul R. *Large-Scale Policy Making*. New York: Elsevier, 1980.

Seitz, Steven Thomas. *Bureaucracy, Policy, and the Public*. St. Louis: C.V. Mosby, 1978.

Selznick, Philip. *TVA and the Grass Roots: A Study in the Sociology of Formal Organization*. New York: Harper Torchbooks, 1966.

Sigal, Leon V. *Reporters and Officials: The Organization and Politics of Newsmaking*. Lexington, Mass.: D. C. Heath & Co., 1973.

Simon, Herbert A., Donald W. Smithburg, and Victor A. Thompson. *Public Admini-stration*. New York: Alfred A. Knopf, 1950.

Sorrentino, Frank M. *Ideological Warfare: The FBI's Path Toward Power*. Port Washington, N.Y.: Associated Faculty Press, 1985.

Stillman, Richard J. *The American Bureaucracy*. Chicago: Nelson-Hall, 1987.

Swenson, Loyd S., Jr., James M. Grimwood, and Charles C. Alexander. *This New Ocean: A History of Project Mercury*. SP-4201. Washington, D.C.: GPO, 1966.

Taylor, L.B., Jr. *For All Mankind: America's Space Programs of the 1970s and Be-yond*. New York: E. P. Dutton & Co., 1974.

Thompson, James D. *Organizations in Action*. New York: McGraw-Hill, 1967.

Trento, Joseph J. *Prescription for Disaster*. New York: Crown Publishers, 1987.

Truman, David B. *The Governmental Process: Political Interests and Public Opinion*. New York: Alfred A. Knopf, 1971.

Tullock, Gordon. *The Politics of Bureaucracy*. Washington, D.C.: Public Affairs Press, 1965.

Turner, Frederick Jackson. *The Frontier in American History*. Huntington, N.Y.: Robert E. Krieger Publishing, 1976.

Van Dyke, Vernon. *Pride and Power: The Rationale of the Space Program*. Urbana: University of Illinois Press, 1964.

von Braun, Wernher. *Space Frontier*. New York: Holt, Rinehart and Winston, 1971.

Warwick, Donald P. *A Theory of Public Bureaucracy*. Cambridge: Harvard University Press, 1975.

Weber, Max. *From Max Weber: Essays in Sociology*. Trans. and ed. H. H. Gerth and C. Wright Mills. Oxford: Oxford University Press, 1946.

Wells, Helen T., Susan H. Whiteley, and Carrie E. Karegeannes. *Origins of NASA Names*. SP-4402. Washington, D.C.: GPO, 1976.

Wildavsky, Aaron. *The New Politics of the Budgetary Process*. Glenview, Ill.: Scott, Foresman & Co., 1988.

Wilford, John Noble. *We Reach the Moon*. New York: Bantam Books, 1969.

Wilson, Andrew. *Space Shuttle Story*. London: Hamlyn Publishing, 1986.

Wilson, James Q. *Bureaucracy: What Government Agencies Do and Why They Do It*. New York: Basic Books, 1989.

Wolfe, Tom. *The Right Stuff*. Toronto: Bantam Books, 1979.

ARTICLES IN ANTHOLOGIES

Almond, Gabriel A. "Public Opinion and the Development of Space Technology: 1957-1960." In *Outer Space in World Politics*, ed. Joseph M. Golden, 71-96. New York: Praeger, 1963.

Beer, Samuel H. "Bureaucracies as Constituencies." In *Bureaucratic Power in National Policy Making*, 4th edn., ed. Francis E. Rourke, 45-56. Boston: Little, Brown & Co., 1986.

Doig, Jameson W., and Erwin C. Hargrove. " 'Leadership' and Political Analysis." In *Leadership and Innovation: A Biographical Perspective on Entrepreneurs in Government*, ed. Jameson W. Doig and Erwin C. Hargrove, 1-23. Baltimore: Johns Hopkins University Press, 1987.

Emme, Eugene M. "Presidents and Space." In *Between Sputnik and the Shuttle: New Perspectives on American Astronautics*, ed. Frederick C. Durant III, 5-138. San Diego: American Astronautical Society, 1981.

Galloway, Eilene. "U.S. Congress and Outer Space." In *Between Sputnik and the Shuttle*, ed. Frederick C. Durant III, 139-55. San Diego: American Astronautical Society, 1981.

Heclo, Hugh. "Issue Networks and the Executive Establishment." In *The New American Political System*, ed. Anthony King, 87-124. Washington, D.C.: American Enterprise Institute, 1978.

————. "One Executive Branch or Many?" In *Both Ends of the Avenue*, ed. Anthony King, 26-58. Washington, D.C.: American Enterprise Institute, 1983.

Holman, Mary A., and Theodore Suranyi-Unger, Jr. "The Political Economy of American Astronautics." In *Between Sputnik and the Shuttle*, ed. Frederick C. Durant III, 161-86. San Diego: American Astronautical Society, 1981.

Lambright, W. Henry. "James Webb and the Uses of Administrative Power." In *Leadership and Innovation: A Biographical Perspective on Entrepreneurs in Government*, ed. Jameson W. Doig and Erwin C. Hargrove, 174-203. Baltimore: Johns Hopkins University Press, 1987.

Long, Norton E. "Power and Administration." In *Bureaucratic Power in National Policy Making*, 4th edn., ed. Francis E. Rourke, 7-16. Boston: Little, Brown & Co., 1986.

McNeal, Sherry Rae. "Public Awareness and Attitude Toward the Space Program." In *Remember the Future: The Apollo Legacy*, ed. Stan Kent, 129-45. San Diego: American Astronautical Society, 1980.

Seamans, Robert C., Jr., and Frederick I. Ordway III. "Lessons of Apollo for Large-Scale Technology." In *Between Sputnik and the Shuttle*, ed. Frederick C. Durant III, 241-88. San Diego: American Astronautical Society, 1981.

Smith, Michael L. "Selling the Moon: The U.S. Manned Space Program and the Triumph of Commodity Scientism." In *The Culture of Consumption*, ed. Richard Wightman Fox and T. J. Jackson Lears, 177-209. New York: Pantheon Books, 1983.

CONGRESSIONAL HEARINGS

U.S. Congress. House. Committee on Appropriations. Subcommittee on HUD—Independent Agencies. *Department of Housing and Urban Development—Independent Agencies Appropriations for 1976*. Part 2. 94th Cong., 1st sess., 4 March 1975.

————. *Department of Housing and Urban Development—Independent Agencies Appropriations for 1977*. Part 2. 94th Cong., 2d sess., 18 February 1976.

————. *Department of Housing and Urban Development—Independent Agencies Appropriations for 1978*. Part 5. 95th Cong., 1st sess., 29 March 1977.

————. *Department of Housing and Urban Development—Independent Agencies Appropriations for 1979*. Part 1. 95th Cong., 2d sess., 25 January 1978.

————. *Space Shuttle Appropriations for Fiscal Year 1979*. 95th Cong., 2d sess., 9 March 1978.

————. *Department of Housing and Urban Development—Independent Agencies Appropriations for 1984*. Part 6. 98th Cong., 1st sess., 22 March 1983.

————. *Department of Housing and Urban Development—Independent Agencies Appropriations for 1985*. Part 6. 98th Cong., 2d sess., 27 March 1984.

————. *Department of Housing and Urban Development—Independent Agencies Appropriations for 1986*. Part 6. 99th Cong., 1st sess., 2 April 1985.

————. *Department of Housing and Urban Development—Independent Agencies Appropriations for 1987*. Part 7. 99th Cong., 2d sess., 13, 15 May 1986.

————. *Department of Housing and Urban Development—Independent Agencies Appropriations for 1988*. Part 6. 100th Cong., 1st sess., 7 April 1987.

————. *Department of Housing and Urban Development—Independent Agencies Appropriations for 1989*. Part 7. 100th Cong., 2d sess., 19 April 1988.

U.S. Congress. House. Committee on Appropriations. Subcommittee on HUD—Space—Science—Veterans. *HUD—Space—Science—Veterans Appropriations for 1975*. Part 3. 93d Cong., 2d sess., 26 March 1974.

U.S. Congress. House. Committee on Appropriations. Subcommittee on Independent Offices. *National Aeronautics and Space Administration Appropriations*, 86th Cong., 1st sess., 29 April 1959.

————. *Independent Offices Appropriations for 1962*. Part 2. 87th Cong., 1st sess., 15 May 1961.

————. *Independent Offices Appropriations for 1965*. Part 2. 88th Cong., 2d sess., 7 April 1964.

————. *Independent Offices Appropriations for 1966*. Part 2. 89th Cong., 1st sess., 5 April 1965.

U.S. Congress. House. Committee on Appropriations. Subcommittee on Independent Offices and the Department of Housing and Urban Development. *Independent Offices and Department of Housing and Urban Development Appropriations for 1968*. Part 3. 90th Cong., 1st sess., April 1967.

————. *Independent Offices and Department of Housing and Urban Development Appropriations for 1969*. Part 2. 90th Cong., 2d sess., 11 March 1968.

U.S. Congress. House. Committee on Appropriations. Subcommittee on VA, HUD, and Independent Agencies. *Departments of Veterans Affairs and Housing and Urban Development, and Independent Agencies Appropriations for 1990*. Part 6. 101st Cong., 1st sess., 25 April 1989.

U.S. Congress. House. Committee on Science and Astronautics. *Full Committee Consideration of H.R. 4990 and S. 1096 with Respect to Authorizing Appropriations to the National Aeronautics and Space Administration*. 86th Cong., 1st sess., 9 March 1959.

————. *International Control of Outer Space*. 86th Cong., 1st sess., 11 March 1959.

————. *1960 NASA Authorization*. 86th Cong., 1st sess., 20, 24 April 1959.

————. *Meeting with the Astronauts*. 86th Cong., 1st sess., 28 May 1959.

————. *Review of the Space Program*. 86th Cong., 2d sess., 27 and 29 January 1960.

————. *To Amend the National Aeronautics and Space Act of 1958*. 86th Cong., 2d sess., 4 April 1960.

————. *1962 NASA Authorization*. Part 1. 87th Cong., 1st sess., 14 April 1961.

————. *1962 NASA Authorization*. Part 3. 87th Cong., 1st sess., 12 July 1961.

————. *1964 NASA Authorization*. Part 1. 88th Cong., 1st sess., 4 March 1963.

————. *1968 NASA Authorization*. Part 1. 90th Cong., 1st sess., 28 February 1967.

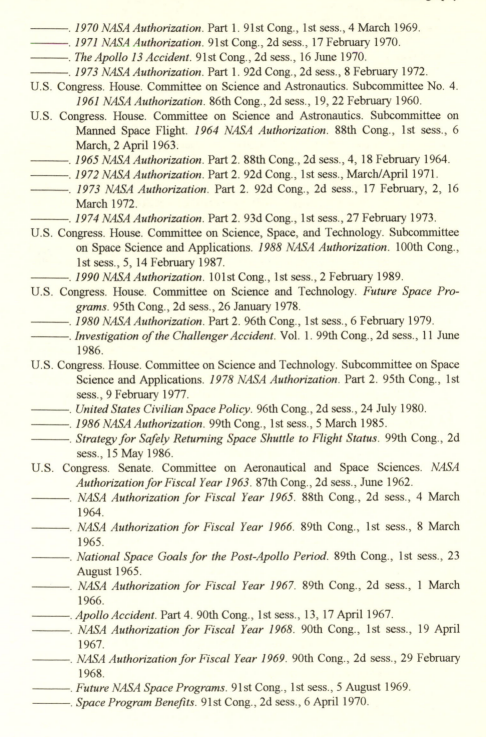

———. *1970 NASA Authorization.* Part 1. 91st Cong., 1st sess., 4 March 1969.

———. *1971 NASA Authorization.* 91st Cong., 2d sess., 17 February 1970.

———. *The Apollo 13 Accident.* 91st Cong., 2d sess., 16 June 1970.

———. *1973 NASA Authorization.* Part 1. 92d Cong., 2d sess., 8 February 1972.

U.S. Congress. House. Committee on Science and Astronautics. Subcommittee No. 4. *1961 NASA Authorization.* 86th Cong., 2d sess., 19, 22 February 1960.

U.S. Congress. House. Committee on Science and Astronautics. Subcommittee on Manned Space Flight. *1964 NASA Authorization.* 88th Cong., 1st sess., 6 March, 2 April 1963.

———. *1965 NASA Authorization.* Part 2. 88th Cong., 2d sess., 4, 18 February 1964.

———. *1972 NASA Authorization.* Part 2. 92d Cong., 1st sess., March/April 1971.

———. *1973 NASA Authorization.* Part 2. 92d Cong., 2d sess., 17 February, 2, 16 March 1972.

———. *1974 NASA Authorization.* Part 2. 93d Cong., 1st sess., 27 February 1973.

U.S. Congress. House. Committee on Science, Space, and Technology. Subcommittee on Space Science and Applications. *1988 NASA Authorization.* 100th Cong., 1st sess., 5, 14 February 1987.

———. *1990 NASA Authorization.* 101st Cong., 1st sess., 2 February 1989.

U.S. Congress. House. Committee on Science and Technology. *Future Space Programs.* 95th Cong., 2d sess., 26 January 1978.

———. *1980 NASA Authorization.* Part 2. 96th Cong., 1st sess., 6 February 1979.

———. *Investigation of the Challenger Accident.* Vol. 1. 99th Cong., 2d sess., 11 June 1986.

U.S. Congress. House. Committee on Science and Technology. Subcommittee on Space Science and Applications. *1978 NASA Authorization.* Part 2. 95th Cong., 1st sess., 9 February 1977.

———. *United States Civilian Space Policy.* 96th Cong., 2d sess., 24 July 1980.

———. *1986 NASA Authorization.* 99th Cong., 1st sess., 5 March 1985.

———. *Strategy for Safely Returning Space Shuttle to Flight Status.* 99th Cong., 2d sess., 15 May 1986.

U.S. Congress. Senate. Committee on Aeronautical and Space Sciences. *NASA Authorization for Fiscal Year 1963.* 87th Cong., 2d sess., June 1962.

———. *NASA Authorization for Fiscal Year 1965.* 88th Cong., 2d sess., 4 March 1964.

———. *NASA Authorization for Fiscal Year 1966.* 89th Cong., 1st sess., 8 March 1965.

———. *National Space Goals for the Post-Apollo Period.* 89th Cong., 1st sess., 23 August 1965.

———. *NASA Authorization for Fiscal Year 1967.* 89th Cong., 2d sess., 1 March 1966.

———. *Apollo Accident.* Part 4. 90th Cong., 1st sess., 13, 17 April 1967.

———. *NASA Authorization for Fiscal Year 1968.* 90th Cong., 1st sess., 19 April 1967.

———. *NASA Authorization for Fiscal Year 1969.* 90th Cong., 2d sess., 29 February 1968.

———. *Future NASA Space Programs.* 91st Cong., 1st sess., 5 August 1969.

———. *Space Program Benefits.* 91st Cong., 2d sess., 6 April 1970.

————. *NASA Authorization for Fiscal Year 1972.* 92d Cong., 1st sess., 30 March 1971.

————. *NASA Authorization for Fiscal Year 1973.* 92d Cong., 2d sess., 14, 15 March 1972.

————. *NASA Authorization for Fiscal Year 1974.* Part 1. 93d Cong., 1st sess., 28 February and 3, 6 March 1973.

————. *NASA Authorization for Fiscal Year 1974.* 93d Cong., 1st sess., 10 April 1973.

U.S. Congress. Senate. Committee on Aeronautical and Space Sciences. Subcommittee on Governmental Organization for Space Activities. *Investigation of Governmental Organization for Space Activities.* 86th Cong., 1st sess., 24 March 1959.

U.S. Congress. Senate. Committee on Aeronautical and Space Sciences. Subcommittee on NASA Authorization. *NASA Supplemental Authorization for Fiscal Year 1959.* 86th Cong., 1st sess., 19 February 1959.

————. *NASA Authorization for Fiscal Year 1960.* Part 1. 86th Cong., 1st sess., 7 April 1959.

————. *NASA Authorization for Fiscal Year 1961.* Part 1. 86th Cong., 2d sess., 28, 29 March 1960.

U.S. Congress. Senate. Committee on Appropriations. *Supplemental National Aeronautics and Space Administration Appropriations, 1960.* 86th Cong., 2d sess., 23 February 1960.

————. *Department of Housing and Urban Development. Space and Science Appropriations for Fiscal Year 1972.* 92d Cong., 1st sess., 23 June 1971.

————. *Department of Housing and Urban Development and Certain Other Independent Agencies Appropriations for Fiscal Year 1976.* Part 1. 94th Cong., 1st sess., 10 March 1975.

U.S. Congress. Senate. Subcommittee of Committee on Appropriations. *Independent Offices Appropriations, 1963.* 87th Cong., 2d sess., 10 August 1962.

————. *Department of Housing and Urban Development, Space, Science, Veterans, and Certain Other Independent Agencies Appropriations for Fiscal Year 1973.* 92d Cong., 2d sess., 12 April 1972.

————. *Department of Housing and Urban Development and Certain Other Independent Agencies Appropriations for Fiscal Year 1976.* Part 1. 94th Cong., 1st sess., 10 March 1975.

U.S. Congress. Senate. Committee on Appropriations. Subcommittee on HUD—Independent Agencies. *Department of Housing and Urban Development and Certain Independent Agencies Appropriations for Fiscal Year 1983.* Part 2. 97th Cong., 2d sess., 5 May 1982.

————. *Department of Housing and Urban Development—Independent Agencies Appropriations for Fiscal Year 1987.* 99th Cong., 2d sess., 16 September 1986.

————. *Department of Housing and Urban Development—Independent Agencies Appropriations for Fiscal Year 1988.* 100th Cong., 1st sess., 9 April 1987.

U.S. Congress. Senate. Committee on Commerce, Science, and Transportation. *NASA Authorization for Fiscal Year 1980.* 96th Cong., 1st sess., 21 February 1979.

U.S. Congress. Senate. Committee on Commerce, Science, and Transportation. Subcommittee on Science, Technology, and Space. *U.S. Civilian Space Policy.* 96th Cong., 1st sess., 25 January 1979.

————. *NASA Authorization for Fiscal Year 1985*. 98th Cong., 2d sess., 28 February 1984.

————. *NASA Authorization*. 100th Cong., 1st sess., 3 February 1987.

————. *NASA Authorization*. 100th Cong., 2d sess., 22 March 1988.

NASA PUBLICATIONS

NASA. *The Challenge of Space Exploration*. Washington, D.C.: GPO, 1959.

————. *Exploring Space . . . Project Mercury*. Washington, D.C.: GPO, 1961.

————. *Exploring Space: Projects Mercury and Apollo of the United States Space Program*. Washington, D.C.: GPO, 1961.

————. *Space: The New Frontier*. Washington, D.C.: GPO, 1962.

————. *Mercury Project Summary*. Washington, D.C.: GPO, 1963.

————. *1-2-3 and the Moon*. Washington, D.C.: GPO, 1963.

————. *Space: The New Frontier*. Washington, D.C.: GPO, 1963.

————. *Ninth Semiannual Report to Congress, January 1-June 30, 1963*. Washington, D.C.: GPO, 1964.

————. *Space Exploration—Why and How*. EP-25. Washington, D.C.: GPO, 1965.

————. *Space and the International Cooperation Year: A National Challenge*. By Arnold W. Frutkin. EP-30. Washington, D.C.: GPO, 1965.

————. *Project Gemini*. Washington, D.C.: GPO, 1966.

————. *Thirteenth Semiannual Report to Congress, January 1-June 30, 1965*. Washington, D.C.: GPO, 1966.

————. *Space: The New Frontier*. Washington, D.C.: GPO, 1966.

————. *NASA Astronauts*. EP-34. Washington, D.C.: GPO, 1967.

————. *Space: The New Frontier*. EP-6. Washington, D.C.: GPO, 1967.

————. *Apollo: Man Around the Moon*. Washington, D.C.: GPO, 1968.

————. *This Is NASA*. EP-22. Washington, D.C.: GPO, 1968.

————. *America's Next Decades in Space*. Washington, D.C.: GPO, 1969.

————. *In This Decade...* EP-71. Washington, D.C.: GPO, 1969.

————. *Man in Space*. By David A. Anderton. EP-57. Washington, D.C.: GPO, 1969.

————. *Manned Space Flight: Apollo*. NF-23. Washington, D.C.: GPO, 1969.

————. *Putting Satellites to Work*. By William R. Corliss. EP-53. Washington, D.C.: GPO, 1969.

————. *Space Physics and Astronomy*. By William R. Corliss. EP-51. Washington, D.C.: GPO, 1969.

————. *Space Station: Key to the Future*. EP-75. Washington, D.C.: GPO, 1970.

————. *Twenty-first Semiannual Report to Congress, January 1-June 30, 1969*. Washington, D.C.: GPO, 1970.

————. *Man in Space: Space in the Seventies*. By Walter Froehlich. EP-81. Washington, D.C.: GPO, 1971.

————. *NASA: National Aeronautics and Space Administration*. Washington, D.C.: GPO, 1971.

————. *Space Shuttle*. EP-77. Washington, D.C.: GPO, 1971.

————. *This Is NASA*. EP-22. Washington, D.C.: GPO, 1971.

————. *Space Benefits and Older Citizens*. Washington, D.C.: GPO, 1972.

————. *Space for Mankind's Benefit*. SP-313. Washington, D.C.: GPO, 1972.

———. *Space Shuttle*. EP-96. Washington, D.C.: GPO, 1972.

———. *Kennedy Space Center Story*. Washington, D.C.: GPO, 1973.

———. *Most Asked Questions About Space and Aeronautics*. Washington, D.C.: GPO, 1973.

———. *Space Shuttle: For Down to Earth Benefits*. Washington, D.C.: GPO, 1974.

———. *New Horizons*. EP-117. Washington, D.C.: GPO, 1975.

———. *Questions About Aeronautics and Space*. Washington, D.C.: GPO, 1976.

———. *Space Shuttle*. SP-407. Washington, D.C.: GPO, 1976.

———. *What's New on the Moon?* EP-131. Washington, D.C.: GPO, 1976.

———. *Space Shuttle*. Washington, D.C.: GPO, 1977.

———. *The Space Shuttle at Work*. By Howard Allaway. EP-156. Washington, D.C.: GPO, 1979.

———. *This Is NASA*. EP-155. Washington, D.C.: GPO, 1979.

———. *Aboard the Space Shuttle*. By Florence S. Steinberg. EP-169. Washington, D.C.: GPO, 1980.

———. *A Meeting with the Universe*. Edited by Bevan M. French and Stephen P. Moran. EP-177. Washington, D.C.: GPO, 1981.

———. *Mission Report*. MR-001. Washington, D.C.: GPO, 1981.

———. *Space Benefits*. By Denver Research Institute. Washington, D.C.: GPO, 1981.

———. *Space Shuttle*. Washington, D.C.: GPO, 1981.

———. *The Next Step: Large Space Structures*. NF-129. Washington, D.C.: GPO, 1982.

———. *National Aeronautics and Space Administration: Twenty-fifth Anniversary, 1958-1983*. NF-200. Washington, D.C.: GPO, 1983.

———. *We Deliver*. Washington, D.C.: GPO, 1983.

———. *Daring What Others Dream*. Washington, D.C.: GPO, 1984.

———. *Space Station: The Next Logical Step*. By James M. Beggs. Washington, D.C.: GPO, 1984.

———. *Space Station: The Next Logical Step*. By Walter Froehlich. EP-213. Washington, D.C.: GPO, 1984.

———. *Space Shuttle: NASA's Answer to Operations in Near-Earth Orbit*. NF-144. Washington, D.C.: GPO, 1985.

———. *Questions & Answers About Aeronautics and Space*. PAM-106. Washington, D.C.: GPO, 1985.

———. *The Partnership: Space Shuttle, Space Science, and Space Station*. By Philip E. Culbertson and Robert F. Frietag. Washington, D.C.: GPO, 1986.

———. *Space Program Spinoffs*. PMS-023. Washington, D.C.: GPO, 1987.

———. *Space Station: Leadership for the Future*. By Franklin D. Martin and Terence T. Finn. PAM-509. Washington, D.C.: GPO, 1987.

———. *Space Station: The Next Logical Step*. By Andrew J. Stofan. Washington, D.C.: GPO, 1987.

———. *Space Station: A Step into the Future*. By Andrew J. Stofan. PAM-510. Washington, D.C.: GPO, 1987.

———. *Agenda for Tomorrow*. Washington, D.C.: GPO, 1988.

———. *Discovering Space for America's Economic Growth*. Washington, D.C.: GPO, 1988.

———. *The Early Years—Mercury to Apollo-Soyuz*. Washington, D.C.: GPO, 1988.

———. *NASA Highlights 1986-1988*. Washington, D.C.: GPO, 1988.

————. *On the Wings of a Dream: The Space Shuttle.* EP-269. Washington, D.C.: GPO, 1988.

————. "Safe Flight NASA's Top Concern." *NASA Activities*, March/April 1988.

————. *Science in Orbit: The Shuttle & Spacelab Experience: 1981-1986.* NP-119. Washington, D.C.: GPO, 1988.

————. *Space Shuttle: The Journey Continues.* By Richard Truly. NP-117. Washington, D.C.: GPO, 1988.

————. *Space Station: A Research Laboratory in Space.* PAM-512. Washington, D.C.: GPO, 1988.

————. *Space Station Freedom: A Foothold on the Future.* By Leonard David. NP-107. Washington, D.C.: GPO, 1988.

————. *STS 26: Flight of Discovery.* PAM-515. Washington, D.C.: GPO, 1988.

————. *Aeronautics and Space Report of the President: 1987 Activities.* Washington, D.C.: GPO, 1989.

————. *Commercial Use of Space: A New Economic Strength for America.* NP-113. Washington, D.C.: GPO, 1989.

————. *NASA.* NP-111. Washington, D.C.: GPO, 1989.

————. *Space Shuttle.* PMS-013A. Washington, D.C.: GPO, 1989.

————. *Space Shuttle: The Renewed Promise.* By Neil McAleer. PAM-521. Washington, D.C.: GPO, 1989.

————. *Exploring the Universe with the Hubble Space Telescope.* NP-126. Washington, D.C.: GPO, 1990.

————. *Agenda for Tomorrow.* Washington, D.C.: GPO, n.d.

————. *National Space Grant College and Fellowship Program.* Washington, D.C.: GPO, n.d.

————. *Sentinels in the Sky: Weather Satellites.* By Robert Haynes. NF-152(s). Washington, D.C.: GPO, n.d.

OTHER GOVERNMENT PUBLICATIONS

U.S. Bureau of the Budget. *Budget of the United States Government.* Washington, D.C.: GPO, 1959-70.

U.S. Congress. Office of Technology Assessment. *Civilian Space Policy and Applications.* Washington, D.C.: GPO, 1982.

————. *Civilian Space Stations and the U.S. Future in Space.* Washington, D.C.: GPO, 1984.

————. *Round Trip to Orbit: Human Spaceflight Alternatives.* Washington, D.C.: GPO, 1989.

U.S. Office of Management and Budget. *Budget of the United States Government: Fiscal Year 1995, Historical Tables.* Washington, D.C.: GPO, 1994.

————.*Budget of the United States Government.* Washington, D.C.: GPO, 1971-77.

U.S. President. *Public Papers of the Presidents of the United States.* Washington, D.C.: Office of the Federal Register, National Archives and Records Service. John F. Kennedy, 1961, 1962.

U.S. President. *Weekly Compilation of Presidential Documents.* Washington, D.C.: Office of the Federal Register, National Archives and Records Service. Ronald Reagan, 12 July 1982, 6 February 1984, 30 July 1984.

U.S. Presidential Commission on the Space Shuttle Challenger Accident. *Report to the President*. Washington, D.C.: GPO, 1986.

NEWSPAPER ARTICLES

Blakeslee, Sandra. "Feynman's Findings: They 'Fooled Themselves.' " *New York Times*, 11 June 1986, B6.
Boffey, Philip M. "Space Agency Image: A Sudden Shattering." *New York Times*, 5 February 1986, A1.
Broad, William J. "Back Into Space." *New York Times*, 3 July 1988, sec. 6, p. 11.
———. "High Risk of New Shuttle Disaster Leads NASA to Consider Options." *New York Times*, 9 April 1989, 1.
———. "Diverse Factors Propel Bush's Space Proposal." *New York Times*, 30 July 1989, 16.
———. "NASA Defends Space Station Building Plans." *New York Times*, 20 March 1990, C8.
———. "Troubles Raising Questions About Space Agency." *New York Times*, 1 July 1990, 14.
———. "Pervasive Decline of Staff Stunts NASA, Critics Say." *New York Times*, 9 September 1990, 1.
———. "Shuttle's Stargazing Disappoints Astronomers." *New York Times*, 11 December 1990, B5.
———. "NASA Budget Cuts Raise Concerns Over Safety of the Shuttle." *New York Times*, 8 March 1994, B5.
Clark, Evert. "Moon Plan Given Backing in Polls." *New York Times*, 15 November 1964, 4.
———. "Key Space Decision in Mid-70's Seen." *New York Times*, 14 October 1965, 8.
———. "Six Months After the Tragedy, the Apollo Program Finds Itself Gaining but 'Still in a Time of Testing.' " *New York Times*, 2 July 1967, 21.
Clymer, Adam. "Public Blames NASA Officials." *New York Times*, 28 January 1987, D27.
Davis, Bob, and Laurie McGinley. "Why a Space Station That Costs $25 Billion May Never Leave Earth." *Wall Street Journal*, 1 September 1988, 1.
Diamond, Stuart. "NASA Wasted Billions on Space Projects." *New York Times*, 23 April 1986, A14.
———. "NASA Cut or Delayed Safety Spending." *New York Times*, 24 April 1986, B4.
Dunn, Marcia. "From 'Gee Whiz' to 'So What' for NASA." *Nashville Tennessean*, 16 December 1990, 2D.
———. "Space Walk Repairs Antenna." *Murfreesboro (Tenn.) Daily News Journal*, 8 April 1991, 10.
Eagleston, Leigh Ann. "Kids Ask and NASA Answers." *Nashville Tennessean*, 20 September 1990, 3B.
"Excerpts from Shuttle Memorandum by Shuttle Chief." *New York Times*, 9 March 1986, 36.

"Fans Stream into Shuttle Landing Area." *Murfreesboro (Tenn.) Daily News Journal*, 19 March 1989, 10A.

Finney, John W. "House Unit Urges Bold Space Plan." *New York Times*, 11 January 1959, 50.

———. "Space Agency's Chief Says U.S. Will Shun Timetable." *New York Times*, 25 January 1959, 26.

———. "President Gives 10-Year Program for Space Probes." *New York Times*, 3 February 1959, 1.

———. "House Space Cuts Called Crippling." *New York Times*, 5 July 1959, 25.

Fisher, James. "America Loves NASA, Budget Writers Don't." *Orlando Sentinel*, 24 November 1987, 12-13.

Fletcher, James C. "Space Program to Aim at Practical Needs." *New York Times*, 4 December 1972, 50.

Gigot, Paul A. "NASA's Flyboys Have Grown Old and Fat." *Wall Street Journal*, 13 July 1990, A8.

"Glennan Warns on Space Work." *New York Times*, 6 October 1959, 2.

Greenberg, Daniel S. "Space Politics and Useless Cargo." *Chicago Tribune*, 5 December 1985, 27.

Harris, Louis. "Public Has Doubts About Space Program." *Washington Post*, 1 November 1965.

———. "Most OK Great Society," *Philadelphia Inquirer*, 3 April 1967.

———. "Space Programs Losing Support," *Washington Post*, 31 July 1967.

———. "49% Oppose Moon Project," *Philadelphia Inquirer*, 17 February 1969.

———. "Public Would Cut Funds for Space," *New York Post*, 18 February 1969.

———. "Public, in Reversal, Now Backs Landing on Moon, 51 to 41 Pct." *Washington Post*, 14 July 1969.

Hotz, Robert Lee. "Lunar Rocks Open Window to Solar System's Birth." *Atlanta Journal & Constitution*, 16 July 1989, B5.

Hoversten, Paul. "World Saw 'Eagle' Land in 1969." *Sunday (Nashville) Tennessean*, 16 July 1989, 3G.

Johnson, George. "The Long Way to Outer Space." *New York Times*, 23 July 1989, sec. 4, p. 5.

Kagay, Michael R. "Poll Finds Increased Support for Nation's Space Program." *New York Times*, 5 October 1988, B4.

Klose, Kevin, and Barry Sussman. "NASA Gets 'Fair Amount' of Blame in Poll." *Washington Post*, 25 February 1986, A3.

Leary, Warren E. "U.S. Advisers Urge Sweeping Change in Shuttle Program." *New York Times*, December 1990, A1.

———. "Space Shuttle Launching Delayed by Navigational Equipment Flaw." *New York Times*, 2 June 1991, sec. 1, p. 36.

Lembede, Mdu. "Fletcher Says NASA Gains Support." *Washington Post*, 19 October 1988, A21.

Moffett, Matt, and Laurie McGinley. "NASA, Once a Master of Publicity, Fumbles in Handling Shuttle Crisis." *Wall Street Journal*, 14 February 1896, 23.

"Moonwalk." *Christian Science Monitor*, 20 July 1989, 11.

Morin, Richard. "A Sea Change on Federal Spending." *Washington Post Weekly Edition*, 28 August 1989, 37.

"Most in U.S. Still Endorse Space Program, Poll Finds." *Wall Street Journal*, 11 February 1986, 29.

"NASA Plan May Put Man on Mars By 2011." *New York Times*, 21 November 1989, C13.

"Nobility, and Knowledge, in Space." *New York Times*, 30 July 1986, A22.

Phillips, Don, and Boyce Rensberger. "Astronaut Says NASA Cut Corners." *Washington Post*, 9 March 1986, A1.

"Poll Finds Backing for Space Spending." *New York Times*, 26 July 1988, C10.

Potter, Michael. "Shuttle's Success Masks Space Program's Troubles." *Atlanta Constitution*, 2 October 1988, 2B.

"Reveille for Sophomores." *New York Times*, 17 January 1990, A24.

"Russian Space Gain Seen by NASA Chief." *New York Times*, 20 May 1966, 51.

Sawyer, Kathy. "Back in Space, But Where to Go?" *Washington Post National Weekly Edition*, 10 October 1988, 7.

Schmeck, Harold M., Jr. "Experts Outline U.S. Space Plans." *New York Times*, 27 May 1961, 10.

"Seddon So Busy with New Baby She Forgot 'Surgery' Anniversary." *Nashville Tennessean*, 13 April 1989, 7B.

"Seddon Targets Education Needs." *Murfreesboro (Tenn.) Daily News Journal*, 15 November 1989, 3.

"Shuttle Liftoff Again Delayed," *Nashville Tennessean*, 2 June 1991, 13A.

"Space Agency Head Warns Moon Mission Might Fail." *New York Times*, 30 June 1969, 16.

"Space Chief Talks." *New York Times*, 5 April 1962, 67.

"Spending on Space Defended by Webb." *New York Times*, 24 October 1963, 14.

Spivak, Jonathan. "NASA's Jim Webb—A Rare Bureaucrat." *Wall Street Journal*, 11 October 1968, 16.

———. "Apathy is NASA's Biggest Foe." *Wall Street Journal*, 25 February 1977, 12.

Spotts, Peter N. "NASA Needs Better Tools for Reducing Shuttle Risks, Study Says." *Christian Science Monitor*, 9 March 1988, 5.

Stevens, William K. "Space Official Talks About Problems on Earth." *New York Times*, 19 May 1969, 31.

"Transcript of Astronauts' Addresses to Congress." *New York Times*, 17 September 1969, 30.

Van, Jon. "Americans Still Back Space Program, but NASA's Goals Remain Sketchy." *Chicago Tribune*, 1 February 1987, sec. 4, 4.

Webb, James E. "America's Role in Space Today." *New York Times*, 8 October 1961, sec. 12, p. 1.

"Webb Expects Faith 7 to End Mercury Program." *New York Times*, 16 May 1963, 18.

Weinraub, Bernard. "President Calls for Mars Mission and a Moon Base." *New York Times*, 21 July 1989, A1.

Wicker, Tom. "Icons and O Rings." *New York Times*, 18 February 1986, 31.

Wilford, John Noble. "Nixon Restates His Support of Space Effort." *New York Times*, 20 April 1970, 1.

———. "NASA, on 15th Birthday Today, Finds Itself in an Identity Crisis." *New York Times*, 1 October 1973, 70.

———. "Astronauts Certain of Shuttle's Safety." *New York Times*, 24 January 1981, 10.

————. "Seminar Envisions U.S.-Soviet Mars Venture." *New York Times*, 17 July 1985, A9.

————. "Challenger and NASA's 8th Casualty." *New York Times*, 14 February 1986, Y11.

————. "Steadier Orbit for NASA," *New York Times*, 11 December 1990, B9.

Wright, Robert A. "NASA Chief Seeks More Funds in '73." *New York Times*, 3 October 1971, 30.

PERIODICAL ARTICLES

Aldrin, Col. Buzz, with Wayne Warga. "Return to Earth." *Good Housekeeping*, October 1973, 212.

Allen, Joseph Baneth. "Mr. Acronym." *Final Frontier*, November/December 1990, 16.

Bamberger, David. "NASA and Watergate: How the Publicists Lost the Public." *America*, 19 July 1975, 33-34.

Begley, Sharon. "Heaven Can Wait." *Newsweek*, 9 July 1990, 48-55.

Bell, Trudy E., and Karl Esch. "The Space Shuttle: A Case of Subjective Engineering." *IEEE Spectrum* 26 (June 1989): 42-46.

Bethell, Tom. "NASA (That's Right, NASA) Is a Good Thing." *Washington Monthly*, November 1975, 5-14.

Biddle, Wayne. "NASA: What's Needed to Put It on Its Feet?" *Discover*, January 1987, 40-47.

Bjerklie, David. "Roots of the Hubble's Troubles." *Time*, 10 December 1990, 78.

Blakely, Steve, and John R. Cranford. "Lawmakers Weigh in on Shuttle Safety Issue." *Congressional Quarterly Weekly Report*, 14 June 1986, 1324-27.

Bloom, Mark. "NASA's Pie in the Sky." *The Nation*, 22 May 1972, 647-49.

Boot, William. "NASA and the Spellbound Press." *Columbia Journalism Review* 25 (July/August 1986): 23-29.

Brown, Stuart F. "20 Years After Apollo: Is the U.S. Lost in Space?" *Popular Science*, July 1989, 63-75.

Budiansky, Stephen. "What's Wrong with America's Space Program." *U.S. News & World Report*, 28 December 1987, 34.

Cloud, David S. "U.S. Space Flight Ambitions Face New Ground Rules." *Congressional Quarterly Weekly Report*, 22 July 1989, 1848-49.

Covault, Craig. "NASA Managers Fear Loss of Space Program Leadership." *Aviation Week & Space Technology*, 2 February 1987, 21-22.

————. "NASA Plans to Fight Threats to Its Role in Space Program." *Aviation Week & Space Technology*, 26 October 1987, 61-62.

————. "Space, the Political Imperative." *Aviation Week & Space Technology*, 11 November 1987, 9.

Cowen, Robert C. "Tough Choices Ahead for NASA." *Technology Review* 89 (August/September 1986): 21.

Cranford, John R. "A New Tone Heard in Congressional Dealings with NASA." *Congressional Quarterly Weekly Report*, 14 June 1986, 1325.

David, Leonard. "NASA at T + 30 Years." *Space World*, October 1988, 7-9.

"Doublespeak at NASA." *Space World*, February 1987, 7.

Downs, Anthony. "Up and Down with Ecology—the " 'Issue-Attention Cycle.' " *The Public Interest* 28 (Summer 1972): 38-50.

Foley, Theresa M. "Departing NASA Manager Criticizes Micromanagement of Space Agency." *Aviation Week & Space Technology*, 4 April 1988, 51-53.

Frieling, Thomas J. "The Reagan Report Card." *Space World*, March 1988, 9-11.

Fries, Sylvia D. "2001 to 1994: Political Environment and the Design of NASA's Space Station System." *Technology and Culture* 29 (July 1988): 586-93.

"The Future of NASA." *Time*, 10 August 1970, 44-45.

The Gallup Report, No. 246, March 1986, 12.

Goldberg, Jeff. "Lunar Reflections." *Omni*, July 1989, 34-40.

Greenberg, D. S. "Space Program." *Science*, 8 March 1963, 890-91.

The Harris Survey, 6 February 1986, 1.

———. 15 September 1986, 1.

"The Heart of the Matter." *Scientific American*, August 1986, 63-64.

C.F. Larry Heimann. "Understanding the *Challenger* Disaster: Organizational Structure and the Design of Reliable Systems." *American Political Science Review* 87 (June 1993): 421-35.

Hines, William. "NASA: The Image Misfires." *The Nation*, 24 April 1967, 517-19.

Holden, Matthew, Jr. " 'Imperialism' in Bureaucracy." *American Political Science Review* 60 (December 1966): 943-51.

Isbell, Douglas. "Space 'Mission' to Study Global Environment." *Washington Flyer*, January/February 1990, 6.

Jaroff, Leon. "Spinning Out of Orbit." *Time*, 6 August 1990, 26-27.

Jones, Charles O. "The Limits of Public Support: Air Pollution Agency Development." *Public Administration Review* 32 (September/October 1972): 502-508.

Kuntz, Phil. "Pie in the Sky: Big Science Is Ready for Blastoff." *Congressional Quarterly Weekly Report*, 28 April 1990, 1254-60.

———. "Bush Goes on the Counterattack Against Mars Mission Critics." *Congressional Quarterly Weekly Report*, 23 June 1990, 1958.

———. "Hubble, Shuttle, and Moon-Mars Add Up to Bad Week for NASA." *Congressional Quarterly Weekly Report*, 30 June 1990, 2054.

Lambright, W. Henry, and Dianne Rahm. "Ronald Reagan and Space Policy." *Policy Studies Journal* 17 (Spring 1989): 515-27.

Lemonick, Michael D. "Goodbye to NASA's Glory Days," *Time*, 22 February 1988, 54.

———. "Back to the Future." *Discovery*, January 1989, 42-47.

Lewis, Richard S. "End of Apollo: The Ambiguous Epic." *Bulletin of the Atomic Scientists* 28 (December 1972): 39-44.

Lewis, Ruth A., and John S. Lewis, "Getting Back on Track in Space." *Technology Review* 89 (August/September 1986): 30-40.

Light, Larry. "One Decade After the Moon Landing, Space Program Gets Little Attention or Interest." *Congressional Quarterly Weekly Report*, 28 April 1979, 780-87.

Logsdon, John M. "The Space Shuttle Program: A Policy Failure?" *Science*, 30 May 1986, 1099-1105.

———. "A Response to Alex Roland." *Space Policy*, May 1987, 113.

Marshall, Eliot. "Academy Panel Faults NASA's Safety Analysis." *Science*, 11 March 1988, 1233.

Matlack, Carol, and Scott Marshutz. "They Fly, We Cry." *National Journal* 19 (11 April 1987): 879-81.

McKean, Kevin. "They Fly in the Face of Danger." *Discover*, April 1986, 48-58.

Miller, Jon D. "Is There Public Support for Space Exploration?" *Environment*, June 1984, 25-35.

———. "The Challenger Accident and Public Opinion," *Space Policy*, May 1987, 122-40.

Morrison, David C. "Vice-President for Space." *National Journal*, 29 July 1989, 1910-15.

"NASA Changes Management Structure." *Aviation Week & Space Technology*, 26 January 1987, 74-75.

"NASA: No Flight Plan." *Scientific American*, February 1987, 58-60.

Naugle, John E. "Research with the Space Shuttle." *Physics Today*, November 1973, 30-37.

"No Free Launch." *Time*, 31 July 1989, 21.

"Opinion Roundup." *Public Opinion* 9 (February/March 1986): 21-40.

Peters, B. Guy, and Brian W. Hogwood. "In Search of the Issue-Attention Cycle." *Journal of Politics* 47 (February 1985): 238-53.

Peters, Charles. "From Ouagadougou to Cape Canaveral: Why the Bad News Doesn't Travel Up." *Washington Monthly*, April 1986, 27-31.

"Pitchman for NASA's Trip to the Moon." *Business Week*, 27 May 1967, 71-72.

"Poll Shows Growing Space Complacency." *Space Business Daily*, 29 July 1966, 153.

"Poll Shows 69 Percent Support of Project Apollo." *Space Business Daily*, 30 November 1966, 143.

"Public Opinion Survey Shows Increase in Support of Space Program." *Langley Researcher*, 21 November 1986, 5.

"Public Support for Space." *Space Futures Newsletter*, March 1980, 3.

"The Public's View." *Newsweek*, 10 February 1986, 37.

Reagan, Ronald. "United States Space Plan." *Weekly Compilation of Presidential Documents* (12 July 1982): 872-74.

———. Radio address of 28 January 1984. *Weekly Compilation of Presidential Documents* (6 February 1984): 113.

———. Radio address of 21 July 1984. *Weekly Compilation of Presidential Documents* (30 July 1984): 1057.

Reed, Bruce. "Rocket Man." *The New Republic*, 15 May 1989, 12-13.

Roland, Alex. "The Shuttle: Triumph or Turkey?" *Discover*, November 1985, 29-49.

———. "Priorities in Space for USA." *Space Policy*, May 1987, 104-14.

Romzek, Barbara S., and Melvin J. Dubnick. "Accountability in the Public Sector: Lessons from the Challenger Tragedy." *Public Administration Review* 47 (May/June 1987): 227-38.

Rosenberg, Tina. "Mission Out of Control." *The New Republic*, 14 May 1984, 18-21.

Schull, Steven A. "Presidential-Congressional Support for Agencies and for Each Other." *Journal of Politics* 40 (August 1978).

Sherrod, Robert. "The Selling of the Astronauts." *Columbia Journalism Review* 12 (May/June 1973): 16-25.

Shifrin, Carol A. "Reagan Backs Space Commerce." *Aviation Week & Space Technology*, 30 July 1984, 16-17.

"Shuttle Lessons." *Science Digest*, September 1986, 18.

"Shuttle Risk High NASA Admits." *Spaceflight*, June 1981.

Skardon, James A. "The Apollo Story: What the Watchdogs Missed," *Columbia Journalism Review* 6 (Fall 1967): 11-15.

————. "The Apollo Story: The Concealed Patterns." *Columbia Journalism Review* 6 (Winter 1967/68): 34-39.

Smith, R. Jeffrey. "Shuttle Problems Compromise Space Program." *Science*, 23 November 1979, 912.

————. "Uncertainties Mark Space Program of the 1980s." *Science*, 14 December 1979, 1284-86.

"Space Shuttle: NASA Versus Domestic Priorities." *Congressional Quarterly Weekly Report*, 26 February 1972, 435-39.

Stoke, Harold W. "Executive Leadership and the Growth of Propaganda." *American Political Science Review* 35 (June 1941): 490-500.

Tumlinson, Rick Norman. "Space in Your Living Room." *Space World*, February 1986, 21-22.

Van Allen, James A. "Myths and Realities of Space Flight." *Science*, 30 May 1986, 1075-76.

"What the Public Thinks." *Space World*, April 1986, 6.

Yarwood, Dean L., and Ben J. Enis. "Advertising and Publicity Programs in the Executive Branch of the National Government: Hustling or Helping the People?" *Public Administration Review* 42 (January/February 1982): 37-46.

Zentner, Joseph L. "Organizational Ideology: Some Functions and Problems." *International Review of History and Political Science* 10 (May 1973): 75-84.

INTERVIEWS

Fletcher, James C. Interview by author, 5 October 1990, Washington, D.C.

Seddon, Rhea. Interview by Al Tompkins, WSMV-TV, 27 July 1989, Nashville, Tennessee.

————. Interview by author, 23 November 1989, Murfreesboro, Tennessee.

SPEECHES

Beggs, James M. "The Wilbur and Orville Wright Memorial Lecture." Speech to the Royal Aeronautical Society, London, England, 13 December 1984. NASA History Office, Washington, D.C.

Dryden, Hugh L. "Safety in the Space Age." Speech to the National Safety Congress, Chicago, Illinois, 31 October 1962. NASA History Office, Washington, D.C.

Glennan, T. Keith. "The Challenge of the Space Age." Speech to Fort Worth Chamber of Commerce, 8 December 1958. NASA History Office, Washington, D.C.

————. Speech at Wright Day Dinner, Washington, D.C., 17 December 1958. NASA History Office, Washington, D.C.

Horner, Richard E. Speech to the annual convention of the Society of Technical Writers and Editors, Chicago, Illinois, 21-22 April 1960. NASA History Office, Washington, D.C.

Low, George M. "Project Mercury Progress." Speech to UPI Editors Conference, Washington, D.C., 9 September 1960. NASA History Office, Washington, D.C.

Seamans, Robert C. "Reliability in Space Systems—A National Objective." Speech to the I.A.S. National Propulsion Meeting, Cleveland, Ohio, 8 March 1962. NASA History Office, Washington, D.C.

Webb, James E. "The Challenge and Promise of the Space Age." Speech at the University of Miami, 25 January 1965. NASA History Office, Washington, D.C.

MISCELLANEOUS

Congressional Quarterly Almanac. Washington, D.C.: Congressional Quarterly, 1958-90.

Cooper, Kenneth Dean. "Mission Control: The Manned Space Program and the Reincarnation of the Frontier Myth." M.A. thesis, Vanderbilt University, 1988.

"The Dream is Alive." IMAX Film, 1985. National Air & Space Museum, Washington, D.C.

General Social Surveys, 1972-1989: Cumulative Codebook. Chicago: National Opinion Research Center, 1989.

Jahnige, Thomas P. "Congress and Space: The Committee System and Congressional Oversight of NASA." Ph.D. dissertation, Claremont Graduate School, 1965.

"Man in Space." ABC-TV, 9 July 1989.

Michener, James A. Foreword to *Beachheads in Space*, by Jerry Grey. New York: Macmillan, 1983.

"The Moon Above, the Earth Below." CBS-TV, 13 July 1989.

"NBC Nightly News." NBC-TV, 6 April 1991.

Petrovic, Nancy. "Design for Decline: Executive Management and the Eclipse of NASA." Ph.D. dissertation, University of Maryland, 1982.

Webb, James E. Foreword to *Managing NASA in the Apollo Era*, SP-4102, by Arnold S. Levine. Washington, D.C.: GPO, 1982.

Index

About the Author

MARK E. BYRNES is assistant professor of political science at Middle Tennessee
State University, Murfreesboro, Tennessee, where he specializes in American
politics, with emphasis on the presidency, Congress, and Tennessee government.
He holds a Diploma in International and Comparative Politics from the London
School of Economics, and a Ph.D. in political science from Vanderbilt University.
He is currently revising his chapter for the forthcoming new edition of
Congressional Quarterly's *Guide to the Presidency*.

ISBN 0-275-94950-8

90000>

EAN

9 780275 949501

HARDCOVER BAR CODE